Campaigns in the 21st Century

CRITICAL TOPICS IN AMERICAN GOVERNMENT SERIES

Alan Abramowitz: *Voice of the People: Elections and Voting in the United States*

David Lowery and Holly Brasher: *Organized Interests and American Government*

Kevin McGuire: *Understanding the U.S. Supreme Court: Cases and Controversies*

Richard J. Semiatin: *Campaigns in the 21st Century: The Changing Mosaic of American Politics*

Campaigns in the 21st Century

The Changing Mosaic of American Politics

Richard J. Semiatin

American University

Boston   Burr Ridge, IL   Dubuque, IA   Madison, WI   New York
San Francisco   St. Louis   Bangkok   Bogotá   Caracas   Kuala Lumpur
Lisbon   London   Madrid   Mexico City   Milan   Montreal   New Delhi
Santiago   Seoul   Singapore   Sydney   Taipei   Toronto

CAMPAIGNS IN THE 21ST CENTURY
The Changing Mosaic of American Politics

Published by McGraw-Hill, an imprint of The McGraw-Hill Companies, Inc.,
1221 Avenue of the Americas, New York, NY 10020. Copyright © 2005 by The
McGraw-Hill Companies, Inc. All rights reserved. No part of this publication may be
reproduced or distributed in any form or by any means, or stored in a database or
retrieval system, without the prior written consent of The McGraw-Hill Companies,
Inc., including, but not limited to, in any network or other electronic storage or
transmission, or broadcast for distance learning.

2 3 4 5 6 7 8 9 0 DOC / DOC 0 9 8 7 6 5

ISBN 0-07-245362-1

Editor-in-chief: *Emily Barrosse*
Publisher: *Lyn Uhl*
Sponsoring editor: *Monica Eckman*
Marketing manager: *Katherine Bates*
Media producer: *Sean Crowley*
Production editor: *Brett Coker*
Production supervisor: *Randy Hurst*
Design manager and cover designer:
  Srdjan Savanovic

Manager, photo research: *Brian J. Pecko*
Compositor: *Interactive Composition
  Corporation*
Typeface: *10/12 Palatino*
Paper: *45# New Era Matte*
Printer and binder: *R.R. Donnelley,
  Crawfordsville*

Cover photos: left, © Reuters NewMedia, Inc./Corbis; center, © AFB/Corbis;
right, © Reuters NewMedia, Inc./Corbis

Library of Congress Cataloging-in-Publication Data

Semiatin, Richard J.
  Campaigns in the 21st century: the changing mosaic of American politics / Richard J.
Semiatin.
    p. cm. - (Critical topics in American government series)
  Includes bibliographical references and index.
  ISBN 0-07-245362-1
  1. Political campaigns—United States. 2. Politics, Practical—United States.
  3. United States—Politics and government—21st century. I. Title: Campaigns
in the twenty-first century. II. Title. Series.

  JK2281.S47 2004
  324.7'0973—dc22

          2003071002

The Internet addresses listed in the text were accurate at the time of publication.
The inclusion of a Website does not indicate an endorsement by the authors or
McGraw-Hill Higher Education, and McGraw-Hill does not guarantee the
accuracy of the information presented at these sites.

www.mhhe.com

Brief Contents

Contents

Preface

Campaigns in the 21st Century examines how campaigns adapt to changes in the political environment. Every presidential, senatorial, gubernatorial, and congressional candidate campaign attempts to stay ahead of the curve in terms of technology and strategy. For example, the 1960 presidential campaign revolutionized political communication as John Kennedy (D-MA) brought television into our living rooms. The second communication revolution is emerging today as the Internet brings campaigns into the hands of voters. This book acquaints readers with the motivations, decisions, and operations of political campaigns in this dynamic environment. The dynamism of campaigns makes them exciting and interesting. They serve as the fulcrum of our political system. Without campaigns and elections, there would be no members of Congress, no president, and thus no appointed members of the Supreme Court.

The book seeks to engage readers to understand the reality of politics. It does not attempt to be a theoretical or behavioral treatise about elections and campaigns. *Campaigns in the 21st Century* provides readers with an unvarnished view of how campaigns work, how candidates campaign, and how staff and consultants serve candidates. The book takes in the most recent developments in campaigns through the early winter campaign of 2004. This is particularly important because each wave of Internet technology occurs in a six-month to one-year cycle. The author trusts that not too much information is dated. The manuscript is written without excessive jargon to give the reader a sense of excitement about the world of political campaigns and candidates today; thus, it is not a history book about political campaigns.

Two important points are worthy of notation in terms of writing the book. The author refers to the 41st President as George Bush, Sr. rather than George H.W. Bush. Many undergrads might confuse George H.W. Bush with the 43rd President George W. Bush. Furthermore, reputable international news organizations including CNN, *Guardian* (Great Britain), *Pravda* (Russia) have referred to the 41st President as Bush, Sr. as has the American *Business Week* magazine.

The second notation regards footnoting in the text. Citations appear at the end of the paragraph, encompassing all references in the paragraph, including quotations. The "Notes" section of each chapter carefully details every citation in order. The author in conjunction with the editorial staff opted for this format to ensure that the text reads smoothly. The author apologizes for any inconvenience this may cause a reader or reviewer.

The author would like to thank Ilene Semiatin who always "fixes" the author's writing style having an innate understanding of how his mind actually works. Her work was invaluable and critical to the success of the book. My sincere appreciation to the following reviewers who provided in-depth analysis for making valuable suggestions that improved the text tremendously: Melanie Blumberg, California University of Pennsylvania; Joseph A. Kunkell, Minnesota State University, Mankato; George Marcus, Williams College; Stacy McMillen, Wayne State University; Charles Prysby, University of North Carolina at Greensboro; Tari Renner, Illinois Wesleyan University; Mark J. Rozell, Catholic University of America; Dick Simpson, University of Illinois at Chicago; June S. Speakman, Roger Williams University; Carolyn A. Taylor, Rogers State University Peter Ubertaccio, Stone Hill College; Clyde Wilcox, Georgetown University; and Richard Witmer, Northern Arizona University. A special and hearty thank you to Mark J. Rozel who went beyond the call of duty submitting detailed edits of the manuscript, which made the final product much better. Please note that any errors that remain are the responsibility of the author. Shannon Clay must be thanked for providing meaningful suggestions for Chapters 4 and 6. The author's colleagues provided encouragement and enthusiasm. Donna Chapman and Meg Weekes receive kudos for keeping the author sane during the final stages of the manuscript. The continuing support of Dean David Brown of American University helped make this book a reality. Everyone should have Dean Brown as a boss. The author would also like to thank Angela Kao at McGraw-Hill for her tireless efforts in shepherding the book towards completion. Brett Coker receives accolades for his efficiency, collegiality, and professionalism. The author would also like to thank his parents, siblings, nieces, and nephews for being his biggest cheerleaders. Most of all, the author would like to thank Senior Editor, Monica Eckman of McGraw-Hill who is not only a wonderful editor but even a better person. We have worked together for five years on a series of monographs about elections. Never has she flagged in her support of me. She merits this writer's greatest appreciation.

  . . . And now on to the world of campaigns. . . .

To my parents Edith and Lionel Semiatin for their unending devotion and love. I'm honored to be your son.

CHAPTER 1

Introduction to Political Campaigns

"Circumstances have changed dramatically since I first called you," Gore told Bush. "The state of Florida is too close to call." Bush replied, "Are you saying what I think you are saying? Let me make sure I understand. You're calling back to retract that concession?" Gore retorted, "Don't get snippy about it!" Gore went on to explain that until the final vote was resolved neither side should claim victory. Bush could not believe that the candidate who had conceded the election to him less than an hour earlier was telling him to calm down. His brother, the governor of Florida, had assured him he had won the state as he related to Gore. According to one observer Gore snapped, "With all due respect to your brother, he is not the final arbiter of who wins Florida." "Do what you have to do," Bush replied and the conversation ended.[1]

The drama that unfolded delivered the Texas governor the necessary electoral votes to win the presidency in 2000. Bush emerged with a razor-thin 537-vote margin from more than 6 million votes cast in Florida. The stressful telephone conversation between the two combatants illustrated the intensity of the closest race in presidential history fought by two tenacious campaigns. The spectacle of campaigns is perhaps the most memorable aspect of them. Campaigns are often part Greek theater, where each campaign portrays itself as good and the opposition as evil. On other occasions, they may resemble a circus, in which the performers entertain the audience with displays of soaring rhetoric and swooning gaffes; or they may remind one of a tight pennant race at the close of a major league baseball season with the lead seesawing back and forth in the polls before the election.

In the best of all worlds, an election contest becomes a thoughtful policy debate about great issues facing the country.

Despite the entertainment value, the fact is that campaigns do matter. Campaign outcomes directly influence how government operates. They are the powerful engine that contour and shape the parameters of partisan and free debate, the hallmark of a thriving democracy. Since each election cycle is new, the process is never static. As political scientist James Thurber says, "Campaigns are dynamic. They do not happen in a vacuum and they are not predetermined by economic and political circumstances." *Dynamic* means that campaigns must continually adapt to changes in the political environment to achieve success. It is this dynamic that serves as the focus of the book. A candidate's failure to understand the political context of an election will almost certainly result in defeat. Former Speaker of the House Tip O'Neill (D) remarked that George Bush, Sr. (R) at the apex of his personal popularity seemed too "distracted" to address the economic recession following the first Persian Gulf War victory in 1991. The sluggish economy resulted in Bill Clinton defeating George Bush eighteen months later. Politicians not paying attention to the present put their future at risk.[2]

ADAPTATION AND CHANGE IN CAMPAIGNS

A well-run campaign makes the necessary adaptations to the changing landscape of the political environment. In the late spring of 1992, Governor Bill Clinton of Arkansas, the prospective Democratic presidential nominee languished in third place behind President George Bush, Sr. and billionaire Independent candidate Ross Perot in public opinion polls. Negative portrayals in the press regarding extramarital affairs and allegations that he "avoided" the military draft tarnished Clinton's character. The campaign test marketed a new message about Clinton stressing his modest personal roots as "the man from Hope" (a small town in Arkansas) with focus groups. Based on focus group feedback, the campaign retooled Clinton's image as a mainstream populist in contrast to the patrician Bush and billionaire Perot. The "new" Clinton could seize the offensive focusing his message on generational, economic, and political change rather than remaining on the defensive by responding to charges about his dubious character. The strategy enabled Clinton to solidify his Democratic base and attract "swing" or persuadable voters necessary to win the election. The example explains how campaigns can reinvent themselves (i.e., adjust tactics and strategy) to win elections.[3]

Campaigns must cope with *political* changes (national or world events), *technological* changes (broadcast and advertising media), and *demographic* changes (shifting population centers in the country). Three short examples illustrate each of these points. President Lyndon Johnson's failure to cope with flagging support for his policies during the Vietnam War within his Democratic party led to his withdrawal from the race in March 1968. Johnson's withdrawal represented a major political change because a little known anti-war senator, Eugene McCarthy of Minnesota, nearly defeated him in the New Hampshire Democratic presidential primary that year.

Technology brought political campaigns into the living rooms of Americans through television during the 1950s. Vice President Richard Nixon's failure to understand television's visual power became apparent during his first presidential debate with John F. Kennedy in 1960. It was the first nationally televised presidential debate in American politics. Nixon appeared on air with a "5 o'clock shadow," looking pale and sallow compared with the debonair Kennedy. Political commentators have often pointed to that debate as the election's turning point although no definitive evidence is available. However, the physical contrast between the two men is the one lasting image from the Kennedy-Nixon campaign replayed even today.[4]

The growing power of non-white minorities reflects the increased demographic diversity in the United States. For example, the Latino population grew from 9 percent in 1990 to 12.5 percent in 2000. In the 2000 election, Vice President Al Gore and Texas Governor George W. Bush understood the rising power of the Latino vote in key states such as Florida and California. The Gore and Bush campaigns targeted Latinos with advertisements, literature, and phone banks messages in Spanish. As a sign of changing times, this was the first presidential election where both party nominees were somewhat conversant in Spanish (Bush more than Gore). Thus, each campaign's choice to expand Spanish-language appeals to voters reflected the emerging power of Latino voters in American elections. Profound political, technological, and demographic changes influencing campaign management also reflect the rise of candidate-centered politics in which individual campaigns are more responsive to change than the massive political party machines of the past.[5]

(THE DECLINE OF POLITICAL PARTY ORGANIZATIONS)

In the early days of our nation, strong party organizations and partisan newspapers personally connected voters to campaigns. Political parties were the organizing principle behind campaigns. Several factors weakened the political party's grasp on voters, according to political scientist Martin Wattenberg. The creation of the federal civil service system in the 1880s replaced political patronage weakening the ability of parties to grant "rewards to friends and financial backers." Next, the introduction of the Australian ballot in the early 1900s provided voters with a secret ballot to choose individual candidates, replacing the open ballot (or ticket). Before the Australian ballot, a voter obtained a ticket from a party official and deposited it in a box. This made it easy for parties to buy votes, particularly in cities where the impoverished lived. Public attention to the buying and selling of votes gradually led to the adoption of the Australian ballot.[6]

The decline of party-line voting and party identification throughout the 20th century marked a third important change. The causes were economic and political. Greater economic wealth in the second half of the century increased population movement to new suburbs and away from urban centers where political machines proliferated. Furthermore, the Vietnam War and the Watergate scandal greatly contributed to distrust in government, political institutions, and political parties in the late 1960s and early 1970s. One outcome was the reform of the presidential nomination system in the early 1970s, which increased the number of state primaries and lessened the number of party-controlled state caucuses. It enabled candidates outside of the Democratic party mainstream such as George McGovern (D-SD) and Jimmy Carter (D-GA) to win the Democratic party nomination in 1972 and 1976.

The growth of television, furthermore, dislocated viewers from political parties providing candidates with a separate avenue to communicate with voters. The cumulative effect of these causes contributed to the decline of parties and resulted in candidates' exercising more control over their own campaigns—a phenomenon called candidate-centered politics. Today, candidates are electoral entrepreneurs entirely responsible for their own campaign operation. Parties play a supporting, but not leading role. Candidates rely on personal staff and consultants to organize, strategize, and promote their campaigns.[7]

CANDIDATES AND MASS COMMUNICATIONS

Political analyst Christopher Arterton says, "modern politics have eviscerated these (party) networks, replacing them with polling and mass communications" because they are time and cost-effective. Candidates from states large and small utilize mass communications, although they play out differently. California characterizes how important mass communications are in a state with an enormous population (35 million) and geographic size. Rallies held on airplane tarmacs provide easy press coverage for the evening news. Massive television advertising covers sizable media markets in Los Angeles, the Bay area, San Diego, Fresno, and Sacramento. However, in small states such as New Hampshire, citizens expect presidential candidates to come knocking on their doors vying for votes in the nation's first primary every four years. Mass communications technology to reach large groups of voters in New Hampshire is important; however, unlike in California, personal campaigning remains an expectation of candidates. Thus, local political culture and campaign resources (staff, volunteers, and money) dictate how a candidate communicates with voters and tries to win their support.[8]

THE REALITY OF POLITICS

The job of a campaign organization is not to win merit badges for civility; instead, the purpose is to win elections. (The conventional wisdom that politics was a noble pursuit when the Founders established our democracy runs contrary to the evidence.) Campaigns, even from the beginning, used messages as blunt instruments to stir up support. John Adams was pilloried as "His Rotundity" by the Republican press, which supported Jefferson in 1796, and the Federalist press sympathetic to Adams warned that electing Jefferson would lead to "murder, robbery . . . and adultery." How campaigns win may not be aesthetically pleasing but it is a reflection of the democratic process. Thus, *Campaigns in the 21st Century* focuses on the realities of how candidates and their campaigns attract votes, instead of pursuing a theoretical treatise on electoral organizational behavior. To win, a modern campaign organization draws on the practical experience of professional consultants to give them an advantage over the opponent.[9]

PROFESSIONALS IN MODERN CAMPAIGNS

The growing number of professional staff and consultants permeating a campaign organization is a phenomenon of the last half-century of American politics. Over 3,000 firms now advertise in *Campaigns and Elections* magazine's "Political Pages," a phone book released annually that lists services offered to candidates. Among the services are paid advertising, polling, fundraising, field operations, speech writing, and web page design. The campaign industry is responsive to the marketplace—always seeking more precise and sophisticated means to target voters. Therefore, new computer-assisted technologies have transformed how campaigns operate in the past two decades. The turnaround time to produce a response ad to an opponent's attack took one full day in the past. Today, computers speed the process of writing, editing, and producing a response ad before beaming the final cut by satellite transmission to a television station. The entire process takes just several hours. The *speed* or pace of change has increased dramatically as technology has brought information to voters, notes media consultant Joe Cerrell. Since campaigns have a shorter time-frame to make decisions, the expertise of a consultant becomes more important to provide shortcuts addressing unexpected problems that arise. A consultant's experience can produce more cost and time efficient solutions than those generated by a less seasoned campaign staff.[10]

The business of politics means that a consultant will place their own self-interest, if necessary, above the interests of their client (i.e., the candidate). For example, political consultant Dick Morris illustrates how a political professional promotes himself. Morris served as a top strategist for Bill Clinton's reelection effort in 1996. Morris resigned when a scandal broke regarding his relationship with a prostitute. Morris' book *Behind the Oval Office: Getting Reelected Against All Odds* details his role in positioning Clinton as a moderate divide-and-conquer force between liberal congressional Democrats and the majority conservative congressional Republicans. The book pays homage to Morris' own strategic acumen following the 1994 midterm elections when Republicans gained control of the House and Senate. Morris portrays himself as the key figure transforming Clinton into a political moderate "triangulating" as a third force between congressional Republicans and Democrats. The goal was to put Clinton above the partisan rancor of politics, positioning him to win reelection. Morris deserves much credit, but he gives little to the formidable political skills of Clinton and his political staff.[11]

On the other hand, Karl Rove the brilliant strategist behind George W. Bush's presidential victory in 2000 devoted most of his career to helping Texas Republicans and the Bush family in politics as a consultant and campaign staff member. Following the election, Rove accepted a White House appointment rather than establish a new consulting business in Washington, D.C., earning him millions. Rove's loyalty to George W. Bush demonstrates that self-interest does not dictate the motivation of all consultants.[12]

Consultants craft messages and political strategy, raise money, conduct surveys, produce advertising, and advise on Internet operations for campaigns. Examining their work as part of the campaign process provides a contextual understanding of the role, and the contributions that consultants make to political campaigns. Furthermore, candidates often profit more from the work of staff, volunteers, family members; their own political skill; and the ineptitude of their opponents. Thus, the book focuses less on consultants and individual staff and more on their organizational roles in political campaigns.

THE CAMPAIGN ROADMAP

Campaigns are a unique political process since they have a definable ending, election day. They unfurl slowly in the beginning stages and then progress at a breakneck pace until their conclusion. Without learning how public leaders win election to public office, understanding how democratic institutions operate is limited because an impending election sometimes motivates officials to act on national issues. Therefore, the book's discussion focuses on the largest playing field of campaigns, the national political arena where campaigns have the greatest long-term consequences for the country and states. Therefore, illustrations from presidential, senatorial, congressional, and gubernatorial elections appear throughout the book demonstrating how candidates pursue public office.

Motivations and Decisions to Run for Office

Chapter 2 explores the dynamic nature of candidate motivation by examining the personal, political, and social forces that produce such candidacies. Important issues, compelling personal reasons, recruitment by political leaders, political experience, political reform, opportunity, and ego all serve as motivations to run for office. The motivation for any given candidate may be singular or plural. Chapter 3 assesses the decision to run for political office. Prospective candidates face the reality of coping with family demands and withstanding personal scrutiny. Running for office takes tremendous stamina, necessitates raising money, and involves seeking political endorsements. Furthermore, Chapter 3 discusses the initial stages of candidate planning as an individual moves from prospect to contender.

Organizing a Campaign Operation

Once a candidate has decided to run for office, the next stage is organizing a political campaign operation. Chapter 4 discusses the campaign operation that has internal roles (all activities managed within the campaign) and external roles (consultants hired to manage aspects of the campaign). The subsequent discussion turns to *strategy* or the overall message and plan for conducting the campaign. For example, George W. Bush's successful strategy of winning the White House in 2000 illustrated how personal morality, compassionate conservatism, and an identity as a Washington outsider contrasted with Vice President Gore's association with President Bill Clinton. *Tactics* or tools such as polling and paid advertising help candidates implement their overall campaign strategy. Note that strategy and tactics often must adapt to changes in the political environment that require altering plans in the midst of an electoral contest.

Polling, Paid Advertising, and the Internet

Important research and communication features such as polling, paid advertising, and Internet technologies, are discussed in Chapters 5–7. Polling provides a snapshot of the political landscape providing information about past voting behavior of the electorate, what issues resonate with voters, candidate support and favorability ratings, and demographic information on the subjects interviewed. The data allow the campaign team to develop or refine strategies to win the election. Polling also shapes the advertising strategy by finding the audiences most receptive to a candidate's message. In national campaigns, the largest portion of a campaign's budget is allocated to paid advertising. For example, Bush and Gore spent

$156 million out of a total $306 million raised in 2000 on television advertising. Advertising also includes direct mail, radio, and newspaper advertising.[13]

Mass communications enable a campaign to reach more viewers with a simple message than any other medium and more cost-effectively. The Internet represents the newest medium to reach voters through online technologies such as websites and e-mail. The Internet is an interactive medium with the voter as an information seeker perusing menus of choices on websites ranging from newspapers to candidates to party organizations acquiring the information they seek. However, campaigns and party organizations are expanding e-mail solicitations to attract volunteers and contributors. *The Washington Post* reported that the Howard Dean (D-VT) presidential campaign raised $4 million in Internet contributions from April through June 2003. The Internet has become a growing electronic grassroots medium for organizing political movements such as *MoveOn.org*, a liberal populist organization with two million members seeking to endorse a presidential candidate. Campaigns in the 21st century will feature faster changes spurred by technology increasing the electronic interaction between candidates and voters.[14]

Campaigning for Public Office and the Implications for Democracy

Campaigning for office involves planning the candidate's schedule, determining where to campaign, holding rallies, making speeches, participating in debates, producing events to earn press attention, and intensifying the pace to attract votes as the election approaches. Chapter 8 discusses how the complexities of campaigning for office require tremendous teamwork and sublimation of egos by staff and consultants, as well as the mounting pressure that candidates and staff face as the election approaches.

The book concludes with an evaluation of the effect of campaigns on democracy. Campaigns are a permanent fixture on the American landscape raising implications about how well politicians govern given a continuous concern for reelection. On the other hand, campaigns provide voters with copious amounts of information to help them discern and make choices. The benefits and costs of the campaign system reveal that voting remains the most important democratic value exercised by citizens and that the ritual of running for office is firmly ensconced in American political culture.

STUDY/DISCUSSION QUESTIONS

Why is it important for campaigns to adapt to the political environment?

What impact did the decline of parties have on the rise of candidate-centered politics?

How significant are political consultants to political campaigns?

SUGGESTED READINGS

Boller, Paul F. *Presidential Campaigns*. New York: Oxford, 1984.

Johnson, Dennis W. *No Place for Amateurs: How Political Consultants Are Reshaping American Democracy*. New York: Routledge, 2001.

Sabato, Larry J. *The Rise of Political Consultants*. New York: Basic Books, 1981.

Thurber, James, and Candice J. Nelson. *Campaigns and Elections American Style*. Boulder, CO: Westview, 1995.

"The Political Pages," *Campaigns and Elections* (annual editions).

NOTES

1. Adapted from David Von Drehle, "The Night That Would Not End," *The Washington Post*, November 9, 2000, A1, 36. Kevin Sack and Frank Bruni, "How Gore Stopped Short on His Way to Concede," *The New York Times*, November 9, 2000, A1. *The New York Times* reports the same story with nearly identical quotes from the candidates.

2. James A. Thurber, "The Transformation of American Campaigns," in *Campaigns and Elections American Style*, ed. James A. Thurber and Candice J. Nelson (Boulder, CO: Westview, 1995), 4; Tip O'Neill with Gary Hymel, *All Politics Is Local* (Holbrook, MA: Bob Adams, 1994), xv.

3. Stanley B. Greenberg, *Middle Class Dreams* (New York: Times Books, 1996), 222–25.

4. Theodore H. White, *The Making of the President 1960* (New York: Pocket Books, 1961), 340–49.

5. "USA Statistics in Brief—Population and Vital Statistics," *U.S. Census Bureau*, accessed June 18, 2003. *www.census.gov/statab/www/poppart.html*.

6. Martin P. Wattenberg, *The Rise of Candidate Centered-Politics: Presidential Elections of the 1980s* (Cambridge, MA: Harvard University Press, 1991), 33 for quote on patronage and the Australian ballot.

7. Ibid. See pages 36–46, on the decline of party identification and party voting. Wattenberg is also credited with the term *candidate-centered politics.*

8. Chris Arterton, "New Relationships," *Campaigns and Elections* (April 2000): 22, quote; U.S. Census Bureau, accessed on July 15, 2003. *www.census.gov/qfd/states/06000.html.* The Census Bureau estimates that California's population in 2001 was 34,501,000; thus, the population total was rounded up to 35 million.

9. David McCullough, *John Adams* (New York: Simon & Schuster, 2001), 462, on the "His Rotundity" quote; Paul F. Boller, Jr., *Presidential Campaigns* (New York: Oxford, 1984), 12, on the "murder, robbery . . . and adultery" citation.

10. Data calculated from *Campaigns and Elections: The Political Pages 2002–2003* (released March 2002); Joseph R. Cerrell, "Ever Increasing Speed," *Campaigns and Elections* (April 2000): 25, quote.

11. Dick Morris, *Behind the Oval Office: Getting Reelected Against All Odds* (New York: Renaissance, 1998).

12. See James Moore and Wayne Slater on *Bush's Brain: How Karl Rove Made George W. Bush Presidential* (Hoboken, NJ: Wiley and Sons, 2003).

13. Candice J. Nelson, "Spending in the 2000 Elections," in *Financing the 2000 Election,* ed. David J. Magleby (Washington, DC: Brookings, 2001). Nelson states that Bush spent $186 million and Gore $120 million in the 2000 presidential election campaign, 29. "2000 Presidential Election," *CMAG Eye Newsletter* December/January 2000, 1. *CMAG* provides the amount of advertising expenditures by Bush and Gore. Accessed June 22, 2003 from *www. politicsontv.com.*

14. Dan Balz, "Surge of Cash Puts Pressure on Insurgent Dean to Deliver Votes," *The Washington Post,* July 2 2003, A1 on the Dean campaign. Go to *MoveOn.org* for the most current list on activists at *www.moveon.org.* The 2-million membership level was mentioned on the home page as of July 15, 2003.

CHAPTER 2

The Motivation to Run for Office

Ambition must be made to counteract ambition.
—*James Madison,* **Federalist No. 51**

What separates politicians from ordinary people is their extraordinary ambition to run for public office. Although the techniques of campaigns change, the motivations to run for office are still very much the same today as when Madison wrote his prophetic words two centuries ago. It takes a great deal of nerve for a candidate to campaign for the votes of 50,000, 500,000, or 100 million people. However, the motivation to seek public office means that candidates select themselves. "Although national parties have recently expanded their efforts to recruit and finance candidates . . . most serious congressional aspirants operate out of choice and necessity as political entrepreneurs." Thus, the candidate-centered politics of today heightens those same individual motivations and ambitions mentioned in Federalist No. 51.[1]

THE MOTIVATION TO RUN FOR OFFICE: AN OVERVIEW

Chapter 2 explains the motivating forces that inspire prospective candidates to run for office. The motivations can be systemic (issue driven, political reform), service-related (best person for the job, political experience) or personal (compelling personal reason, opportunity, and ego). Overlap among these typologies also exists. For example, Congressman David Price (D-NC) points toward his strong religious belief rooted in the Baptist Church and tenure as Democratic state party chair as two instrumental factors motivating him to run for the U.S. House in 1986. Price exemplifies how the normative and cognitive values of an individual, based on personal experiences, serve as inspirations for a candidacy. Furthermore, the altruism of public service is an intrinsic and positive component not divorced from any motivation. Many candidates abandon the private sector to run for public office, which is not self-serving. Motivations are often interrelated, complex, and not mutually exclusive, although our examination categorizes them individually. One aspiration this chapter does not discuss is the incumbent motivation—getting reelected—since that incentive is self-explanatory.[2]

Systemic Motivations

Issues often lead an individual into the political arena to fight for or against a particular cause. A candidate may be a lifetime advocate of or a newcomer to a cause who decides to run for office to bring about change. For example, former Representative Pat Schroeder (D-CO) first ran for public office in 1972 to advance environmental, women's, and defense spending reduction issues. Issues serve as a noble or an idealistic motivation to run for public office to bring about change and better people's lives.[3]

Reforming the political system harkens back to Thomas Jefferson's saying that "a little rebellion now and then is a good idea." The explicit meaning of Jefferson's adage seems to be extreme by today's standards but the implicit desire to end perceived corruption or scandal in the political system provides strong motivation for a reformer. A "populist" (or a candidate of the people) may work from outside the two-party system (or within the two-party system) to bring about political change. Thus, the dynamic from an outside third-party force and within the two-party system illustrates reform as a candidate motivation.[4]

Service-Related Motivations

Party leaders and (or) citizens recruit public figures of great stature to run for office because they view that leader as the best person for the job. Leadership demonstrated by great military generals such as Dwight D. Eisenhower and Ulysses S. Grant provide instances of war heroes who run for president on "honor and country." These candidates believe in the transferability of skill from one enterprise (the military) to another (governing). Popular local politicians, such as mayors, sometimes become governors (e.g., George Voinovich of Ohio) because leadership is seen as a transferable political skill. However, there is no guarantee of success even for an "annointed" candidate. For instance, the White House and leading Republicans persuaded former Los Angeles Mayor Richard Riorden to seek the 2002 GOP nomination for California governor because of his popularity in opinion polls. Riorden's bid failed because of missteps in his campaign and charges that he was a RINO (Republican In Name Only). In other instances, political novices run when citizens recruit them to be leaders (e.g., Ross Perot who ran as a third-party presidential candidate in 1992 and 1996). Candidates with prior public service, such as Riorden, may be less idealistic but run because of a sense of duty to their political party. Elevated self-esteem based on prior military, business, or public service success characterizes this type of candidate.[5]

Political experience often encourages an elected politician to run for higher office, or it spurs a losing candidate to try again. Furthermore, political experiences can inspire an individual immersed in politics from family connections to become a candidate. For example, a scion of a well-known political family such as President George W. Bush or his brother Governor Jeb Bush (R-FL) gained insights into the machinations of politics through their father President George Bush, Sr. Politically experienced candidates possess the confidence and understanding of the give-and-take of politics that inexperienced candidates usually lack.

Personal Motivations

A traumatic experience or a tragedy provides a *compelling personal reason* to run for office. Congresswoman Carolyn McCarthy (D-NY) elected to the U.S. House in 1996 was motivated to run for Congress when her husband and several others were slain on a Long Island railroad passenger car by a psychopath wielding a firearm. Gun control advocacy became her newfound mission. She ran for Congress to tighten restrictions on handguns and other firearms.

Opportunity indicates an opening created by reapportionment, retirement, or a political misstep that provides a fertile environment inviting a challenger bid. Congressional reapportionment can create opportunities for favored candidates of political parties. The

Republican state legislature created an Orlando congressional district for Republican Florida State Senate Leader Tom Feeney in 2002, who won the election with 62 percent of the vote. Senator Daniel Patrick Moynihan's retirement provided an heir apparent, Hillary Rodham Clinton with an opportunity to run for an open U.S. Senate seat. Political miscalculations can create an opportunity for a challenger to defeat an incumbent such as the 1996 rematch between David Price (D-NC) and Fred Heineman (R-NC) in North Carolina's Fourth Congressional District. The recall election of Democratic Governor Gray Davis in California provided an unexpected opportunity for actor Arnold Schwarzenegger, a Republican, to win the governorship in October 2003. Previously, Schwarzenegger had turned down an opportunity to run for California governor in the 2002 election. Thus, opportunistic motivations result when the benefits of running outweigh the costs.[6]

Ego is the most identifiable reason that candidates run for office. One Republican media consultant who wished to remain anonymous stated, "I don't care what anyone says I have never known a candidate who *didn't* run for office because of ego." While some politicians have self-destructive and insecure egos termed "active negative" by political scientist James David Barber in his study on presidents (e.g., Presidents Richard Nixon and Lyndon Johnson), others have healthy or "active positive" egos. Active positive egos make the engagement in politics affirmative and enjoyable (e.g., as Presidents Franklin Roosevelt or John Kennedy). A singular egocentric motivation would probably be self-destructive. However, most motivational aspects of running for office, as previously mentioned, are interrelated. The case studies that follow demonstrate how each motivation illustrates a candidate's desire to run for office.[7]

ISSUES

"I calculated at one time that if my grandson was a dentist and we kept going the way we were going, he'd have to do 900 crowns just to pay his part of the interest on the national debt." Congressman Charlie Norwood (R-GA) articulated this point as his motivation for running for Congress. Norwood was a dentist who practiced in Augusta, Georgia (a city famous for hosting the Masters golf tournament). The dentistry practice that Norwood operated made him wary of government spending and regulations put on small businesses.

Norwood sold his dentistry practice to run for the U.S. House in 1994 believing that taxes on business had become so onerous that they were driving people out of professions such as his. His goal was to change government tax, regulatory, and budget policy as part of the larger agenda from the "Republican revolution" of 1994. Charlie Norwood's election illustrates that issue-driven campaigns often feature common citizens turning to politics in order to bring about substantive policy change. Candidates may be motivated by single issues, multiple issues, and (or) the party's national platform.[8]

Single-Issue Motivation

Candidates motivated by one issue tend to be ideological. An issue such as abortion, the death penalty, family values, gay rights, the environment, lower taxes, or national security may be the primary focus of a candidate. Senator Eugene McCarthy's (D-MN) opposition to the Vietnam War led to his 1968 Democratic presidential nomination bid when he almost defeated President Lyndon Johnson in the New Hampshire primary. Billionaire magazine publisher Steve Forbes (R-NJ) ran for the 2000 Republican presidential nomination supporting a flat-tax rate system to replace the current progressive system (tax rates increase with income) arguing that it promoted fairness.

The motivational force is singular; however, candidates may change course during the campaign and expand their agenda to broaden their base of support. Universal health care served as the initial motivation for Dr. Howard Dean, former Vermont governor, to run for the Democratic presidential nomination in 2004. Dean's issue portfolio expanded once war with Iraq became imminent when he announced his opposition in the fall of 2002. Thus, a single issue may not sustain a campaign through an entire election season.

Multiple-Issue Motivations

More than one issue can impel an individual to run for office. Groups of similar issues (e.g., jobs/economy) or different issues (e.g., foreign policy and the environment) develop from personal interests, concerns, or experiences and provide aspirations to run for office. Patricia Schroeder, a homemaker from Denver, Colorado exemplifies someone motivated by multiple-issue concerns. Schroeder ran for the U.S. House at a time (1972) when few professional women or women working at home even tried. The impetus to run emanated from a conversation between Schroeder and her husband Jim. Both were well-known local political activists. Patricia's community activism and local reputation as an adjunct constitutional law professor (she was a Harvard Law School graduate) provided her standing in the community. Jim served as a member of an ad hoc committee searching for a candidate to challenge one-term Republican incumbent, Arch McKevitt. McKevitt had established his public reputation by shutting down a well-known pornographic movie called *I Am Curious Yellow* when he was the local district attorney. Jim mentioned to Patricia that her name had come up at an ad hoc committee meeting as a possible challenger to McKevitt. She replied, "why should I be the designated kamikaze?" Her husband said, "you think that the government's policies about the Vietnam War and the environment are wrong-headed, and you're always urging your students to get involved. It's an opportunity that may not come again." Ms. Schroeder recounts in her book that these policy reasons convinced her to run for Congress.[9]

The Norwood and Schroeder stories demonstrate how potential candidates relate national issues to concerns affecting citizens in their own congressional districts. Ideological compatibility between the candidate and the constituency should correlate closely in most instances to win election. However, the motivation to run does not prevent third party candidates from running for office. Third party candidates tend to be issue or ideologically driven wherever they appear on the political continuum, from the American Taxpayers Party on the right to the Socialist Workers Party on the left. Even in an era of candidate-centered politics, major political parties may unite on a coherent party platform of issues as Republicans did in 1994.

Party Platform

"If we break this contract, throw us out." Newt Gingrich (R-GA), the House Minority Whip spoke these words on the House steps on September 27, 1994, as 367 House Republican candidates, incumbents and challengers, signed the Republican "Contract with America." The "Contract" was a platform or series of 11 promises that Republican candidates pledged they would vote on if elected during the first 100 days of the next session. Republicans needed to win a majority of

U.S. House seats in the election in order to enact their agenda. Among the "Contract's" provisions were a $500 per child tax cut, lower business taxes, welfare reform, term limits for members of Congress, an anti-crime package, limits on punitive damages in lawsuits, and a balanced budget amendment. The agenda of the "Contract with America" motivated the Republican party's conservative base to turn out on election day. Republicans won simultaneous control of the U.S. House and Senate for the first time in 40 years. Republicans presented a philosophical belief system that was an alternative to that of Democrats, based on a less intrusive federal government. Although the contract provided only part of the explanation for why Republicans triumphed, it was important in stimulating the party's base to get out and vote.[10]

REFORMING THE POLITICAL SYSTEM

The American tradition of reform is part of our historical political culture. Fighting corruption, ending patronage, reducing money interests in politics, and promoting public health and safety are among the common attributes of reform politics. Reform took center stage in the late 19th century when Eastern railroad owners systematically overcharged small Midwestern farmers to transport their produce to market. These events set the stage for the emergence of James B. Weaver's "People's Party" as a potent political force in the rural Midwest and South winning 13 percent of the vote in 1892.

The "Age of Reform" continued from the late 19th into the early 20th century as fighting political corruption and promoting a safer workplace motivated a slew of reformers to run for political office. Sam "Golden Rule" Jones—elected mayor of Toledo, Ohio, in 1897— and Eugene V. Debs—a labor activist, who was five times the Socialist party's presidential nominee (1900–1920)—were two famous reformers bent on fighting corruption and special interests. The reform movement reemerged in the 1970s when the Watergate scandal forced President Richard Nixon to resign. Furthermore, scandals such as Koreagate and ABSCAM involving the corruption and bribery of congressional members following Watergate spawned a wave of reform. The first wave of modern federal campaign finance reforms emerged during the 1970s. The Ethics in Government Act of 1978 required public appointees to disclose their personal finances.

As a result, reform politicians became more active in the political process.[11]

Reform politicians often thrive on controversy and seek to promote change, either as an external force (e.g., Jesse Ventura) or within the two-party system (e.g., John McCain). Other reformers want change but approach the process as conciliators (e.g., Angus King). Unlike an issue motivation, reform is often part of a larger social movement to bring about systemic change.

Reform as an External Political Force

Third party or independent candidacies serve as *external* forces to change the status quo represented by the two-party system. Third party candidates can change the dynamic of a political contest when they are articulate, innovative, and able to mobilize grassroots support. Jesse Ventura's (I-MN) successful gubernatorial campaign as the Reform Party candidate in 1998 provides an excellent illustration of how changing the status quo to bring about change is a major impetus for a candidacy. Ventura believed that the bitter partisanship between Democrats and Republicans in Minnesota politics could be resolved only by interjecting the force of his personality as a counterweight against both Democrats and Republicans. Ventura's large physical presence was imposing. His extraordinary life included military service as a Navy SEAL, a decade-long career as a professional wrestling star, and a long stint as a television commentator for the World Wrestling Federation. Ventura later served as mayor of Brooklyn Park, Minnesota, a suburb of Minneapolis, and was credited for opening up city council meetings to the public airwaves and for providing individual citizens more access to the city council.[12]

Ventura's gubernatorial bid was, in part, premised on his campaign refrain that "I am no career politician" (a line from a rap song he had recorded). His distaste for the two major parties was evident throughout the campaign. In one off-beat campaign commercial, a Ventura-like action figure beat up "Evil Special Interest Man" and said, "I don't want your stupid money!" The commercial symbolized Ventura's view that both political parties were tools of special interests, and this helped characterize his motivation: to shake up the political establishment.[13]

Not all reformers are polarizing political forces like Ventura. Political reformers running as conciliators such as independent gubernatorial candidate Angus King (ME) elected in 1994 stress reducing political polarization as part of their appeal. King an environmental activist, a former U.S. Senate staff aide, and a television talk show host articulated his campaign as a bid to break the deadlock that existed between a squabbling Democratic legislature and a Republican governor in Maine. King saw himself as an external mediator seeking to change the political discourse in Maine by positioning himself between both parties. As a polarizing or a conciliating force, political reform reveals itself as a potent and vital motivation for candidates to run locally, statewide or nationally.[14]

Reform Within the Party System

Reformers sometimes develop their political interests through formative life experiences. The events of the 1960s such as the movement to attain civil rights or to protest the Vietnam War, served as an impetus to get many Baby Boomers involved in politics. The late Senator Paul Wellstone's (D-MN) career symbolized how a protester became involved in Democratic party politics to bring about political change.

Wellstone's personal background was unusual for a populist because as a high school student he was more interested in wrestling than politics. However, the civil rights movement and the Vietnam War kindled Wellstone's interest in politics as a college student. Wellstone continued with his studies, received a Ph.D in political science, and then accepted an appointment as a political science professor at Carleton College in Minnesota at the height of the Vietnam War. Wellstone taught a course on the politics of protest that was popular among students. The dynamic and controversial professor was soon living out his academic dreams by demonstrating with Hormel meatpacking strikers in Texas and participating in other protests including one leading to his arrest. Seeking an alternative means to bring about change, Wellstone ran for State Auditor as a Democrat. His statewide candidate experience enabled him to become Reverend Jesse Jackson's (D) Minnesota presidential campaign manager in 1988. Jackson lost the primary but the experience emboldened Wellstone to take his own long-shot bid running for the U.S. Senate in 1990 as he defeated incumbent Republican Rudy Boschwitz.[15]

Wellstone and Ventura represent two Minnesotans illustrating different variations of political reform: *externally* as a third-party force as illustrated by Ventura or *internally* through the two-party system as demonstrated by Wellstone. The nature and dynamic of reform may change over time, but the motive to make the political system fairer, more open, and less corrupt is timeless.

"THE BEST PERSON" FOR THE JOB

Imagine the scenario as politicians, academics, businesspeople, and other opinion leaders approach you at home, at your official place of business, or at social functions and tell you that *your country needs you*. *Newsweek* magazine's cover story from November 1994 featured the most popular public figure in America, former general and Persian Gulf hero Colin Powell. The headline of the issue was "Can this man save America?" Powell declined to run for the Republican presidential nomination in 1996 and 2000, even though early polls showed him leading other prospective Republican candidates for his party's presidential nomination in both years. Powell said he did not have the "passion and commitment" to run for the presidency. Almost a half-century earlier, military hero Dwight D. Eisenhower had come to a different conclusion. In 1949, the Republican governor of New York, Thomas Dewey, secretly met with Eisenhower. Dewey lost the 1948 presidential election by a very narrow margin to President Harry S. Truman. Dewey snuck in through a back entrance to Eisenhower's private office at Columbia University where the former general and World War II hero was serving as the university's president. Dewey made a dramatic pitch by telling Eisenhower he was the "only" man who could "save this country from going to Hades in the handbasket of paternalism, socialism, and dictatorship." Eisenhower resisted all public and private pleas to run for the presidency until the groundswell of public support overwhelmed him in early 1952. Eisenhower relented to public pressure and gave his assent to a presidential bid. Imagine how difficult it is to resist flattering appeals such as the one articulated by Dewey to Eisenhower feeding the ego and fueling the ambition for a prospective candidate. He later said, "the presidency is something that should never be sought, (but) could never be refused."[16]

Recruiting Candidates with Public Standing

Candidates recruited to run for public office by parties may include political notables (e.g., Ted Kennedy's 1980 presidential bid),

HILLARY RODHAM CLINTON: FIRST PRESIDENTIAL
SPOUSE ELECTED TO THE SENATE

The portrayal of Hillary Rodham Clinton as a valuable policy player by supporters and as an ambitious opportunist by opponents characterized most of her tenure as the nation's first lady. The impeachment and trial of her husband on charges of lying under oath and obstructing justice concerning his affair with former White House intern Monica Lewinsky resulted in a reexamination of the first lady's public persona. Public opinion polls at the time showed that Hillary Rodham Clinton's personal approval rating skyrocketed upward because of sympathy for her plight as a woman betrayed and deceived by her husband. Mrs. Clinton treated the Lewinsky affair as a private matter not subject to public discussion. This "gentler" image of Hillary Rodham Clinton seemed to soften her controversial image as an intrepid policy player in the White House.

During the winter of the impeachment trial, speculation about a successor to New York's revered senior Senator Daniel Patrick Moynihan (D) had begun in earnest. The Clintons were planning to move to New York at the conclusion of his presidency. Speculation that Democrats might draft Hillary Clinton to run for Moynihan's senate seat was predicated on four factors: She had universal name recognition; she demonstrated fundraising skills matched by few in politics; she had acquired international and domestic policy credentials as first lady; and she engendered public sympathy (due to the Lewinsky affair) making her a less viable target of the political right. Clinton also faced the challenge of answering criticisms that she was a "carpetbagger" and opportunist by moving to New York.

Clinton waited for Democratic party leaders to approach her. Professional politicians privately urging her to run received a significant boost in the winter of 1999 when Harlem's powerful congressional representative Charles Rangel made a surprise announcement. He said that the state Democratic party "'pulled together an offer that the First Lady can't refuse,' including a guarantee that the nomination for senator of New York would be hers for the asking, without a primary." Rangel, one of

New York's top power brokers, had undermined the only other prospective Democrat running for the Senate, Congresswoman Nita Lowey. Lowey quickly deferred to Clinton knowing that she had no chance to win the party nomination. Rangel's prophetic words helped deliver the nomination to Hillary Rodham Clinton, who strode to a comfortable victory over Republican Congressman Rick Lazio of Long Island in the fall election by a 55–43 percent margin.[17]

entertainment celebrities (Ronald Reagan's 1966 California gubernatorial bid), and even presidential spouses. For example, when Democratic Senator Daniel Patrick Moynihan (D-NY) announced his retirement leaders and activists from the Democratic party in New York state started a "draft Hillary" Clinton movement to succeed Moynihan in 2000. Talk of a draft coincided with President Clinton's impeachment trial in the Senate during the winter of 1999 (see the box on Hillary Rodham Clinton). Drafted candidates run to fill a void within the leadership structure of a local, state, or national party. The drafted candidate believe that their participation may stave off their party's defeat on election day.[18]

POLITICAL EXPERIENCE

Experience through public office or public service can fuel candidate aspirations. Name recognition heightens the attractiveness of candidates to their community or state electorates. Public service experience builds self-confidence as officials practice the rituals of success they have learned. Success breeds ambition and many politicians seek higher office. Of the eight new U.S. senators elected in 2002, four were House members, one an attorney general, one a former mayor, one a former U.S. senator, and one a former cabinet official.[19]

Suffering political defeat and being the scion of a well-known political family represent experiences unique to the understanding of campaign politics. Defeat by an opponent in a close contest can quash an individual's ambition or can energize them to run again. Growing up in a prominent political family provides insight concerning the campaign process and public service. Mark Pryor (D-AR) and John E. Sununu (R-NH) both elected to the U.S. Senate in 2002 were children of famous politicians. Pryor's father served as Arkansas governor and U.S. senator, whereas Sununu's father was a New Hampshire governor and White House chief-of-staff. Few receive this intimate experience and political schooling. No matter how political experience manifests itself as a motivation to seek office, it is characteristic of power-seeking politicians' possessing great faith in their abilities.

The Experience of Losing Motivates a Candidate to Run Again

Political experience can enhance a candidate's personal drive to succeed. One of the great experiential lessons for politicians is that if they fail to succeed at first, they might try again. The experience of losing helped Richard Nixon and Ronald Reagan achieve their goal of winning the presidency. More recently, the election of John Ensign (R-NV) to the U.S. Senate in 2000 after losing his first attempt in 1998 provides an excellent illustration of how political experience benefits a second-time candidate.

Ensign was an active born-again Christian and veterinarian, represented Las Vegas in the U.S. Congress winning election by a narrow margin in 1994 and 1996. The Congressman challenged incumbent Senator Harry Reid (D-NV) in 1998. The socially conservative Ensign ran a hard-fought campaign against Reid known for his prodigious ability to bring federal projects back to Nevada. Ensign lost one of the closest senate races in recent history to Reid by a razor-thin margin of 428 votes out of 216,872 total votes! The recount took several weeks and the results took a tremendous personal toll on Ensign. Fate took a positive turn for Ensign when Nevada's senior Senator Richard Bryan (D-NV) announced in 1999 that he would not be a candidate for reelection in 2000. Ensign immediately jumped into the race where he faced a less formidable opponent compared with 1998. Ensign's tremendous propensity to raise money ($4.9 million) in a small state combined with his high name recognition enabled him to defeat Democratic attorney Ed Bernstein by a substantial margin (55–40 percent). Reflecting on his victory, Ensign thought back to his loss against Harry Reid in 1998. "That loss was one of the better things that ever happened to me. . . . Your greatest victories in life come from your greatest defeats. You can learn so much about yourself. I think I needed a good dose of humility back then. It was good for me." Losing deflates an ego and enables a politician to become a better public servant according to Ensign because the loser can rationally evaluate his or her strengths, weaknesses, and dedication to public service upon reflection.[20]

Politics by Immersion

Scions of aristocratic political families such as Adams, Kennedy, Roosevelt, and Bush learned politics by immersion from an early age. Such immersion can breed great self-esteem (e.g., Franklin Roosevelt, John Kennedy, George W. Bush) and can ensure that proper political connections are made to advance one's career. Franklin Delano Roosevelt (FDR) illustrates how personal political experience benefits a politician. Roosevelt was the scion of a well-known political family, which had already produced a president (his cousin Theodore). FDR served as the Secretary of the Navy during the Wilson administration (appointed), and then was selected to be the vice presidential running mate for Democratic nominee James M. Cox in 1920 (they lost to Warren G. Harding and Calvin Coolidge).

Roosevelt parlayed his family connections and previous political experience to run successfully for Governor of New York in 1928 following his partial recovery from polio. Four years later, FDR won the presidency defeating Herbert Hoover at the height of the "Great Depression." Presidential scholar James Barber said that Roosevelt's parents "had infused a deep confidence . . . a self-esteem so strong that it could overcome the apparent end of his career when he was toppled by polio." Roosevelt's parents had inculcated an expectation of public service from an early age, and his life might have been far different if he had been raised in an environment without emotional support, financial advantage, and political connections.[21]

COMPELLING PERSONAL REASON

An event or a tragedy that profoundly affects an individual can provide a compelling personal reason to run for office. This goes beyond a personal interest in an issue. Compelling personal reasons are life-altering experiences that provide an altruistic motivation—to make a difference in people's lives, not to satisfy one's ego. In this section, we examine three contemporary women politicians who faced unusual hurdles and overcame them in their pursuit to win public office. Carolyn McCarthy, Olympia Snowe, and Patty Murray illustrate how tragedies and other events motivate someone to win public office.

Personal Tragedy

Carolyn McCarthy was a dedicated professional nurse with a happy home life in suburban Long Island. All of that changed one morning in 1993 when a deranged gunman named Colin Ferguson opened fire on a Long Island railway car, killing her husband and severely wounding her son. In all, six people died and 19 were wounded that morning. The horror of that day is still palpable for McCarthy. As she has said, "don't let anyone tell you that it will go away." Her son, whom many doctors believed would die from head wounds managed to survive. The tragedy turned McCarthy into a gun control advocate. She tried unsuccessfully to lobby her Congressman, Daniel Frisa (R-NY) to vote against the repeal of the assault weapons ban. McCarthy was so angry at his decision that she decided to run against him in 1996. Although she was a registered Republican, the Long Island nurse-turned-politician decided not to run in the Republican primary because Frisa had sewn up his party's nomination. McCarthy then switched parties and challenged the incumbent in the general election as a Democrat. The Long Island nurse was such a political novice that when informed House Democratic Minority Leader Dick Gephardt wanted to meet her she replied, "Who's Dick Gephardt?" McCarthy's naïveté about politics only made her motivation seem more genuine to voters. She triumphed over Daniel Frisa on election day 1996 by a 16-point margin.[22]

Senator Olympia Snowe's (R-ME) compelling personal journey shaped by tragedy differed from Carolyn McCarthy's experience. Both of Snowe's parents died when she was nine years old. She and her older brother (John) went to live with her Aunt Mary and Uncle Jim. In the tenth grade, Olympia lost her beloved Uncle Jim to a premature death. However, the sequence of tragedies in Snowe's life did not end. After completing college, she married Peter Snowe. Peter ran successfully for the Maine state legislature in 1972. Driving home in a snowstorm following a state legislative session one evening in 1973, Peter was killed when his car crashed. Friends, family, and state Republican politicians urged Snowe to run for the seat to fill her husband's unexpired term. Snowe recalled, "I have always tried to turn negatives into positives. . . . With the tremendous devastation of Peter's death came a sensitivity to the tremendous difficulties that other women in similar situations face—such as raising children alone." Motivation stemming from tragedy has enabled Snowe to become an effective advocate for women and children during her tenure in the Senate.[23]

Gender-Bias Motivations

Gender bias can immobilize or can motivate an individual to change the political system because its effects are so personal. Cultural roles and mores are barriers that sometimes impede opportunities for women. Senator Patty Murray (D-WA) recounts the event that prompted her involvement in politics:

> My kids attended the preschool program (at a local community college), and I took courses and did volunteer work. One day I went to class and the teacher said, "I'm sorry. The program is going to end. The state legislature is taking the funding away". . . . I decided to go to the state capitol in Olympia, to talk to some legislators and convince them of their mistake. . . . Finally, one legislator I'd pigeonholed listened to my story and then let me know what he really thought. . . . "Lady, that's a really nice story but you can't get the funding restored. . . . You can't make a difference. You're just a mom in tennis shoes."[24]

The transforming event of Murray's life leading to public service is hardly as traumatic as that of Carolyn McCarthy or Olympia Snowe, but it is a life-changing experience. This conversation crystallized a perception—rarely stated in public—that the opinions of homemakers are not important.

Murray said she was "seethed" by the experience. The lack of sensitivity and indifference to mothers provided the impetus for Murray to becoming a full-time political activist. Murray lost her first race for the Shoreline School Board in Washington state where she resided. However, when a vacancy appeared on the school board, she received an appointment. Her career moved forward with her election to the State Senate (1998) and then the U.S. Senate (1992). Patty Murray like Olympia Snowe took a negative and turned it into a positive. Compelling personal reasons often motivate candidates to run for office to improve the welfare of citizens at home and across the nation.[25]

OPPORTUNITY

"Is the race winnable?" This is the essential calculation that most challengers consider before deciding whether to be a candidate. Opportunity avails itself through open-seat contests (featuring no incumbent), races featuring electorally vulnerable incumbents, and elections in which incompetence, missteps, or scandal enhance the opportunity for a challenger.

Open-Seat Contests and Incumbent Vulnerability

Open-seat contests where no incumbent runs for reelection provide the best opportunity to seek public office. In 2002, 49 out of 435 U.S. House seats were open at the beginning of the election year. Seven U.S. Senate seats featured no incumbent (out of 34 contested), and most importantly, 20 out of 36 Governor's races were open-seat contests. (Most states term-limit governors, resulting in more open-seat contests.) The 1992 election year, often dubbed "the Year of the Woman," showed women increasing their representation in the U.S. Senate from two to seven seats and in the U.S. House from 28 to 42 seats. The substantial number of open-seats that year contributed to victories by women candidates.[26]

Senate incumbents tend to be more vulnerable than their U.S. House counterparts are. Reelection rates of house incumbents from 1978–2000 exceeded 94 percent compared to 82 percent for senate incumbents. Senate races tend to attract better-known, wealthier, and more experienced challengers. Furthermore, senate races receive more press exposure than local house races. The resources and (or) public standing of a challenger can weaken an incumbent's chances of winning reelection. Personal wealth or the prodigious ability to raise money help a challenger buy name recognition, the first step toward building public support. Department store heir Mark Dayton (D) of Minnesota and RealPlayer vice president Maria Cantwell (D) of Washington used their personal wealth to fuel their successful 2000 senate campaigns. Weak or vulnerable incumbents may motivate quality challengers to oppose them such as governors. Former Governor George Allen of (R-VA) and Governor Thomas Carper (D-DE) defeated incumbent U.S. Senators in 2000. Incumbent vulnerability increases with the stature of the office. As a result, senate races have a greater likelihood of being competitive than house races.[27]

Incompetence or Missteps Provide Opportunity

Incumbent vulnerability through incompetence, misstep, or scandal enhances the opportunity for an opponent. If any of these conditions is present, then opportunity becomes a much stronger motivation because the perceived benefits of possible victory (public office) outweigh the costs (time and money) of running. Senator Ted Kennedy (D-MA) challenged President Jimmy Carter (D-GA) for the 1980 Democratic presidential nomination because he believed that the president was responsible for the nation's economic recession. In addition, four prominent Republicans including former Governor Ronald Reagan (R-CA), Senate Minority Leader Howard Baker (R-TN), former U.N. Ambassador George Bush, Sr. (R-TX), and Senator Robert Dole (R-KS) challenged for the Republican presidential nomination that year to face President Carter. Negative voter attitudes regarding Carter's competence to manage the economy out of recession and his failure to bring home American hostages held in Iran undermined his candidacy and led to his defeat.[28]

Congressman David Price's (D-NC) 1996 campaign illustrated how an opponent's electoral vulnerability and verbal misstep translated into an opportunity to win back the U.S. House seat he lost in 1994. Price had served four terms in the House when the "Republican revolution" of 1994 swept him out of office.

Fred Heineman (R-NC), a former Raleigh, NC police chief, defeated Price by 1200 votes (or less than one percent of the total vote). Soon after his defeat, Price decided to run for his former seat believing that Heineman would be a weak incumbent given the strong two-party competition in the district. Heineman made matters worse when he was quoted in the *Raleigh News and Observer* on October 21, 1995. The reporter asked Heineman where he stood on the "income scale." Heineman's salary and pensions added up to $184,000 per year. Heineman replied, "when I see someone making $300,000 to $750,000 a year, that's middle class." The implication that somehow he was less than "middle class" did not play well with his constituents. Heineman's foible enabled Price to have both a *motive* and an *issue* in his election bid. Price's "Earth to Fred" ads asked whether Heineman dwelled in the real world of middle-class citizens. Heineman helped make the race winnable for Price with his comments in the *News Observer* demonstrating how out of touch he was with ordinary constituents. The result was a victory for Price by a 54–44 percent margin. A challenger must possess good political instincts to seize an opportunity, which is rare given the prodigious reelection rate of incumbents.[29]

EGO

Ego enables a politician to appeal to thousands or millions of voters. It fuels ambition and generates a single-minded desire to run for office. According to famous psychoanalyst Sigmund Freud, the ego deals with external reality. That external reality is on display when candidates seek the presidency or other high offices because voters have so much exposure to their personalities. A politician is often self-centered but also self-confident, believing that *he or she* is the best candidate. Ego is not inherently evil or Machiavellian; it can be positive as Barber noted in the cases of Presidents Theodore and Franklin Roosevelt. Both men regarded politics as an affirmative pursuit, and their well-considered opinions of their own abilities did not make them maniacal or self-destructive.[30]

Ego and Ambition

In this context, ego and ambition are inseparable. As political scientists Fowler and McClure write in their book, *Political Ambition*, "there are those who have spent most of their lives on the edges of politics but have long hankered for public office. Suddenly, this desire flames up under the heat of an explosive public issue or the glow of a noteworthy career success." Furthermore, a viable candidate is not on the fringes of politics, but someone with a single-minded approach and strategic ambition to win election.[31]

Positive Self-Confidence Can Breed Success

A single-minded desire to win illustrates how an improbable underdog triumphed in a special congressional election held in Jefferson Parish (New Orleans). David Vitter's underdog status did not undermine his self-confidence that he could win election. Congressman Bob Livingston (R-LA), slated to become the next Speaker of the House, suddenly resigned his congressional seat in December 1998.

Livingston admitted to marital infidelities after Larry Flynt's *Hustler* magazine conducted an investigation into his personal affairs. Livingston's resignation led to a special election to fill his vacant congressional seat in 1999.

What ensued was a circus-like primary campaign of well-known, controversial, and unusual candidates, including former Grand Wizard of the Ku Klux Klan and former gubernatorial candidate David Duke, wealthy ophthalmologist Monica Monica, former governor David Treen, and State Legislators Bill Strain and David Vitter. Of the candidates who were running in the non-partisan primary, Strain was the only Democrat; Democrats and Republicans run alike in the same primary in Louisiana. The veteran Treen (age 70) was supported by the Republican party establishment in his bid. Duke had run competitive senatorial and gubernatorial races in the recent past. Monica Monica's entry was ironic given that the special election was taking place at the height of President Clinton's impeachment trial concerning his affair with Monica Lewinsky. Finally, David Vitter, a young state legislator representing a district within New Orleans filled out the candidate field.[32]

The 1999 special election was an atmosphere of huge egos and political appetites. Vitter's ambition seemed greater than his ability to win against better-known opposition. But, as he said, "We need a younger congressman, *like me*, so we can start building up the seniority we lost when Bob Livingston resigned" (emphasis added). Vitter portrayed himself as a younger face in politics, but also as a skilled and energetic legislator. Thus, Vitter's ambition, self-esteem, age, and focus enabled him to set himself apart from his opposition. The top two vote-getters Vitter and Treen, made it into the runoff since no candidate received 50 percent of the vote in the first round of voting. Not intimidated by his more well-known and experienced opponent, Vitter defeated Treen by a 51–49 percent margin in the May runoff election. Compare Vitter's positive self-confidence with David Duke's negative and racist beliefs calling for white supremacy. In an autobiography published at the time, immodestly titled *My Awakening*, Duke reaffirmed his white supremacist views by saying the "belief in racial equality is the modern equivalent of believing the earth is flat." The book's release date coincided closely with the special election campaign. Duke's articulation of racial superiority proved to be self-destructive and ultimately led to his defeat.[33]

Presidential Ambition

No one expects a presidential candidate to have a small ego. The world's most important job requires requisite ambition. Taming that ambition remains the more difficult task because the motivation to run for president can come across as an egomaniacal pursuit with candidates selling themselves to the exclusion of ideas. Rarely does that occur, but the perception of it can have a profound effect on a presidential campaign because the candidates are so visible.

Ross Perot running as the Reform party candidate in 1992 often came across as an intense egomaniac. Despite his folksy charisma, Perot had let his guard down about his ambition in a much more revealing way earlier in the campaign. The billionaire businessman-turned-politician dismissively said, "the American people don't care about issues. . . . I've talked to *my people,* and they don't care" (emphasis added). The volunteers who surrounded Perot sometimes seemed more dazzled by the Dallas billionaire's personality than by his views. Perot saw himself as the leader of his army of volunteers who would take the nation out of its economic troubles into the land of prosperity, despite never having held any elected or appointed public office. In essence, Perot saw his movement as an extension of his own persona.[34]

John F. Kennedy personified ego in a more refined and elegant way than the folksy Perot. He was handsome, bright, immaculately coiffed and dressed; he was a polished speaker; and he had an engaging personality. Kennedy radiated confidence in himself and those around him. In 1959, Kennedy was a 42-year old Massachusetts senator moving forward with his own plans to pursue the Democratic presidential nomination the following year. Although Kennedy was young, his charisma was unmistakable, and he attracted top people to work for him. In *The Making of the President 1960,* author Theodore White recalls how Kennedy hired staff to reflect his own self-confident image:

> In the personal Kennedy lexicon, no phrase is more damning than 'He's a common man' or 'That's a very ordinary type.' Kennedy, elegant in dress, in phrase, in manner, has always required quality work; these men by his standards were extraordinary; they were his choices.[35]

Kennedy, unlike Perot, did not have to draw sustenance from a cadre of supporters. What characterized his ego was a serene regard for his own abilities, as well as security in his own judgment. Candidate self-confidence is instrumental in motivating and leading a party to victory. Whether or not ego is on public display, most candidates have a healthy belief in their own abilities, because campaigning takes such nerve and determination to campaign, which are important requisites for governing.

CONCLUSION

Candidate motivations to run for office are often the stuff made for psychology books. The reasons candidates run for office are usually not singular but rather, multiple, and the examples in this chapter show the different facets of candidate motivation. Congressman David Price (D-NC) demonstrated opportunity as a motive. Moreover, Price could have served as an illustration for issue motivation because of his concerns to protect small businesses, and to provide greater educational and work opportunities for minorities. Governor Jesse Ventura (I-MN) exemplified why reforming the political system is important, yet his case study could also have illustrated ego as a manifestation to run for public office.

Charismatic national figures such as Dwight Eisenhower, or Hillary Rodham Clinton and John Kennedy demonstrate that public service itself transcends many motivational aspects. Public service as a civic duty is one aspect. Another is the realization that a heightened standing in society can attract quality people to help an Eisenhower or a Kennedy run for office. Furthermore, candidates' confidence can inspire those around them. There are dozens of additional motivations or variants of motivations that one could examine in addition to those presented in this chapter. The case studies examined in this chapter reveal the nuances of understanding an office-seeker's character.

An understanding of what makes a candidate "tick" is one of the great anomalies of politics because it remains somewhat elusive. However, political scientists Fowler and McClure provide some insight into the bond between candidates and constituents: "(A) good congressional candidate must have a burning desire to serve in Washington. . . . such ambition helps tie federal lawmakers more closely to their constituents." Ambition ties candidates to the responsibilities of their congressional district, their state, or the nation. The bond remains intact as long as ambition is commensurate with the interests of the people they represent. The philosophical or ego-driven

beliefs of candidates must also be tempered by the practical con-
straints of running for office as they consult family, friends, and
political colleagues. Those consultations and assessments take into
account the family, economic, and political realities that can impinge
on their motivation to run. Such discussions take place, both formally with supporters and informally among friends, as candidates
plot their quest for public office.[36]

STUDY/DISCUSSION QUESTIONS

What motivated your congressman to run for office? Research and
report.

Do the motivations of candidates who run for President of the
United States differ demonstrably from those who run for the
House or Senate? Please explain.

Explain why motivations of running for public office are complex
rather than simple.

What do the examples of David Vitter and John Kennedy explain
about how ego manifests itself in a political campaign?

Compare and contrast two areas of candidate motivation using examples. For instance, how did the motivation of Hillary Rodham
Clinton to run for the U.S. Senate differ from that of Jesse Ventura
to run for Minnesota governor? Are there any similarities you can
draw as well?

What are the implications of candidate motivation for the electoral
process?

SUGGESTED READINGS

Ehrenhalt, Alan. *The United States of Ambition: Politicians, Power and
the Pursuit of Power*. New York: Times Books, 1992.

Fowler, Linda L., and Robert D. McClure. *Political Ambition: Who
Decides to Run for Congress*. New Haven, CT: Yale University
Press, 1989.

Kazee, Thomas A. *Who Runs for Congress? Ambition, Context, and
Candidate Emergence*. Washington, DC: Congressional Quarterly
Press, 1994.

Mikulski, Barbara, et al., with Catherine Whitney. *Nine and
Counting*: The Women of the Senate. New York: Perennial, 2001.

Price, David E. *The Congressional Experience*. Boulder, CO: Westview, 2000.

Schroeder, Pat. *24 Years of House Work . . . and the Place is Still a Mess: My Life in Politics*. Kansas City, MO: Andrews McNeel, 1999.

Wattenberg, Martin P. *The Rise of Candidate-Centered Politics: Presidential Elections of the 1980s*. Cambridge, MA: Harvard University Press, 1991.

NOTES

1. Gary Jacobson, *The Politics of Congressional Elections*, 3rd ed. (New York: HarperCollins, 1992), 7, for quote on candidate aspirations. For a discussion on policy entrepreneurs or candidates or politicians who advance their own policies, rather than that of a political party see David E. Price, *The Congressional Experience* (Boulder, CO: Westview, 2000).

2. Price, chapters 1, 2, and 10. For an extensive theoretical discussion on candidate motivations, see Linda K. Fowler, *Candidates, Congress, and the American Democracy* (Ann Arbor, MI: University of Michigan, 1993). Chapters 2 and 3 integrate a discussion of the socialization process.

3. Pat Schroeder, *24 Years of House Work . . . and the Place Is Still a Mess: My Life in Politics* (Kansas City, MO: Andrews McNeel, 1999), 42.

4. C. Cullen, J. P. Boyd, and Heizer, eds., *Thomas Jefferson. "Letter to James Madison—January 30, 1787." Jefferson Papers, vol. 11* (Princeton, NJ: Princeton University Press, 1955). See also James L. Sundquist, *Dynamics of the Party System: Alignment and Realignment of Political Parties in the United States* (Washington, DC: Brookings, 1983), chapters 6 and 7 on the 1896 realignment.

5. Robert D. Novak, "Fall of a RINO," *The Washington Post*, March 7, 2002, A 21.

6. Jonathan Allen, "Florida Remap Gives GOP Edge on Seats," *Congressional Quarterly*, March 22, 2002. Accessed on April 12, 2000 at *www.washingtonpost.com/wp-dyn/politics/elections/redistricting/A5492-2002Mar22* on the Feeney seat.

7. Republican media consultant speaking on background to a seminar of Washington Semester students Washington, DC, American University, Dunblane House, Washington, DC (September 8, 1999), quote concerning ego. James David Barber, *The Presidential*

Character: Predicting Performance in the White House (Englewood Cliffs, NJ: Prentice-Hall, 1992).

 8. Michael Barone and Grant Ujifusa, *The Almanac of American Politics 2000* (Washington, DC: National Journal, 1999), 485, quote on Norwood. See also "Career Paths: How They Got Where They Are"—Charlie Norwood, *Campaigns and Elections* (September 2001), 16.

 9. Schroeder, 5–6.

10. Jeffrey Gayner, "The Contract with America: Implementing New Ideas in the U.S.," Heritage Lecture No. 549, The Heritage Foundation, Washington, DC (October 12, 1995), quoting Gingrich on Capitol steps; Richard E. Cohen, *Changing Course in Washington: Clinton and the New Congress* (New York: MacMillan, 1994), 156.

11. See James L. Sundquist, *Dynamics of the Party System*, rev. ed. (Washington, DC: Brookings, 1973), chapters 6 through 8 on Populist reform of the late 1800s and early 1900s.

12. David Hanners, "Who Did We Elect?" *St. Paul Pioneer Press*, November 7, 1998.

13. Gregg Aamot, "The Man Behind Ventura's Unique Approach," *Associated Press*, November 8, 1998; Jesse Ventura, *I Ain't Got Time to Bleed* (New York: Villard, 1999), 159, quote on "Evil Special Interest Man."

14. Michael Barone with Richard E. Cohen, *The Almanac of American Politics 2002* (Washington, DC: National Journal, 2001), 691, about King as a conciliator between Democrats and Republicans.

15. Barone and Ujifusa, 867.

16. "I Will Not Run, Says Powell," *Time for Kids*, November 17, 1995. Accessed on April 15, 2002 at *www.timeforkids/TFK/magazines/story/0,6227,97683,00.htm*. Humphrey Taylor, "The Republican Nomination for President," *Harris Poll #40*, August 5, 1998; Stephen E. Ambrose, *Eisenhower: Soldier and President* (New York: Touchstone, 1990), 247, regarding Dewey's remarks. Eisenhower quote appears on page 262 of Ambrose. See 259–65 for the entire discussion concerning the Eisenhower campaign.

17. Gail Sheehy, *Hillary's Choice* (New York: Ballantine, 2000), 340, all references.

18. Jack W. Germond and Jules Witcover, *Blue Smoke and Mirrors* (New York: Viking Press, 1981), 53 and chapter 3.

19. House members, Chambliss (R-GA), Talent (R-MO), Sununu (R-NH), and Graham (R-SC). The former mayor was Norm Coleman (R-MN) of St. Paul. The former attorney general was Mark Pryor (D-AR). The former senator was Frank Lautenberg (D-NJ), and the former cabinet official was Elizabeth Dole (R-NC).
20. Barone and Cohen, 946, 950; Scott Sonner, "Nevada makes Ensign first GOP senator in 12 years; Bernstein concedes," *Las Vegas Sun*, November 7, 2000. Accessed on April 16, 2002 at *www.lasvegassun.com/sun/bin/stories/test/2000/nov/07/511005214. html*, quote on lessons learned from losing.
21. Barber, 287.
22. Jeffrey Zaslow, "Straight Talk: Carolyn McCarthy," *USA Today Weekend*. Accessed on April 17, 2002 at *www.usaweekend.com/ 98_issues/98503/98503talk_mccarthy.html;* Barone and Ujifusa, 1109.
23. Barbara Mikulski et al. with Catherine Whitney, *Nine and Counting: The Women of the Senate* (New York: Perennial, 2001), 70, for quote. See pages 64–70 for discussion; Phil Duncan, ed., *Politics in America 1998* (Washington, DC: Congressional Quarterly, 1997), 629.
24. Mikulski et al., 40.
25. Ibid, 41.
26. "The Green Papers Governor's Chairs, Senate, and House Seats up for Election on 5 November 2002 with no incumbent running for them." Accessed on June 10, 2003 at *www.greenpapers.com;* for compilation of election rates 1998–2002, see Richard J. Semiatin, *The 2002 Midterm Elections* (Boston: McGraw-Hill, 2003), 8. See Sue Thomas, Clyde Wilcox, and Elizabeth Cook, eds., *Year of the Woman: Myths and Realities* (Boulder, CO: Westview, 1994) for an excellent examination of women and the 1992 election.
27. Data from the *Cook Political Report* (October 3, 1998) quoting Norman J. Ornstein, Thomas E. Mann, and Michael J. Malbin, *Vital Statistics on Congress 1997–1998*. Washington, DC: (Congressional Quarterly Press, 1997) for 1978–1996 reelection rates; Semiatin on 1998–2002 reelection rates.
28. Anthony Downs, *An Economic Theory of Democracy* (New York: Harper and Row, 1957), chapter 2, on costs and benefits of voting.
29. Price, 36 as cited from James Rosen, "Heineman Says He's Not Middle Class," *Raleigh News and Observer,* October 21, 1995, A14,

for Heineman interview; Price, 38, for additional commentary on the race.

30. Sigmund Freud, *The Ego and the Id* (New York: Norton, 1990) on the ego. See the framework of active positive and active negative presidents in Barber, chapters 1 and 3.

31. Barber, ibid.

32. Barone and Cohen, 671; Kristin Brainerd, "Three Davids, No Goliath and Plenty of Slingshots: How Reformer David Vitter Won the Special Election to Fill Bob Livingston's Vacant Louisiana House Seat," *Campaigns and Elections*, September 1999, 35–47.

33. Barone and Cohen, 671 (both quotes); Brainerd.

34. "Superhero," *Newsweek Special Election Issue*, November/December 1992, 75. See pages 72–76 for more detail.

35. Theodore H. White, *The Making of the President 1960*. (New York: Pocket Books, 1961), 63.

36. Linda L. Fowler and Robert D. McClure, *Political Ambition: Who Decides to Run for Congress* (New Haven, CT: Yale University Press, 1989), 238, quote on political ambition.

CHAPTER 3

The Decision to Run for Office

Being a politician is a tough job. If you do it right, it means long hours, constant interruptions, tension-filled debates, stressful decisions and surrendering your privacy.[1]
—Former House Speaker Tip O'Neill (D-MA)

Running for public office is the world's most difficult job interview. It means that a candidate's past and present are in the public domain, scrutinized by voters who will decide whether they will hire that person or someone else for the position. A politician's public service motivation is distinct from whether that individual can stomach the travails of campaigning for elective office the way Tip O'Neill described it. Congresswoman Pat Schroeder of Colorado was considering a run for the Democratic presidential nomination in 1988 when "a moment of truth" dawned on her before a receptive audience while traveling through the South. As she was introduced, a Democratic state party chair told the crowd "glowing things: that he admired my style, that he'd love to have a woman in the White House, that I knew more about national defense than all of the other candidates combined. . . . Then the bubble burst. 'Of course I can't vote for her,' he said, 'because I have a problem with a man being the first lady.'" Even though the politics of 2004 differs from 1988, the Schroeder example illustrates that a desire to run for office is tempered by reality. Understanding this reality enables a prospective candidate to decide whether a race is viable.[2]

ASSESSING THE POTENTIAL RACE

"Politics was war without bloodshed," former Republican House Speaker Newt Gingrich often repeated, quoting a maxim from Mao

Tse Teng, the founder of Communist China. Candidates prepare for
political combat with the opposition in both the primary and the
general elections, arming themselves with sufficient resources
(i.e., money) to compete, recruiting volunteers to build a small army
of supporters, and seeking political endorsements within their
party to build momentum toward victory. Flexibility is an important personal trait because candidates cannot always dictate the
direction of a long campaign. Problems within the campaign environment or external events may require candidate adaptation. Challengers, who have not been through a long campaign for national
office, should understand that the realities of a 12–24 month campaign require great patience because the emotional effort can be
overwhelming.[3]

No matter how much any candidate prepares to run, it seems inadequate upon reflection. John Kline (R-MN), a former Marine
colonel bemoaned his own naïveté after entering his first congressional race in 1998. "Sometimes I ask myself, 'What the heck were
you thinking?'" For a candidate has to consider a myriad of questions: "Will I be able to balance family demands with campaigning?"
"Do I have the personal stamina and enthusiasm to campaign effectively?" "Am I willing to invest the time and effort to raise lots of
money?" "Can I attract enough political endorsements to make my
campaign credible?" "Is there anything in my background that could
potentially cause me profound embarrassment?" "Am I flexible and
adaptable enough to change course during the campaign?" Although the answers to these questions are not all those that a candidate needs, they do provide a list of important factors candidates
often consider and serve as the basis for the first section of the chapter. If the answers are positive, a candidate moves forward to the
planning stages of a campaign. The chapter's second part discusses
how a candidate seeks friends and associates for advice, consults
with party pros, and conducts prospective research on the race.[4]

Will I Be Able to Balance Family Demands with Campaigning?

Balancing family demands with campaigning means that candidates have to consider whether the time and effort put into the effort
could have a detrimental effect on spouses and children, which in
turn harms their own campaign. Candidates have to deal with family

matters such as alcoholism, divorce, health, and personal tragedies. For example, Senator Al Gore's (D-TN) life changed when a car driving through the Baltimore Orioles stadium parking lot hit his six-year old son Albert III in 1989. The accident was nearly fatal, although his son made a full recovery. According to authors David Maraniss and Ellen Nakashima, Gore "promised himself that he would spend more time with his wife and children, (and) worry less about trivial political matters." The accident prompted Gore's decision not to run for the presidency in 1992 and provided a better opportunity for another southern candidate named Governor Bill Clinton (D-AR), to win the Democratic presidential nomination. Ironically, Clinton selected Gore to be his running mate in 1992.[5]

The choice between family and career is more vexing for women candidates because society still regards women as the primary caregivers of children. Senator Mary Landrieu (D-LA) remarked that women in the past had to choose between a public service career and family. "Now these women are retired, and they have no children, no grandchildren. In some cases . . . they were forced to sacrifice one great joy for another. . . ." Today, she says women should not have to make that choice. "It just doesn't seem right. . . . If I can do it, other women can." The anecdotal evidence whether attitudes have changed toward electing women with children is mixed. Senator Blanche Lambert Lincoln (D-AR) left the U.S. House in 1996, had twins, and within two years was running for the Senate. On the other hand, Governor Jane Swift (R-MA) gave birth to twins while serving in office. Some critics accused the governor of doing too much: raising two children, managing the state, and running for election in 2002 (she later dropped out of the race). Although Swift's unpopularity stemmed from miscues in office, she accused the press of having a double standard for women with children who run for office.[6]

Balancing family demands with the copious *amount* of time it takes to campaign deters not only potential challengers from running but also some incumbents from seeking reelection. House members spend nearly half their time in campaign mode given their two-year term of office. During a typical week, an incumbent U.S. House member spends Tuesday through Thursday in Washington, D.C. and Friday through Sunday working in the district meeting with constituents. For example, California members fly home most weekends by taking the "red-eye" flight to the state on Thursday evening and returning on the "red-eye" to Washington, D.C. on

Monday morning. This grueling pace means that members must decide whether to keep their family back in the district or in the Washington, D.C. area. Whatever their decision, the existence is dysfunctional.

Do I Have the Stamina and Enthusiasm to Run an Effective Campaign?

Running for a national public office is a prelude to the long hours of service once elected. The 12–15 hours days spent on Capitol Hill are reflective of the daily schedule a candidate works while running for office. Senators Hillary Rodham Clinton (D-NY) and John McCain (R-AZ) are indefatigable campaigners who can operate on little sleep and campaign 16 hours or more a day. McCain held "court" aboard his bus, the *Straight Talk Express*, in his fight to win the 2000 Republican presidential nomination. The *Express* carried top campaign aides and reporters as it barnstormed through New Hampshire in the month preceding the February 2000 presidential primary. The candidate, staff, and reporters munched on powdered donuts every morning and drank lots of black coffee aboard the bus. McCain was a tireless and energetic campaigner, going full-tilt all day speaking enthusiastically at events, greeting voters in the streets or just talking to reporters on the campaign bus where no subject was off-the-record. As one reporter said about McCain, "And he talks. And talks. And talks." McCain's personality traits matched his well-honed populist campaign message of running against the influence of "special interests." Extroversion is not required, but an individual who *enjoys* campaigning is better suited to the job of candidate where long hours, bad weather, and bad diet are part of daily life.[7]

Candidates who embrace local customs when campaigning do better than those who eschew them. No task may appear too menial or undignified that a candidate will not perform to win support. The New Hampshire presidential primary of 2000 featured a pancake-flipping contest among the Republican contestants. The event held in late January of 2000 showed the ineptitude of one of the candidates, which left an indelible image. Social conservative family activist and presidential candidate Gary Bauer slipped backwards off the stage as he was flipping a pancake. Bauer allegedly caught it in the pan as he was falling down proclaiming, "I'm a fighter!" However, the impression Bauer made was embarrassing when it appeared on the evening news. If Bauer had used self-deprecation to make fun of himself, as did John McCain and Bill Clinton, he could have turned a negative into a plus. Candidates who connect as real people doing common things have a tremendous advantage over candidates who feel awkward and defensive.[8]

Enthusiasm means feeling at ease with audiences large and small. Bill Clinton reveled not only in large crowds but in private conversation. In private conversation, "he treats you like you are the most important person he could talk to at the moment. . . ." One staff member reported Clinton would focus his eyes on his subject, nod his head, and listen. While he tended to do this with everyone, a Clinton staffer said, "it cheapens it, but I love him." For extroverted candidates, the act of campaigning is joyful because they feed off the crowd's enthusiasm. When politics is fun, candidates connect more closely to their audience, enhancing their personal appeal.[9]

While some candidates have enjoyed success by disdaining the campaign trail for television (e.g., Richard Nixon and Ross Perot), most congressional, senatorial, and gubernatorial candidates understand that direct and personal contact with voters is a necessary part of the process of winning election. As political scientist Samuel Popkin says, "American media coverage of politics, and of American culture in general is becoming more personalistic." Running an ideas-based campaign devoid of personality can have detrimental consequences.[10]

Am I Willing to Invest the Time and Effort to Raise Lots of Money?

Politicians often find raising money the most distasteful aspect of running for office, but necessary in order to win. Total spending for the 2000 presidential, senatorial, and congressional elections totaled a record $3 billion, a 50 percent increase from 1996. The cost to run a competitive U.S. House race runs from $500,000 to $1 million depending on the size of the media market. Competitive Senate races cost more than $5 million in small states to $15 million or higher in large states. Members spend more time raising money than any other campaign activity. U.S. Senators and House members emerge from

TEDDY ROOSEVELT GIVES SPEECH AFTER BEING SHOT

Former President Teddy Roosevelt was a true extrovert. Running as the candidate of the Bull Moose Party in 1912, Roosevelt's enthusiasm was infectious. Whether the setting was intimate or in front of a large audience, Teddy Roosevelt loved people. Following his return from an African safari, Roosevelt decided to challenge his Republican successor, William Howard Taft for the presidency. The two had had a personal falling out because Roosevelt thought Taft vacillated in carrying out a reform agenda. However, Roosevelt was unable to garner the Republican party nomination and ran on a third party ticket called the "Bull Moose." (Roosevelt told reporters, "I'm feeling like a Bull Moose!" and supporters adopted the name for the party.)[11]

On October 14, 1912, Roosevelt emerged from his hotel in Milwaukee, Wisconsin began walking a short distance to a car that would drive him to a downtown hall to deliver a speech. Suddenly, an anarchist named John Shrank approached Roosevelt and shot him. When the bullet was fired, Roosevelt clutched his speech to his body. By a stroke of luck, the text absorbed some of the bullet's impact. Supporters urged Roosevelt to go to the hospital but he insisted on delivering his speech and ordered his car to proceed to the hall. Roosevelt's oratory commenced only five minutes after the shooting. Still wearing his blood-stained vest, Roosevelt delivered a 90-minute address that was one of the most rousing speeches of his career. Roosevelt waved his bullet-marked manuscript and emphatically told the crowd, "You see it takes more than that to kill a Bull Moose!" Roosevelt accepted medical attention at a local hospital following the speech suffering broken ribs from the bullet wound.

When a candidate connects with voters, that individual *wants* to be with them, and voters *want* to be with the candidate. The adrenaline and stamina to deliver a 90-minute speech following an assassination attempt and wounding makes Teddy Roosevelt's feat unique in American campaign annals. Roosevelt did not win the election, but he did finish second to New Jersey Democratic Governor Woodrow Wilson marking the last time a major party candidate (Taft) finished third in a presidential election.[12]

the west front of the Capitol, facing the reflecting pool, and call campaign donors on their cell phones. Members are prohibited from soliciting donations inside the Capitol. Although raising money is time-consuming and difficult for incumbents, it is even more daunting for challengers. Incumbents have a stronger fund-raising base (with a pre-existing list of donors), and long-term support from political action committees (PACs). On the other hand, a Senate challenger needs to raise an average of $60,000 *every* week for two years to remain competitive in a state the size of Connecticut. Congressman David Price (D-NC) explained the difficulties challengers face raising money. "I will never forget how difficult it was to raise the first dollars. I understand quite well why many potentially strong challengers and potentially able representatives simply cannot or will not do what it takes to establish financial viability and why so many who reach that point do so only on the basis of personal wealth."[13]

Candidates considering a run for the House or Senate often seek advice from a national party organization such as the Democratic Congressional Campaign Committee (DCCC) or the National Republican Congressional Committee (NRCC). Senate candidates will contact political staff from the Democratic Senatorial Campaign Committee (DSCC), or National Republican Senatorial Committee (NRSC) depending on their party affiliation. The common question asked by a party organization official of a challenger is: "do you have the money or can you raise enough money to run a competitive race?"

No candidate under normal circumstances can be competitive without raising hundreds of thousands (for a house race) or millions of dollars (for a senate race). Money buys name recognition through expensive mass media such as television and direct mail. National party organizations recruit candidates who have personal wealth or statewide elective political experience because they already maintain a fundraising list. Wall Street financier Jon Corzine (D-NJ) was encouraged to run by national Democratic officials because of his great wealth. Corzine spent $63 million on his winning U.S. Senate campaign compared with his opponent Congressman, Bob Franks (R-NJ) whose expenditures were one-tenth that amount. Corzine was a political novice but his enormous wealth helped him win an open seat in New Jersey.[14]

Political experience enhances the ability of a challenger to raise money. To run a competitive race means that a well-known candidate on the state or local level has a greater likelihood of raising the

money needed to win a competitive election. Sherrod Brown's
(D-Ohio) 1992 election to the U.S. House exemplifies how political
experience and contacts makes a candidate formidable. Brown
served as Ohio's secretary of state for two terms before being defeated in 1990. Brown states that his elective service was invaluable
in raising money as his book *Congress from the Inside* explains:

> My eight years as Ohio secretary of state, and my experiences
> as an officeholder and both as a successful (six times) and
> unsuccessful candidate (once) helped me substantially. I spent
> approximately $150,000 and won the primary by almost
> 25 percent.[15]

Name recognition as an established public figure means that
building a fund raising base is easier than for an unknown political
novice. Community activists, successful business people, prosecu-
tors, and college professors are examples of non-elected public figures attracting financial support to run competitively for office
because of high name recognition in a district or state. Public standing in a community enhances the credibility of such individuals. The
late Walter Capps (D-CA), a religion professor at the University of
California at Santa Barbara, used his standing in the wealthy Santa
Barbara community as a respected educator and ethicist to raise
money from wealthy liberals needed to run a competitive race
against his well-funded opponent, conservative legislator Andrea
Seastrand (R-CA). The two matched off in 1994 with Seastrand
winning, and again in 1996 resulting in a Capps victory.[16]

Celebrity provides instant name recognition and an instant base
of support to run for office. Famous public figures often have personal
wealth and (or) connections to wealthy donors, which makes a competitive race plausible. Celebrities, unlike "ordinary" candidates, can
raise money in large increments from donors who want to rub elbows
with them. Former New Jersey senator and NBA Hall-of-Famer Bill
Bradley held a fundraiser for his presidential campaign in Madison
Square Garden on November 15, 1999. The event raised $1 million as
former NBA greats such as Kareem Abdul-Jabbar, Julius Erving, Bill
Walton, and Bill Russell trooped before the microphone to praise
Bradley. In other cases, celebrities can bring their own financial resources to bear. Arnold "the Terminator" Schwarzenegger gave serious consideration to run for California's Republican gubernatorial

nomination in 2002. In an April 2001 poll of prospective Republican candidates, Schwarzenegger was running second behind Bush National Security Advisor, Condoleeza Rice by a 24–18 percent margin. (Neither individual ran for the governorship.) Schwarzenegger's exceptional wealth could have bankrolled his campaign. Nevertheless, the action star declined to run because of a financial agreement with the producers of his next film *Terminator III* requiring that he owe millions of dollars upon breaking his contract. Celebrity candidates such as Schwarzenegger, and well-known public servants such as Condoleeza Rice have fewer financial barriers to attaining public office than unknown local congressional challengers who lacks such status or wealth of someone famous. Ironically, Schwarzenegger ran in fall 2003 when Governor Gray Davis (D-CA) was recalled from office and the actor was elected in his place.[17]

Do I Have the Ability to Attract Political Endorsements?

Endorsements can help a candidate ward off primary competition, solidify their political base, and attract campaign volunteers. For example, Democrats tend to seek endorsements from labor unions (e.g., AFL-CIO), teacher's unions (e.g., National Education Association), women's groups (e.g., National Organization for Women), and environmental groups (e.g., Sierra Club). Republican candidates often look for endorsements from business organizations (e.g., U.S. Chamber of Commerce), religious and family-values organizations (e.g., Christian Coalition), and gun rights organizations (e.g., National Rifle Association). Candidates from both parties vie to win the support of farmers, medical organizations, and law-enforcement groups. Interest group support entails both campaign contributions and (or) field organization support of the endorsed candidate. Both the AFL-CIO (11 million members) and the National Rifle Association (3 million members) can provide organizational muscle, money, and support.

One illustration of attracting endorsements is exemplified by Congressman Eric Cantor (R-VA), elected in 2000. Cantor represents a district that extends westward from Richmond (the former capital of the Confederacy) to historic Charlottesville (where Thomas Jefferson dwelled and built the University of Virginia). Tobacco interests such as Philip Morris reside in Cantor's district. Further-more, many Philip Morris employees live in the district as well. Prior to his congressional election, Cantor served in the Virginia House of Delegates for nearly a decade and sponsored legislation limiting the liability of tobacco companies in lawsuits. Cantor received $24,800 in campaign contributions from tobacco companies in his congres-sional campaign. Most often, an interest group contributes to a cam-paign when the interest and candidate reside in the *same* district. Outside interests with no economic stake in the district are less likely to contribute money to a candidate, particularly a challenger.[18]

Failure to win an endorsement from a key constituent or an ide-ological group can cripple a candidacy. Gary Bauer, former presi-dent of the Family Research Council (a conservative, family-values organization) failed to win the endorsement of any major pro-life or pro-family organizations in his 2000 bid for the Republican presidential nomination. Those organizations supported Governor George W. Bush's (R-TX) candidacy for pragmatic reasons because he was electable. Bush's pedigree and political standing (Texas gov-ernor) represented greater potential to win the election. Since reli-gious conservatives were keen on recapturing the White House, Bush presented a far more appealing alternative than the more ideo-logical Bauer.

Candidates considering a run for office benefit if they have the ability to attract endorsements from major political figures. Potential candidates cultivate personal relationships with party figures or celebrities to bring credibility to their candidacy. Heading into the 2000 Democratic presidential primaries, former Senator Bill Bradley's (D-NJ) campaign was flagging until retiring Senator Daniel Patrick Moynihan (D-NY) endorsed his candidacy. Moynihan was a major political figure in the U.S. Senate representing New York for 24 years. Bradley had served with Moynihan in the Senate from neighboring states (New Jersey and New York) for nearly two decades. Furthermore, the two men had worked together for many years as members of the Senate Finance Committee. Moynihan be-lieved Bradley's electability made him the better candidate to en-dorse (as opposed to Al Gore). Moynihan said, "Nothing is the matter with Mr. Gore except that he can't be elected President." An endorsement from a respected party leader such as Moynihan enhances the credibility of the endorsed candidate and helps them raise money to remain competitive.[19]

Is There Anything in My Background That Would Cause Profound Embarrassment to Me and Damage My Candidacy?

Any political consultant will tell you that *this* question is at the top of their list when interviewing a prospective client. After all, such a revelation may not only embarrass or destroy a candidate, but also damage a political consultant's business. However, stories abound how many politicians hide details of their background from their political operatives and their families. During the 2000 election campaign, John McCain admitted that he had had affairs with women during his first marriage. However, the revelation had little effect on McCain's candidacy because no one prompted him to say it. Al Gore's admission that he had smoked marijuana as a young man barely caused a ripple when he sought the 1988 Democratic presidential nomination. McCain and Gore demonstrate that personal indiscretions from the distant past result in little political fallout when the candidate addresses the issue promptly.

History demonstrates that candidates attempting to hide personal embarrassments can suffer catastrophic consequences. Perhaps the most devastating example concerned Senator Gary Hart's (D-CO) bid to win the Democratic presidential nomination in 1988.

Early polls showed Hart leading potential rivals, largely due to his strong showing in the 1984 Democratic primaries. Hart's cool, calm, and reassuring demeanor reminded some of John Kennedy. He evoked Kennedy with his call for "new ideas" to imbue politics. In the spring of 1987, rumors circulated about Hart's having an extramarital affair. Fed up with the innuendoes, Hart told a *New York Times* reporter: "Follow me around. . . . I'm serious. If anybody wants to put a tail on me, go ahead. They'd be very bored." Hart apparently was not serious because the *Miami Herald* took him at his word and staked him out. Several days later, model Donna Rice emerged from his Washington, D.C. townhouse near dawn. The revelation reported in the *Herald* destroyed Hart's credibility as a presidential candidate. Hart's stock in a pre-primary poll in New Hampshire plummeted from 32 to 17 percent almost overnight. On May 8, 1987, Hart withdrew from the race just three weeks after formally entering the contest. Candidates taking the initiative to come clean about their background have a much greater chance of withstanding public scrutiny than those who prevaricate.[20]

Am I Flexible and Adaptable to Change Course During the Campaign?

Building a winning coalition and appealing to diverse constituencies means that candidates must understand their audience and adapt their message accordingly. Campaign strategy and tactics might undergo revision because of internal (campaign-related) or external pressures that often affect candidacies. Al Gore never seemed quite comfortable trying to be more folksy and personal and less like "Clark Kent" as he often appeared in his White House bid in 2000.

On the other hand, Bill Clinton seemed to play the role of a method actor, adapting his political persona to fit the audience. He could appear hip on the *Arsenio Hall* talk show jamming on the saxophone with the show's band members. Clinton could then transform himself into a family-values advocate chastising rap artist Sista Souljah before Reverend Jesse Jackson's Rainbow Coalition for making racially insensitive remarks. These manifestations of Clinton's personality were both an advantage and a disadvantage. Critics questioned Clinton's sincerity given his espousal of liberal policies such as universal health coverage, while appearing to protect the poultry industry in Arkansas from environmental regulations as governor. In the end, the electoral payoff of winning two terms appeared to exceed the cost of criticism as a politician who "morphed" before audiences. Clinton's ability to communicate what his audience wanted to hear demonstrated his formidable political skills.[21]

National or world events can change in a moment transforming the political landscape. As a result, candidates try to cope with a reality they never expected and adapt to the circumstance. The Virginia gubernatorial election of 2001 between Mark Warner (Democrat) and Mark Earley (Republican) provides an excellent case study of how candidates adapt or fail to change to world events.

Warner was a high-tech multimillionaire businessman and former U.S. Senate candidate who lost his 1996 election contest to incumbent Republican John Warner by a narrow 52–47 percent margin. Earley elected as state attorney general in a 1997 landslide was a close confidant of Governor Jim Gilmore. With Gilmore's support in the primary, Earley defeated Lieutenant Governor John Hager to win the Republican party gubernatorial nomination. Warner maintained a consistent lead (5 to 10 points) over Earley as summer was ending when the tragedy of September 11, 2001 took place at the World Trade Center in New York and at the Pentagon in Arlington, Virginia. In fact, the candidates and "the consultants at first seemed at a loss as to what to do." Both campaigns decided on a moratorium of campaigning for a week. Then Earley's campaign decided to proceed as if nothing had happened. Earley went on the attack about a week later, claiming that Warner was going to raise taxes. Pollster John McLaughlin serving as Earley's strategist changed tactics based on the outcome of the New York mayoral primary. He said, "right after 9/11, right at ground-zero (New York), Mark Green won the Democratic nomination on racial politics. It didn't change anything." However, Warner's pollster argued that, "if he (Earley) had switched to a campaign emphasizing experience with protecting the public, he probably would have made more headway." Commercials attacking Warner contrasted with the bi-partisanship on display between Democrats and Republicans on Capitol Hill providing President Bush with a united political front in the wake of the terrorist attacks. The aggressive tactic of attacking Warner provided no traction for Earley.[22]

Warner modified his strategy following September 11 from being a skillful and fiscally competent manager to a non-partisan public conciliator. The ads went positive, drawing a deliberate contrast to Earley's attacks. Warner ran ads "urging the support of President Bush in the time of peril. An accompanying endorsement spot reminded voters that more than 40 sheriffs and police chiefs— including a few Republicans—were backing the Democrat." The ad underscored "the freeze" on the hiring of law enforcement officers because of a budget shortfall, a subtle reminder that the Republican governor and state legislature were responsible for the problem. The September 11 tragedy should have benefited Earley who was the state's top law-enforcement official (i.e., attorney general). However, Warner adapted more effectively to the events of September 11 by advertising himself as a conciliator at a time when a quieter and gentler campaign was more appealing to voters. He won the election by a 52–47 percent margin. Although the Warner-Earley story discusses an election campaign rather than the preparation to run for office, it explains how a candidate's adaptation under adverse circumstances can meet with success.[23]

PLANNING THE POTENTIAL RACE

Running for national office requires extensive consultation and planning. For an incumbent, the task of running for reelection is much easier than for challengers because there is already an organization in place or one that is easy to rebuild. The process of establishing a campaign organization often begins at home for a challenger. For example, Mark Sanford (R) of Myrtle Beach, South Carolina began his race for the U.S. House on his kitchen table. Later, Sanford and his wife cleared out "the dungeon" (i.e., the basement) to establish a base of operations. Candidates contact friends, family, and political stalwarts in the community or state to seek advice about running for public office. At the same time, the candidate does some exploratory research regarding the demographics of the jurisdiction that they wish to represent. Research enables the challenger to understand how their ideology, demographic background, and personality "fit" the jurisdiction (i.e., from local congressional to statewide senatorial and gubernatorial races).[24]

Contacting Friends for Advice

Candidates benefit from friends providing unbiased advice, candid opinions and analysis as they prepare to run for office. Personal advisors play a particularly important role in the early campaign stages. In his book, *The Congressional Experience*, David Price (D-NC) relates how a group of friends called the "Wednesday night group" convened to plot his campaign race for the U.S. House. Price said the group was a "fertile source of campaign ideas, good and bad." Each week the group met to discuss "campaign strategy, parcel out key contacts and tasks, and bolster one another's morale." A candidate needs peers who are political insiders from the jurisdiction to share personal thoughts about the campaign. Frank Hunger, Al Gore's brother-in-law, was the Vice President's closest confidant during his 2000 presidential campaign. They were so close that Gore thanked Hunger in his presidential nomination acceptance speech. Relatives and friends can help the candidate screen potential campaign staff and consultants by perusing through resumes, sitting in on interviews, and lending frank advice and opinions about whom to hire.[25]

Advice from Party Professionals

Smart candidates go outside their personal circle of friends to seek advice from political pros in the party. Political pros play an invaluable role because their advice is not only free, but also based on years of political experience and success. Leading political figures such as Robert Strauss, the former Democratic National Committee party chair from the 1970s and Haley Barbour, the former Republican National Committee party chair from the 1990s provide shrewd advice for candidates seeking statewide or national office. Both individuals rebuilt their parties to compete more effectively on the presidential level (Strauss) and the congressional level (Barbour). The downside is that the advice can become generic when many contenders for a party nomination consult with the same political pro.

Candidates seeking the White House court former presidents given their experience at winning election. One of the finest political strategists was former President Richard M. Nixon. Republican presidential candidates actively courted Nixon less than 14 years after he left the White House disgraced by the Watergate scandal. Senator Bob Dole of Kansas visited former President Richard Nixon at his home in New Jersey when contemplating a bid for the White House in 1988. It was as if a former student had gone back to his favorite professor for a mentoring session:

> For hours the old campaigner, now in exile [Nixon] held forth on
> politics and policy. The deficit, he advised, had never been an
> effective issue. Dole needed to talk about something that
> conveyed the sense that he had a larger purpose. But Nixon did
> not have this something at hand to give Dole.[26]

However, it is possible that Nixon did have "something at hand" but reserved judgment to remain uncommitted and stay above the fray. Political stalwarts lend an understanding about the issues, voters, and strategy that provides an overview of the political environment. General election candidates may receive explicit advice on message and strategy. Bill Clinton provided advice to many 2004 Democratic candidates in off-the-record conversations because he loves politics and is a shrewd political strategist.

Political pros are fallible too so prospective candidates may go with their gut instinct, if it differs from the pros' advice. Orrin Hatch was an attorney in Salt Lake City, Utah representing opponents of government regulation in court. Having no public office experience, Hatch planned to launch an anti-Washington campaign for the Republican nomination for the U.S. Senate in 1976. He courted Vernon Romney, Utah's attorney general, a leading Republican. He then courted State Senator Warren Pugh, another leading Republican. "All responses were negative. They centered on the fact that all the Republican candidates were well known, while Hatch was a newcomer, that Moss (the Democratic incumbent) was probably unbeatable . . . ," Yet, Hatch disregarded their advice and ran successfully. The judgment to discern whether a race is winnable should include valuable advice from political pros. However, a candidate's political instinct and drive can lead to a different conclusion. Some candidates solicit too much advice, which only leads to confusion rather than wisdom. Candidates are best served when political pros provide them context about the political environment that clarifies how they can best run for office.[27]

Understanding the Political Environment

Candidates perform their own informal assessment of their race before assembling a campaign organization. The assessment takes into account electoral strengths and weaknesses in different areas of the jurisdiction. For example, a candidate running in economically depressed Harlem against incumbent Congressman Charles Rangel (D-NY) would be well-advised by friends not to run on a theme of smaller government. Furthermore, candidates need to gather intelligence about the jurisdiction or state where they plan to campaign by asking themselves the following questions: Who are the constituents? What parts of the district are rural or urban? What parts are wealthy or poor? What issues concern voters? Are those concerns the same across the district or state?

California provides an interesting example of different political environments because it is almost a nation unto itself. No state has greater demographic diversity, yet many congressional districts are rather homogenous. California is the size of a European country, with 35 million people, definable geographic regions, and the fifth largest economy in the world. The enormity and expense of campaigning in the state means that candidates exploring a statewide bid tend to be well-known public figures such as California Secretary of State Gray Davis (D) and State Attorney General Dan Lungren (R) who ran for governor in 1998. California is home to the entertainment industry, where many celebrities have won statewide election. For-mer Senator John Tunney (D), son of former heavyweight boxing champion Gene Tunney, and Governor Ronald Reagan (R), a former movie actor and, actor-turned-Governor Arnold Schwarzenegger (R) were elected statewide. Candidates must spend tens of millions of dollars to run statewide because of California's geographic and de-mographic diversity. The truism that a well-known public figure with deep pockets and substantial name recognition has a substantial advantage is magnified in California due to its size.[28]

Running for the U.S. House in California is a far different story than campaigning statewide given the variety found among its dis-tricts. California has fifty-three congressional members or 12 percent of the entire House of Representatives. For instance, staunch conser-vative Dana Rohrabacher (R) represents Orange County, a suburb of Los Angeles (home of the International Surfing Museum). Compare his district to House Minority Leader and liberal Nancy Pelosi (D) representing San Francisco (home of the Haight-Ashbury neighbor-hood, which was the center of the Hippie movement of the late 1960s). California also abounds in agricultural districts. Moderate Cal Dooley's (D) district in central California is one of the largest agricultural producing areas in the country. Thus, California has tremendous ideological, urban-rural, ethnic, and racial diversity. The state has large Anglo, Hispanic-American, African-American, and Asian-American constituencies. In fact, over half of California's population is non-white. California's representation differs substan-tially from a smaller and more homogenous state such as Utah where 85.3 percent of the population is white.[29]

Candidates grasp a greater understanding of the district or state by driving around visiting coffee shops, churches, farms, restaurants and visiting small retail outlets. This enables a prospective office-seeker to hear the opinions and concerns of fellow citizens without the filter of an opinion poll. Arkansan Blanche Lambert Lincoln (D) explains how important it was for her to drive around the district and talk to citizens when running for the U.S. House in 1992: "The district was twenty-five counties but the largest city had only about sixty thousand people . . . and that presents a challenge if you're going to reach the grass roots. You've got to be out there in the coffee shops, the farms, the lunch counters at noon." Candidates use such information for an intelligence-gathering operation to understand the issues and political dynamics of a jurisdiction.[30]

CASE STUDY: DON SHERWOOD AND PENNSYLVANIA'S
10TH CONGRESSIONAL DISTRICT

Understanding the political environment goes beyond ideology and demographics. To outside observers, which candidate best "fits" a district can be deceiving at first glance. The case of Republican Don Sherwood's victory in Pennsylvania's 10th Congressional District (C.D.) in 1998 is illustrative of how a candidate "fits" a district even though the district was deemed "Casey country," named for his opponent Democrat Pat Casey.

The 10th C.D. traverses the coal country region in eastern Pennsylvania. The district's largest city Scranton suffers from a flagging economy in recent years in part due to a declining coal mining industry. Sherwood's district has 17.5 percent of its residents over the age of 65 compared to a 12.6 percent national average. Social Security, Medicare, and other entitlement programs for the elderly take on greater significance in the 10th C.D. because the seniors vote in greater numbers than any other age group. On paper, the odds should have favored Pat Casey because the 10th C.D.'s demographics seemed a better natural fit for a Democrat. The Democratic administrations of Franklin Roosevelt (Social Security) and Lyndon Johnson (Medicare) created the entitlement programs that benefited the district's seniors. In addition, strong union representation (United Mine Workers of America) maintained a strong presence in the district.[31]

Republican Don Sherwood seeking to succeed McDade did not fit the mold of a young telegenic candidate at age 57. Sherwood's trusting and reassuring business reputation as a Scranton auto dealer for nearly 30 years played well in the 10th C.D. In fact, the auto dealership was a family business started by his father. An indefatigable campaigner and personable individual, Sherwood had many Democratic friends. His general election opponent 32 year-old Democrat Pat Casey, son of the former governor, "was often disappointed to find that longtime family friends were Sherwood supporters because of old personal and business connections" . . . even though the district should have been "Casey country." Although Casey had been born in the district to a prominent political family, Sherwood maintained advantages based on his age, experience, and business reputation. Sherwood's experiences reflected years of personal interactions with families purchasing cars from his dealership and his serving on the county school board. These experiences gave him a vast understanding of voters and their concerns. It more than equalized any inherent potential advantage that Pat Casey had in the district as Sherwood triumphed by a narrow 49–48 percent margin.[32]

Family as a Campaign Resource

Family plays an intrinsic role in helping a candidate promote his or her candidacy, particularly in the early stages of a race. A husband, wife, or sibling can serve as campaign manager or press secretary. Whom can a candidate better trust than a family member to manage a campaign? Bay Buchanan served as her brother's (Pat's) campaign manager for the Republican presidential nominations of 1992 and 1996. Congressman Ted Strickland's (D-Ohio) wife Frances has served as his campaign manager in his competitive southeastern Ohio district. The family home can serve as a temporary or even permanent campaign headquarters. Relatives who have served in office can provide invaluable advice.

Al Gore's first election campaign to the House of Representatives in 1976 was a family affair from the beginning. The Gores were anything but political neophytes, they were the most powerful political family in Tennessee. Albert Sr. (Gore's father) served in the U.S. Senate representing Tennessee from 1950–1968. The conversation between Gore, Jr. and his father is related in the book *The Prince of Tennessee*: "As he explained to his father when he first talked about the race, he felt he had to run on his own identity, not simply as the heir to a famous Tennessee name. . . ." However, his parents would still be involved in a less visible way. "In the morning, Gore Senior . . . would strategize with whoever was there, then leaf through his battered old black leather book . . . calling out names of small-town mayors and vice mayors and judges and their wives and telephone numbers." His mother Pauline involved herself by quizzing staff members about calls and contacts as she served them lunch.[33]

An experienced and engaged political family can make a difference in jump-starting a challenger's effort by contacting potential supporters and serving as a sounding board. However, there is no guarantee of success as noted in the case study of Pat Casey and Don Sherwood. Both Gore and Casey were scions of well-known political families in their states. However, Gore faced no opponent of the caliber that Casey faced with Sherwood. Furthermore, Gore demonstrated a campaign work ethic to meet and greet voters that few candidates possess.[34]

CONCLUSION

An individual's desire to run for public office often gets a rude awakening when they confront the reality of a political campaign. Many fine people decide not to seek public office because of family issues, an inability to attract endorsements, or have no desire to spend time raising hundreds of thousands of dollars. Motivation alone does not cure the problem. Candidates must take a hard look at their own strengths and weaknesses because their opponent will certainly seek to exploit any negatives. Given the candidate-centered landscape of American politics today focusing on personality and mass politics, such self-examinations become more important. In a perfect world, all potential candidates would strive to be adaptively rational, changing seamlessly to events in the most rational way to maximize their own support. Mark Warner of Virginia adapted his message to the new political realities following the tragedy of September 11 and won, whereas his opponent Mark Earley continued to run the same attack campaign and lost. The prospect of endorsements, political experience, and the enjoyment of campaigning are important factors that calculate into the decision to run for office. Family and close friends can help prospective candidates make this imperfect but useful choice. Most successful candidates are individuals who not only have a desire to hold public office but also have a vision of how to get there. This is all part of the dynamic of running for office. The next step is to build a campaign organization, the engine that drives a candidate's election campaign.[35]

STUDY/DISCUSSION QUESTIONS

In what ways does the reality of running for office differ from its motivations? Explain.

What practical consideration has the greatest impact on the decision to run for national or statewide public office? Elaborate why that consideration is more important than any other.

Describe the process a candidate uses to assess the viability of running for national office.

Why was Al Gore able to capitalize effectively on his family connections, whereas other candidates, such as Pat Casey, were unable to do so? Explain.

What reality-based factors that candidates consider may deter them from running for office? Is that good or bad for democracy?

SUGGESTED READINGS

Barone, Michael, and Richard E. Cohen. *Almanac of American Politics 2002*. Washington, DC: National Journal, 2001.

Brown, Sherrod. *Congress from the Inside: Observations from the Majority and the Minority*. Kent, OH: Kent University Press, 1999.

Maraniss, David, and Ellen Nakashima. *The Prince of Tennessee*. New York: Simon & Schuster, 2000.

Sanford, Mark. *The Trust Committed to Me*. Washington, DC: U.S. Term Limits Foundation, 2000.

NOTES

1. Tip O'Neill, *All Politics Is Local: And Other Rules of the Game*. (Holbrook, MA: Bob Adams, 1994), 174.
2. Pat Schroeder, *24 Years of House Work . . . and the Place Is Still a Mess* (Kansas City, MO: Andrews McNeel, 1999), 183.
3. Eleanor Clift and Tom Brazitis, *War Without Bloodshed: The Art of Politics* (New York: Touchstone, 1997), 14.
4. Alan Greenblatt, "A Tale of Two Underdogs," *Campaigns and Elections,* October/November, 1999, 27.
5. David Maraniss and Ellen Nakashima, *The Prince of Tennessee* (New York: Simon & Schuster, 2000), 246.

6. Barbara Mikulski et al., with Catherine Whitney, *Nine and Counting* (New York: HarperCollins, 2001), 25, on Landrieu remarks. The last set of references regard former Governor Jane Swift (R-MA). Andy Hiller, "Swift Exit." Script of on-air report. WHDH-TV Boston (March 19, 2002). Accessed on May 5, 2000 at *www.whdh.com/features/articles/hiller/119;* "Massachusetts Acting Gov. Jane Swift Drops Out of GOP Governor's Race; Romney to Run," *Associated Press,* March 19, 2002.

7. David Von Drehle, "McCain's Freewheeling 'Straight Talk Express.'" *The Washington Post,* January 31, 2000, A6.

8. "Bauer Flips Out," *ABCNews.com* (January 31, 2000). Accessed on April 24, 2002 at *www.abcnews.go.com/sections/politics/DailyNews/BRIEFS201.html.*

9. "The Specter of Scandal," *Newsweek Special Election Issue,* November/December 1992, 32.

10. Samuel Popkin, *The Reasoning Voter* (Chicago: University of Chicago Press, 1991), 223.

11. Paul F. Boller, Jr., *Presidential Campaigns* (New York: Oxford University Press, 1984), 193.

12. Boller, 195; R. J. Brown, ed. "Teddy Roosevelt Shot by Anarchist— Manuscript of Speech Saves His Life,"Accessed on April 25, 2002 at *www.historybuff.com/library/refteddy.html;* Teddy Roosevelt, "The Leader and the Cause," speech, October 14, 1912, Milwaukee, Wisconsin.

13. David Price, "The House of Representatives: A Report from the Field," in *Congress Reconsidered,* 4th ed., eds. Lawrence C. Dodd and Bruce Oppenheimer (Washington, DC: Congressional Quarterly Press, 1989), 417.

14. The Center for Responsive Politics estimates that Bob Franks (R-NJ) spent $6.6 million, compared with $63.2 million for Jon Corzine (D-NJ). Accessed on July 10, 2003 at *www.opensecrets.org.*

15. Sherrod Brown, *Congress from the Inside: Observations from the Majority and the Minority* (Kent, OH: Kent University Press, 1999), 5.

16. Phil Duncan, ed., *Politics in America 1996* (Washington, DC: Congressional Quarterly Press, 1995), 134, 1510; Phil Duncan, ed., *Politics in America 1998* (Washington, DC: Congressional Quarterly Press, 1997), 150–51. Capps raised $498,000 to Seastrand's $630,000 in 1994 and raised $968,000 to Seastrand's $1.223 million in 1998.

17. "Bradley's Biggest Game," November 15, 1999. *ABCNews.com.* Accessed on May 9, 2002 at *www.abcnews.go.com/sections/politics/*

DailyNews/billbradley991114.html; WISH *List Poll*, April 24–26, 2001. Conducted by American Viewpoint of 800 registered voters for the California gubernatorial primary. Reported in the *National Journal*. Accessed on April 25, 2002 at *www.nationaljournal. qpass.com/members/polltrack/2002/races/gov/ca*; "Terminator III Stopped Schwarzenegger Governor Bid," *NewsMax*, June 20, 2001. Accessed on April 25, 2002 at *www.NewsMax.com/showinside/ schtml?a=2001/6/2074809*.

18. Michael Barone and Richard E. Cohen, *Almanac of American Politics 2002* (Washington, DC: National Journal, 2001), 1577; Center for Responsive Politics, "Candidate Profile: Eric Cantor, 2000 Race." Accessed on April 26, 2002 at *www.opensecrets.org/races/ indus.asp?ID=VA07&cycle=2000&special=N*.

19. "Moynihan Endorses Bradley, Says Gore, 'can't be elected,'" *CNN.com*, September 23, 1999. Accessed on July 25, 2003 at *www. cnn.com/ALLPOLITICS/stories/1999/09/23/president.2000/bradley. moynihan* on Gore being unelectable.

20. James R. Dickenson and Paul Taylor, "Newspaper Stakeout Infuriates Hart: Report on Female House Guest Called 'Character Assassination,'" *The Washington Post*, May 4, 1987, A1. All quotes and references from the *New York Times* and *Miami Herald* appear in this story; polling information was reported in the *tvrundown.com* website. Accessed on May 1, 2002 at *www. tvrundown.com/polhart1.htm*.

21. See James Ceaser and Andrew Busch, *Upside Down and Inside Out: The 1992 American Elections and American Politics* (Lanham, MD: Rowman & Littlefield, 1993), chapter 3; Tom Rosenstiel, *Strange Bedfellows: How Television and the Presidential Candidates Changed American Politics, 1992* (New York: Hyperion, 1993), chapters 3 and 11; *Newsweek Special Election Issue*, November/ December 1992, in passim.

22. David Beiler, "Mark Warner's Five-Year Plan," *Campaigns and Elections*, December/January 2002, 40.

23. Ibid, 41.

24. Mark Sanford, *The Trust Committed to Me* (Washington, DC: U.S. Term Limits, 2000), 31.

25. Price, 10.

26. Sidney Blumenthal, *Pledging Allegiance: The Last Campaign of the Cold War* (New York: HarperPerennial, 1990), 54.

27. Phil Duncan, *Politics in America 1998*, 1452; Richard Vetterli, *Orrin Hatch* (Chicago: Regnery Gateway, 1982), 5.

28. California population can be found from the following link at
    the U.S. Census Bureau, accessed on July 10, 2003 at *www.census.
    gov/census2000/states/ca.html*. California's GDP ranking of fifth
    comes from the Department of Finance, State of California.
    Accessed on July 10, 2003 at *www.dof.ca.gov/HTML/FS_DATA/
    LatestEcondata/Data/Miscellaneous/Bbrank.xls*.
29. Barone and Cohen, 180, 209–10, 274, refers to California members.
    U.S. Census Bureau 2000 information on California and Utah.
    Accessed on June 24, 2003 at *www.census.gov/census2000/states/ca.
    html* and *www.census.gov/census2000/states/ut.html*.
30. Mikulski et al., Whitney, 91.
31. Michael Barone and Grant Ujifusa, *Almanac of American Politics
    2000* (Washington, DC: National Journal, 1999), 64; Michael
    Barone and Grant Ujifusa, *Almanac of American Politics 1982*
    (Washington, DC: Barone and Company, 1981), 957.
32. Barone and Ujifusa, *Almanac of American Politics 2000*, 64 regard-
    ing district data; Mary Clare Jalonick, "Mighty Casey Strikes:
    How the GOP Bucked a Democratic Turnout Tide to Win an Open
    Seat in Pennsylvania," *Campaigns and Elections*, April 1999, 32.
33. Maraniss and Nakashima, 169.
34. Ibid.
35. Charles A. Lave and James G. March, *An Introduction to Models in
    the Social Sciences* (Lanham, MD: University Press of America,
    1993). The premise of the author's argument is that people are
    adaptively rational, that they learn by doing and that their envi-
    ronment constrains their responses. This builds off earlier work
    by March and his long-term colleague, Herbert Simon. Simon's
    pioneering work on the limits of behavioral rationality—Herbert
    A. Simon, "A Behavioral Model of Rational Choice," *Quarterly
    Journal of Economics* (February 1955): 99–118—was part of the
    body of work for which he was awarded the Nobel Prize in
    Economics (1978).

CHAPTER 4

The Campaign Organization

Winning isn't everything, it's the only thing.[1]
—Hall of Fame football coach Vince Lombardi

"Three chattering TV sets, a wire-service machine, copying gear and computers gave the War Room its combat hum. Day and night, Carville's operatives tracked everything Bush and his surrogates said." Clinton campaign manager James Carville created a "War Room," which on a moment's notice responded to any charge thrown at the campaign during the 1992 presidential campaign against President George Bush, Sr. The Clinton campaign recognized that the growth of cable news and the emergence of the 24-hour news cycle made running for office increasingly responsive. Utilizing technology to their advantage enabled the Clinton campaign to keep the Bush campaign on the defensive almost the entire fall. The Clinton campaign typified a tightly run political organization built for flexibility and adaptation. Effective campaign organizations adopt technological innovations, engage in rapid response, take calculated risks, and adjust tactics to meet political exigencies.[2]

Winning is the essential reality of politics. Candidates do not hire staff and consultants to run the most altruistic or virtuous campaign. Since campaign organizations exist for the sole purpose of electing candidates, they last for an intense but short duration time-period. Today, national and statewide campaigns resemble small corporations. Divisions of campaign operations consist of fundraising, polling, advertising, and voter contact. The organizational and managerial skill to run a campaign has become more complex in the past decade because of greater technological sophistication and responsiveness to a more discerning public. Campaigns need structure

63

to campaign effectively because time and effort represent a candidate's most precious commodities.

EXAMINING CAMPAIGN ORGANIZATIONS

Reigning in the egos of staff and providing structure make campaign organizations more effective. When Clinton Commerce Secretary William Daley was selected to replace Tony Coehlo as Al Gore's campaign manager on June 15, 2000, a top House Democrat anonymously told *The Washington Post* that: "Daley brings good managerial skills to the campaign that are needed in an operation where 'there are already too many strategists.'" Daley could bring discipline to a campaign that lacked strong leadership. Effective campaigns plot ahead, plan for contingencies, and recognize their own strengths and weaknesses.[3]

Exploring how a candidate organization functions and how that organization develops a strategy to win serve as the main purpose of this chapter. Presidential campaigns have elaborate organizations while those of congressional candidates are more modest. Cooperation among the staff, the consultants, and the candidate enable the organization to maximize its effort. Popular incumbents with overwhelming resources can win no matter how dysfunctional their organization may be; however, for challengers and incumbents facing strong opposition a vital and coherent organization is essential for victory. Effective organizations develop a clear, direct, and focused strategy that builds voter support during the campaign season. That strategy features a message or theme articulating a reason to elect a candidate or defeat an opponent. While the strategic principle is simple, the execution is quite complex.

ORGANIZATIONAL MODELS OF CAMPAIGNS

A campaign organization is like a small business with a Chief Executive Officer (CEO)—the candidate, a Chief Operating Officer (COO)—campaign manager, a research division chief—a pollster, a public relations chief—a media advisor, and a director of fundraising. A hierarchical structure is the most common model used by campaigns. Power flows from the campaign manager at the top of the pyramid down to the broad base of operatives in the campaign. The major advantage is that accountability and control of information reside at the top. The major disadvantage is that one or two people can restrict the input of ideas that might be valuable to the candidate.

Fewer campaigns operate with a *collegial* or spokes-of-the-wheel operation where no single person has overall authority to direct the campaign. The collegial operation shares management among a number of individuals. The major advantage of a collegial operation is that it provides a freer flow of information directly to the candidate from multiple sources. Multiple sources provide a greater diversity of opinions to draw on to make choices compared with the hierarchical model. The greatest disadvantage is the difficulty of making decisions by committee, which is often slow to respond to the demands of day-to-day campaign operations.

Diffused Authority and Organizational Problems

The dramatic contrast between the hierarchical and collegial campaign styles was apparent in the 1992 presidential campaigns of Bill Clinton and George Bush, Sr. as seen in figure 4-1. Authority clearly rested with James Carville in the Clinton campaign (as of June 1992). Diffused authority characterized the Bush team. Robert Mosbacher served as general chairman, Robert Teeter as campaign chairman,

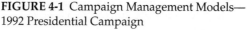

FIGURE 4-1 Campaign Management Models—
1992 Presidential Campaign

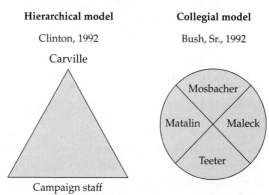

Hierarchical model	Collegial model
Clinton, 1992	Bush, Sr., 1992
Carville	
Campaign staff	

Fred Maleck as campaign manager, and Mary Matalin as political director.

Bush's campaign was nicknamed "Mary and the Boys." Despite the cute nickname, "Mary and the Boys" complained about the lack of coordination with the White House. Most presidents run their reelection campaign out of the White House (e.g., Terry McAuliffe managed Clinton's 1996 reelection campaign from the Office of Political Affairs). However, the chief Bush strategist from the 1988 campaign, James Baker was serving as Secretary of State. Unlike most other presidential reelection campaigns, no direction emanated from the White House. Mary Matalin said the campaign was "in disarray" because memos from the campaign on field organization and campaign strategy sent to the White House went unanswered. Samuel Skinner, the White House Chief-of-Staff, was "not politically attuned to the opportunities of incumbency, or geared to exploit them. And proposals submitted from the campaign (to the White House) seemed to be going down a black hole." According to Matalin the campaign staff repeated a daily mantra seeking Baker's return as chief strategist: "He [Baker] has to come back. We can't do without him." When the campaign appeared to be sliding away from Bush in early September, Baker reluctantly agreed to run the campaign reassuming his old position as White House chief-of-staff. Baker supervised the campaign while managing President Bush Sr.'s schedule at the same time. The chief-of-staff's tremendous organizational skills came too late to rescue Bush from defeat. The lesson from the Bush collegial model was that decentralized authority damaged the reelection effort because the organization lacked coherence. This is why the collegial model of managing campaigns, while very democratic is terribly difficult to execute successfully.[4]

Governor George W. Bush (R-TX) running eight years later learned from the experiences of his father's campaign. The 2000 Bush presidential campaign represented a model of hierarchical organization with Bush as the CEO and strategist Karl Rove as the COO. No detail was too small to plan. For example, Bush's campaign schedule was color-coded green and his official business (as governor) was color-coded black. The color-coding scheme provided Bush a visual picture of time-management to provide focus and discourage over-scheduling. The same organizational imprint followed Bush into the White House in 2001.[5]

THE CAMPAIGN ORGANIZATION—
CONSULTANTS AND STAFF

National and statewide campaigns feature two important human elements: consultants and staff. Candidates hire consultants to provide advice and services. Consultants retain multiple clients; thus, unless the circumstances are unusual, they do not work exclusively for one candidate. Consultants provide fundraising, polling, paid advertising, Internet, and legal services to a campaign. Campaigns also hire consultants to provide other important services including opposition research, candidate training, and targeting services for get-out-the-vote (GOTV) operations. On occasion, the campaign manager is an outside consultant hired to run a campaign such as James Carville for Bill Clinton (1992) and Mike Murphy for John McCain (2000). Carville, Murphy, and other consultants hired to manage campaigns work as chief strategists and sometimes run day-to-day operations.

On the other hand, staff refers to individuals who work exclusively for the campaign. Campaign positions include press secretary, director of scheduling, advance operations, speech writing, and the campaign manager (for most races). These same roles typically appear in races for state and local office across the country. Termination of all staff positions occurs at the end of the campaign meaning that staff members search for gainful employment. However, victorious candidates often bring key campaign staff members to work for them on Capitol Hill or at the White House.

Political Consultants

Consultants assist numerous campaigns during an election season. The list of prestigious clients for a well-known consultant can be quite impressive. For instance, Shrum, Devine and Donilon, a Democratic media firm worked for Al Gore (strategy and advertising), and U.S. Senate candidates Mark Dayton (Minnesota), Jon Corzine (New Jersey), Joseph Lieberman (Connecticut), Bill Nelson (Florida), Ted Kennedy (Massachusetts) and Paul Sarbanes (Maryland) in the 2000 elections. The firm attracts top clients but also takes on very difficult races and produces results. Each of the previously mentioned U.S. Senate candidates won election or reelection demonstrating a level of achievement reached by few other firms.[6]

The breadth of services available to modern campaigns is as-
tounding. *Campaigns and Elections* magazine provides 36 categories
of campaign consultants in its yearly directory to subscribers. Modern campaigns have ten to twenty different operations trying to
mesh like cogs of a machine. The failure to integrate different functions into a cohesive effort can have disastrous implications. Promising campaigns have imploded because of internal strife (e.g., George
McGovern for President—1972), disorganization (e.g., Lynn Yeakel
of Pennsylvania for U.S. Senate—1992), bad advice (e.g., Rick Lazio
of New York for U.S. Senate—2000) and, lack of accountability (e.g.,
George Bush, Sr. for U.S. President—1992). Even worse, some have
been plagued by bad advice and poor decision making. For example,
John Warner (R-VA) came close to losing his 1996 U.S. Senate reelection campaign over charges of ethical misconduct by his media consultants, Greg Stevens and Company. Greg Stevens and Company
produced a commercial that superimposed the head of his opponent
former state party chairman Mark Warner (D) on the body of Senator Chuck Robb (D) making it appear he was shaking hands with
President Bill Clinton who was unpopular in Virginia. The incumbent nearly lost reelection upon the revelation of the subterfuge es-
caping with a 52–48 percent victory.[7]
　　The pollster, media consultant, and the campaign manager serve
as the core *strategists* for major statewide and national campaigns.
Strategists work together developing a plan how to run the campaign. For example, Karl Rove (the boss), Karen Hughes (communications), Stuart Stevens (general consultant), and Mark McKinnon
(advertising) constituted the inner circle of George W. Bush's 2000
strategy team. Tad Devine (strategy director), Bob Shrum (advertising and lead consultant), Mike Donilon (advertising and polling),
and Carter Eskew (advertising) formed the inner circle of Al Gore's
2000 strategy team. Note that strategists sometimes overlap in the
roles they play, such as two consultants working on advertising
strategy. More important, are the chemistry, the teamwork, and the
results the strategists produce.

The Role of Political Consultants in Campaigns   Consultants are
experienced professional campaign people who have worked in
dozens of campaigns. Many consultants apprentice at national party
committees. Others work as staff members on congressional, senatorial, and gubernatorial races. Martin Hamburger is a media consultant

with the firm Laguens, Hamburger and Stone. His firm helped Deborah Stabenow (D) win election to the U.S. Senate from Michigan in 2000. Hamburger's background included service as the deputy political director for the Democratic Congressional Campaign Committee (DCCC). Greener and Hook, a Republican media firm, features Bill Greener, former deputy director and communications director for the Republican National Committee (RNC). His partner, Michael Hook, served as director of issue advertising for the National Republican Campaign Committee (NRCC) and later as chief-of-staff at the RNC before becoming an independent consultant. Greener, Hook, and Hamburger illustrate that a comprehensive campaign background is vital to providing the experience necessary to attract clients and work on important campaigns.[8]

The other major attribute that consultants can bring to a campaign is *expertise.* According to political scientists James Thurber and Candice Nelson, "consultants have taken the place of parties in most areas of campaigning, and are spending vast sums of money to make sure that candidates are competitive and win." Larry Sabato in his book, *The Rise of Political Consultants* quotes the late Matt Reese (the grandfather of the political consulting business): "The whole political world has changed. . . . It's unbelievable what is available to Ted Kennedy in 1980 as opposed to what was available to his brother [John Kennedy] in 1960." Imagine the vast array of services available today compared to 1980! It includes database management, fax services, fundraising software, Internet and web consulting services, online information specialists, opposition research services, and satellite transmission services.

The degree of specialization continues to increase. The number of different categories of consulting services grew from 21 to 36 between the years 1993–2002, as calculated from the categories listed in *Campaigns and Elections* magazine's "Political Pages," an annual directory of political consulting firms. New industries and companies continue to sprout. The growing number of resources available to candidates demonstrates that targeting voter appeals with greater precision is a premium that campaigns must afford. Just a slight advantage can make a tremendous difference. Changing the mind of one voter out of 10,000 would have delivered Al Gore the state of Florida and a presidential victory in 2000.[9]

Hiring a consultant is not always a marriage made in heaven according to consultant Tony Payton: "An Arkansas candidate once

A LARGE-SCALE ELECTION CAMPAIGN ORGANIZATION

Candidate

Campaign Manager

Consultants   Staff

Fundraising   Scheduling/Advance
Polling   Press Secretary
Legal   Research/Issues
Paid Advertising/Media   Speechwriting
General Consultant/Strategist   Field Organization
Opposition Research Consultant   Finance Director
Internet Consultant
Additional Consultants

Consultants

Fundraising—An outside vendor hired to raise money through direct mail, telephone solicitation, and events for the campaign.

Polling—A consultant providing survey research and focus groups on voting attitudes and behavior regarding the electorate. The pollster works with other strategists on message and targeting key demographic voter groups for support.

Legal—Attorneys hired who specialize in compliance with laws, particularly the Federal Election Campaign Act (FECA) which covers contribution and expenditure laws for all campaign for federal and state elections.

Paid advertising/media—A paid advertising firm hired to make television commercials for the candidate. The media strategist works with the pollster, general strategist, and other designated campaign officials to develop the message or theme of the campaign. Candidates often hire a separate direct mail consultant to do targeted mailings.

General consultant/strategist—The general strategist may also double as the campaign manager, media consultant or pollster. This individual is responsible for devising a communication strategy and disseminating it through paid advertising and earned media (news coverage). The general strategist and the pollster create the demographic strategy to target key voter groups for get-out-the-vote (GOTV) operations on election day.

Opposition research consultant—The "Oppo" research consultant utilizes data bases of news stories and public records to perform research on every aspect of the opponent's and client's career. Such information yields weaknesses to attack the opponent's record and (or) character. Oppo research also enables the campaign to understand the weaknesses of its client.

Internet consultant—The campaign "geek" designs, sets up, and maintains the candidate's web site.

Additional consultants—Campaigns hire phone consultants specializing in setting up phone banks for voter contact. They also hire field consultants concentrating on voter mobilization efforts. Many senatorial, gubernatorial, and presidential campaigns hire field consultants.

Staff

Scheduling/advance—The scheduling/advance officials are responsible for setting up candidate events, and ensure that every detail is planned to make the events reflect well on the candidate.

Press secretary—The press secretary is the official spokesperson of the campaign communicating campaign news, information, and statements to the press.

Research/issues—The research staff develops policy positions for the candidate and often provides the research to rebut the opposition's attacks.

Speechwriting—The speechwriter pens official campaign addresses and shorter messages that a candidate wants to convey to voters; they usually involve a policy or a special message for a particular interest, ethnic, or religious group.

Field organization—The Field Director is responsible for operating the largest unit of the staff. The field organization contacts voters on behalf of the candidate through phone banks and literature drops in the weeks preceding the election. On election day, they function as the get-out-the-vote (GOTV) team for the candidate.

Finance director—The financial team is responsible for ensuring that all money received is accounted for on-record. It files financial reports to the Federal Election Commission (FEC), and makes certain that all bills are paid. They work closely with the legal team to assure the accuracy of campaign spending reports filed with the Federal Election Commission.

Campaign manager—The campaign manager supervises day-to-day operations and often develops the campaign's strategy, particularly for house and some senate campaigns.

told me it was important for the candidate and consultant to match noses. . . . Things should smell the same to both of them." In other words, chemistry must exist between the candidate and the consultant for them to have a successful partnership. Without such a bond, trust is elusive. A consultant must demonstrate that commitment means sufficient time and attention will be allocated to a particular campaign. Selecting "the best consultant money can buy" is not the object, says veteran strategist and consultant Joe Napolitan. Napolitan notes that many congressional campaigns can hire excellent consultants without having to pay top dollar—for those who routinely handle statewide campaigns in California, New York, and Texas. Some consultants specialize in local or congressional races such as Nordlinger and Associates (a Democratic media firm) and, Hammond and Associates (a Republican fundraising firm). Whether a campaign is small (e.g., for the U.S. House) or large (e.g., for governor), the most common consulting services hired by a candidate include polling, paid advertising and fundraising. In the past several years, Internet consulting services have become routine as well.[10]

Pollsters   *Pollsters* provide office-seekers an understanding of the political environment to assess voter attitudes toward issues, candidate personalities, and parties through surveys. Surveys have multiple parts to them: 1) "screening" questions to get access to the appropriate respondents who vote in the jurisdiction; 2) attitudinal questions to ascertain the important issues in the campaign; 3) behavioral questions on voting preferences; and, 4) demographic questions to ascertain the profile of each voter (age, income, education, party identification, etc.). The research obtained enables the campaign to construct a "message" to target key voter groups through understanding important voter concerns about the issues and the candidate.

Polling services often include focus groups to help campaigns acquire qualitative information from voters through discussions. Unlike an objective questionnaire, a focus group is a wide-ranging interview of eight to 12 individuals with a moderator. The focus group provides a campaign with in-depth information that might be unavailable from a survey. Most focus groups are video taped and last one to two hours. The polling staff writes summary reports evaluating the attitudes and opinions of the participants. The next chapter explains how campaigns utilize polling and focus groups.

Paid Advertising   An effective *paid advertising* or *media* campaign can secure a candidate's base of support or expand their appeal to more voters. Advertising can take the form of television, radio, newspaper, or direct mail. The purpose of a television or radio ad is to deliver a message in a 30–60 second bloc, which resonate with the voter at home. Often the most potent advertisements tug at emotions, whether it is the little girl counting flower petals as an announcer ticks off the seconds to a nuclear explosion (Daisy Girl) or a true story about a convicted murderer out on parole committing rape (Willie Horton). Nevertheless, credibility has become a more important attribute of modern political advertising given the glut of ads making claims on television.

Campaigns now source the information of political ads at the bottom of the television screen to give them greater veracity to a discerning audience. Campaign advertisements for the general election often go beyond the party base to target "undecided" voters. Business advertising produces commercials to attract consumers who are not brand-loyal. For example, adolescents are the focus of Coca-Cola and Pepsi-Cola advertising because they have not yet established brand-loyalty as have older consumers. The same strategy applies to campaign advertising. Campaigns seek to attract voters to the brand (i.e, the candidate). Chapter 6 explores how advertising works in political campaigns including a discussion of the Daisy Girl and Willie Horton commercials.

Internet Consultants   The 2004 election marks a major change in campaigns because the Internet plays an increasingly important role. Internet services do more than provide design and maintenance of a web page. Campaigns now use email to build grassroots organizations. Internet services provide campaigns with the ability to play commercials on their websites, create chat rooms for supporters, and raise money. Former Governor Howard Dean (D-VT) used this strategy aggressively to build his contributor and volunteer base in his presidential bid. Internet consultants build a grassroots electronic organization to attract the increasing number of visitors to campaign websites. The latest data show that 46 million people use the Internet to get political information. A subsequent discussion (Chapter 7) examines the growing phenomenon of the Internet and future campaign technologies.[11]

FUNDRAISING

"Money is the mother's milk of politics." Forty years ago, Jesse Unruh, Speaker of the California State Assembly, stunned an audience by making this remark. Forty years later, money's importance has increased because of the skyrocketing cost of advertising, consulting services and the increasing duration of political campaigns. Candidate-centered politics have made the *fundraiser* critical to the operation of any viable campaign operation. Presidential candidates who fail to raise $20 million by December of 2003 are likely to be less competitive in the 2004 presidential race because money buys the necessary national name recognition that every candidate covets. Candidates spend a greater proportion of their time fundraising than performing any other campaign activity.[12]

The following short primer explains how fundraising works. Fundraising represents the first crucial step that a candidate takes to run an effective race. Money builds an organization, can buy publicity, and encourage more donors to contribute to a campaign. Campaigns for congress may occasionally succeed on a small budget, but that is the exception rather than the rule. Most candidates find fundraising distasteful because of the disproportionate time they spend calling prospective contributors for money. Nevertheless, any competitive candidate recognizes that success may depend on their ability to raise money. The ensuing discussion provides an overview of how fundraising works, explains the importance of direct mail, discusses how candidate-sponsored events raise money, demonstrates how money is raised through phone banks, and explains the concept and usage of bundling campaign contributions.

How Fundraising Works

"There are two important things in politics. The first is money and I can't remember what the second one is." Mark Hanna, the Republican party boss from Ohio, orchestrator of William McKinley's rise to the presidency made this remark in 1895. The premise of the remark that money fuels political campaigns has greater validity today.

Challengers have a particularly daunting task since it takes more than a half million dollars to run competitively for a U.S. House seat and at least $5 million for a U.S. Senate seat. Candidates who cannot raise sufficient capital cannot research, poll, advertise, and mount aggressive get-out-the-vote (GOTV) efforts with few exceptions. However, campaign spending does not guarantee victory. New York's Libertarian candidate Thomas Golisano spent $73.9 million in his losing election bid for New York governor in 2002. Nevertheless, running for office is far easier when a campaign has the financial resources to compete effectively, meaning that the candidate has a real chance to win.[13]

Fundraising begins with the candidate. Incumbents work off existing lists of contributors whom they personally solicited for contributions during their previous campaign. Challengers face the unenviable task of raising substantial contributions that go far beyond any fundraising effort undertaken in the past. Even if a challenger is a state legislator, he or she may have raised $25,000 or $75,000; but not the $500,000 or $1 million required to run a competitive U.S. House race. Party officials talk to challengers about how to raise money because a competitive race against an incumbent is expensive.

The first fundraising chore for a challenger is to compile a list of possible contributors that includes family members, friends, business associates, and acquaintances. A challenger must raise a respectable amount of money on their own to attract contributions from PACs and other interest groups. The financial assistance that PACs provide is crucial for challengers to compete. As a result, candidates must reach fundraising benchmarks they set. For example, a U.S. House challenger pledging to raise a respectable $125,000 by the end of 2003 for a November 2004 election must meet or exceed that total or face the consequence that a sympathetic PAC may rate their race as non-competitive for lack of resources. According to political consultant Marty Stone, "the first step of a campaign is for the fundraiser to pull out of the candidate's mind the name of every person a candidate has met who can give money." The fundraiser then augments the candidate's personal list with a solicitation plan that targets possible donors. Campaigns use direct mail, events, and phone banks to attract supporters. Competitive campaigns then attract resources from national parties and political action committees (PACs) which serve as clearinghouses to solicit and "bundle" contributions to a campaign.[14]

Direct Mail

Direct mail operations are quite complex and sophisticated. Direct mail is a high-stakes poker game. A good direct-mail operation costs only 40 cents to raise each dollar. Successful direct mail operations yield a one to two percent return rate on solicitations. Of course, the response rate depends on the audience to whom a candidate is appealing, the message articulated, and the number of previous appeals. The payoff can be exceptional for well-known candidates. Former Iran-Contra figure Oliver North (R) raised $20.7 million in his 1994 senate bid. Richard Viguerie, the "king" of direct mail in conservative circles, raised approximately 85 percent of North's money. Direct mail is also used for advertising as discussed in Chapter 6.[15]

Direct mail solicitations that succeed "hook" (or interest) the reader generate a higher response rate according to Chuck Muth, a Republican direct mail consultant. The "hook" begins not with the letter, but with the envelope. People put their mail into two categories: "A" (which they read) and "B" (which they discard as junk mail). Muth's advice is to "mail first class and use a 'live' first-class stamp. Don't meter your mail.... Don't use 'teaser copy'—such as 'Your Help is Urgently Requested' on the envelope. This tips your hand before the envelope gets opened." Muth argues that a personalized strategy is most effective.[16]

Events

Event fundraising is an old but reliable method of soliciting contributions on behalf of a candidate. High profile figures, such as presidents, can raise millions of dollars in one evening. An evening gala for Republican candidates at the Washington Convention Center featured President George W. Bush. The event took place on May 14, 2002 and raised a record $33 million. Contributors who donated $150 received a matted-limited edition photograph montage entitled "The First Year." The fundraising prospect for most mortals running for national office is more modest. Cocktails, dinners, barbecues, coffees and breakfasts are all part of the package of event fundraising. Fundraising night takes place on Tuesday evening in Washington, D.C. when the Congress is in session. East Capitol Street, located behind the Capitol teems with cocktail events to raise money in the quaint townhouses that populate the street. Most fundraising events benefit incumbent members of the U.S. House and Senate. Senior members of both parties stop by these events to add some luster to the event.

For example, one might see House Majority Leader Tom Delay (R-TX) drop-in at a fundraiser for House member Anne Northrup (R-KY) who runs in a highly competitive district from Louisville, Kentucky.[17]

Phone Banks

Phone banks have been a valuable source to raise money from donor lists. Donor lists might include party contributors (national, state or local), magazine subscribers (such as *The Nation* for liberals and *The National Review* for conservatives), or local, religious, business, and ideological organizations. For example, a pro-environmental candidate might buy a list of local contributors to the Sierra Club, the nation's largest environmental lobby; a pro-gun candidate might buy a list of local contributors to the National Rifle Association.

Raising money from telephone banks has become far more difficult given the plethora of calls from telemarketers today. Cathy Allen, a Democratic party fundraiser, suggests that the phone solicitor quickly establish a rapport with the potential donor. "Explain the purpose you are calling and how you got her name. . . . If a person has not contributed to you before, then add a few comments about your key issues." Next, "ask for a specific amount of money." Make sure you stop talking "even if the pause is seemingly forever." If asked, "explain why you need the money" and where it is going to go in the campaign. "Donors prefer to contribute to media buys . . . direct mail expenses . . . anything they can directly see or touch." Local congressional campaigns, especially challengers, delegate this function to volunteers. Fundraising consultants work with a candidate to develop a strategy to raise money. However, they do not always provide a phone bank operation to raise money. Instead, the fundraiser may only write the fundraising script, recruit, and train volunteers.[18]

Bundling

The Federal Election Commission (FEC) defines bundling as a procedure where an "intermediary . . . solicits and forwards (i.e., 'bundles') an earmarked contribution to a candidate or authorized committee." Campaigns frequently work with interest groups to help raise money through events and mail solicitations. One of the most innovative techniques was initiated by a pro-choice Democratic women's group called EMILY's List founded by Ellen Malcolm. The acronym, EMILY, stands for Early Money Is Like Yeast. "Why yeast? Because it makes the dough rise."[19]

EMILY's List provides contributors with a list of recommended candidates. Donors pay $100 to join the "List" and then donate an additional $100 apiece "earmarked" to two candidates the organization has endorsed. EMILY's List provides background material regarding endorsed candidates, including biographical information, issue stances, and an evaluation of the race. Today, EMILY's List raises more money during the election cycle than any other PAC in the nation. "In the 2002 elections, almost 73,000 EMILY's List members contributed nearly $9.7 million directly to pro-choice Democratic women running for the Senate, the House and Governor, by sending more than 101,000 contributions averaging $91." Bundling has become a very effective tool for fundraisers because it provides one-stop shopping for donors. Bundling PACs such as EMILY's List and its pro-choice Republican counterpart WISH List (Women in the Senate and House) only recommend candidates who have a chance to win. Incumbents and competitive challengers are attractive investments for donors because the money they contribute has a higher probability of paying off on election day.[20]

CAMPAIGN STAFF

Party insiders managed campaigns before the growth of the political consulting industry late in the 1950s. Ohio party boss Mark Hanna recruited William McKinley to run for President in 1896. James Farley, the Postmaster General under Franklin Roosevelt, managed the national Democratic Party. The political party provided technical assistance to various campaigns serving as the primary political consultant. The growth of the campaign consulting industry coincided with the decline of parties and the emergence of candidate-centered politics; however, staff still play a crucial role in the day-to-day operations of the campaign. Core staff functions such as press secretary, finance director, field organization director and, the campaign manager work exclusively for the campaign except in rare cases.

Press Secretary   *Press secretaries* filter information through public channels to the press enabling a candidate to earn media access to voters. Managing the news by putting a "spin" on the day's events is a major job function. The stylistic approach, conciliatory or aggressive, the press secretary uses can influence reporters' coverage of the campaign. Howard Wolfson who served as press secretary to

Hillary Rodham Clinton (D-NY) in her 2000 U.S. Senate race exemplified the conciliatory style. Wolfson portrayed the first lady as a team player and an unwarranted victim of opposition attacks. For instance, party officials were concerned that Clinton might upstage Al Gore's nomination at the Democratic Party Convention in Los Angeles. The first lady was delivering a speech on the first night of the convention, which was the main source of their concern. Wolfson, in his typically calm demeanor, attempted to assuage those fears. Wolfson stated to the press that it was "Al Gore's convention," and that Mrs. Clinton was devoted to making sure that that remained "the goal." Contrast Wolfson's reassuring style with Chris Lehane, press secretary to Vice President Gore during the 2000 presidential campaign. Lehane was an aggressive, combative, and extremely energetic press secretary self-nicknamed "the master of disaster." Lehane constantly few information to the press that was harshly critical of the opposition. He eventually wore out his welcome during the Florida recount. In a press briefing, Lehane referred to Florida Secretary of State Katherine Harris as a "Soviet commissar." The Gore campaign quickly replaced Lehane with "the more diplomatic Doug Hattaway."[21]

The press secretary works on the front lines with the news media every day answering inquiries, explaining the candidate's schedule, and strategically "leaking" information that the campaign wishes to feed the press. The press secretary or the campaign's communication director serves as the damage control officer fielding press inquiries about scandals, blunders, and revelations such as George W. Bush's DWI arrest on the weekend before the 2000 presidential election or Bill Clinton's affair with Gennifer Flowers revealed two weeks before the New Hampshire primary in 1992. Press secretaries attempt to "spin" the story in the most positive light. "Spinning" provides the campaign's version of a news story. The campaign uses the press as a conduit to transmit that message or story to voters. In today's world, polished press secretaries who understand public relations appear to have greater success with reporters than do combative press secretaries.

Finance Director   The *finance director* has one of the most difficult jobs in the entire campaign because they are responsible for paying the bills on-time, and for filing campaign finance reports. The complicated nuances of federal election law require the finance director should have intimate knowledge of federal campaign regulations. Campaigns often commit violations because the reporting requirements are so stringent and complex. One campaign finance expert said, "don't ever take the job as a finance director for a campaign because it isn't worth the headache." Campaign finance directors for challengers in U.S. House races are often unaware of the detailed reporting requirements of the Federal Election Campaign Act of 1971, subsequent amendments, the Bipartisan Campaign Reform Act (BCRA) of 2002, and the Internal Revenue Code. Mistakes and errors result in embarrassment when an opponent or reporters peruse these publicly filed reports, which now appear online.[22]

Field Operation   The *field operation* includes planning, scripting and running a campaign event (often known in campaign parlance as "advance" work), stuffing direct mail packets, establishing voter contact through literature drops or phone calls, and serving as the field army to get-out-the-vote (GOTV) on election day. The size of a field organization can vary tremendously from a couple dozen people (most of whom are volunteers) in a congressional race to thousands in a presidential race. For example, an army of young volunteers known as the "Bod Squad" traveled across the state of Minnesota on behalf of independent gubernatorial candidate Jesse Ventura. The effort was so successful that it helped Ventura win the governorship of Minnesota in 1998. Field operations are expanded enormously as candidates attempt to get their supporters (whom they have identified through phone banks) to the polls on election day. For example, wealthy candidate Jon Corzine (D-NJ) spent $2 million on his 2000 GOTV operation to win his New Jersey senate election.[23]

Unions and interest groups provide supplemental organizational muscle for key races. The mammoth AFL-CIO can exhort its 11 million members how to vote. The AFL-CIO uses its considerable resources to direct its own GOTV drive across the nation. The Christian Coalition produced 45 million voter guides in 2000 distributed on the weekend before the election, "educating" voters where candidates stood on issues that concerned fundamentalist Christian pro-family values. These "extended families" provide crucial strength and support for a candidate because no campaign has the budget to run such an extravagant operation.[24]

Targeting is the process of identifying key voter groups of support. Veteran Democratic consultant Will Robinson explains how campaigns target registered voters for GOTV operations: 1) Target the campaign's message to "key groups, areas and individuals to persuade them to support your candidate"; 2) "Create programs to identify key demographic groups, geographic areas or individuals"; 3) Develop a program to get "those identified supporters" to the polls on election day. On election day, the field organization contacts voters, offers rides to the polls, and then redoubles its efforts. A central location is needed to manage voter contact efforts to determine where turnout is lagging on election day (through information from poll watchers), and how to redirect resources if necessary.[25]

Canvassing identifies voters and their level of commitment to a candidate (called Voter ID). For example, hypothetical U.S. House candidate Sally Jones may find voter "a" strongly committed to her, voter "b" weakly committed to her, voter "c" undecided, voter "d" weakly committed to her opponent, and voter "e" strongly committed to her opponent. Campaigns prioritize leaning supporters ("b") as a GOTV target since strongly committed supporters ("a") tend to be self-motivated to vote. Campaigns use demographic, street, or topographic maps locating patterns of "b"-types to concentrate their resources for voter contact and later, GOTV.[26]

The suburban vote has become the biggest battleground for swing voters (leaners and undecided) in statewide and presidential elections. New York State features suburban Westchester (north of the Bronx), Nassau and Suffolk counties (Long Island) where many elections are won and lost statewide. About 20 percent of the statewide vote resides in these three suburban counties. Democrats perform well in New York City and Republicans in upstate New York (with the exception of the cities of Buffalo and Rochester). Since Republicans have a greater propensity to win the suburban vote, any Democrat winning more than 45 percent in the three suburban counties will likely win statewide.

National patterns emerge where Democratic and Republican core constituencies reside. African-Americans, Jews, teachers, manual labor workers, environmentalists, urban city dwellers, and working women identify with the Democratic Party. Geographically, the strongest regions of Democratic support reside in the Northeast, Mid-Atlantic, or on the Pacific Coast. White males, religious conservatives, rural citizens, and business proprietors represent core Republican party constituency groups. An L-shaped bracket drawn on a map from the Mountain States, turning right and cutting across the deep South characterize the Republican Party's base regions of political support. The substantial number of swing states and congressional districts makes the Midwest the most contested geographic region for Democrats and Republicans from congressional races up to presidential campaigns.

THE CAMPAIGN MANAGER: MANAGING CONSULTANTS AND STAFF

The campaign manager's job is akin to being a circus ringmaster featuring the candidate, consultants, and campaign staff. The manager may serve as the campaign's frontline general, the candidate's alter ego, the resident arbitrator to resolve internal conflict, and strategist. The campaign manager is in charge of the day-to-day operations of the campaign, but may also serve as the campaign's strategist. Karl Rove served as the de facto campaign manager of the 2000 Bush presidential campaign. Rove focused on strategy whereas the day-to-day management of campaign personnel, was handled by Joe Albaugh. On the other hand, house campaigns are more likely to feature the campaign manager in the dual role of chief strategist and daily operations manager.

The General

Supervising the day-to-day operations of a major campaign means that the manager serves as commander-in-chief of the ground war of the campaign. A campaign manager must respond immediately to changes in the political environment. The 1992 Clinton campaign headquarters featured a nerve center called "The War Room" with campaign manager James Carville, a former Marine, in the role of general.

> Each morning at 6:45, Carville arrived in his T shirt and jeans and a worn fatigue coat marked SEABEES. He ran the War Room like a drill sergeant, bellowing, "Run, don't walk" and "I'm going to be irritated all day" and "I am about to erupt" at his young recruits.[27]

Carville's combative leadership style infused the Clinton staff with the urgency to remain on the offensive against incumbent President George Bush, Sr. to win. Carville imposed a disciplined regime on a free-wheeling campaign when given the authority in June of 1992. One unidentified campaign staffer told *Newsweek* magazine: "Thank God. He's [Carville] the only one who knows how to play in this league." Clinton promoted Carville at a time when his campaign was struggling and falling behind both President Bush and independent candidate Ross Perot in the polls. Carville understood that the political climate was dynamic and often required the campaign to change tactics on a moment's notice without incessant debate among staffers. A campaign general has the authority to operate in this manner.[28]

Alter Ego and Arbitrator

The campaign manager serves as the resident alter ego for the candidate. An intimate understanding of a candidate's personality traits, stamina, intellect, and moodiness enables the campaign manager to advise and pace the candidate in the field. Candidates such as John McCain and Bill Clinton need little pacing given their extraordinary energy level—they can make five to ten campaign stops a day, travel thousands of miles, eat on the run, and need little sleep. Such a torrid pace for weeks would trip up most normal candidates leading to verbal mistakes on the campaign trail.

The campaign manager must also serve as an arbitrator or mediator among the staff, consultants, and candidate. Presidential candidate Bob Dole (R) consented to campaign manager Scott Reed's plan to demote media advisors Don Sipple and Mike Murphy just three weeks before election day in 1996. Dole gave Reed the authority to bring the "ad operation more directly into the campaign structure." Sipple and Murphy quit. Reed and Dole's displeasure with the advertising led to their de facto dismissal. Campaign managers carry out difficult personnel decisions and ensure that their candidate keeps a distance from the politics within the campaign. Candidates face enough distractions on the campaign trail.[29]

Strategist

Campaign managers doubling as strategists should understand that the scope and vision of a campaign operation go beyond management. Familiarity with important issues and the political environment of a congressional district or state makes a campaign manager invaluable. Hillary Rodham Clinton hired veteran New York politico Bill DeBlasio in November of 1999 as her Senate campaign manager because of his intimate knowledge of state politics. DeBlasio could provide an outsider such as Hillary Clinton an understanding of the nuances of New York politics. Her opponent, Rick Lazio, a Republican house member from Long Island hired national media strategist

Mike Murphy as his de facto campaign manager for an entirely different reason. Lazio needed to boost his name recognition and raise
his stature to equal that of a national political figure such as Hillary
Clinton. Murphy had experience working with nationally renowned
politicians such as Bob Dole (R-KS) and John McCain (R-AZ); thus,
the choice made sense.

The campaign manager works with the lead political consultants as a strategist. Strategists are responsible for developing the
"message" that the campaign wishes to communicate to voters. The
campaign manager is responsible for ensuring "message discipline"
focusing on one or two major ideas the candidate needs to articulate
to win voter support, and for reminding the candidate to stay "on
message." Ronald Reagan was a master of message discipline. His
1980 presidential campaign message of "peace through strength"
implied that the Carter administration vacillated on foreign policy
toward the Soviets and mishandled the Iran-hostage crisis. John
Sears and James Baker who played integral roles managing the campaign ensured that Reagan remained message-disciplined on the
campaign trail, briefing him on the audience and reminding him to
articulate key themes in his speeches. Reagan was the most disciplined candidate of the past quarter-century because his background
as a Hollywood actor enabled him to memorize and articulate ideas
with great clarity.

CAMPAIGN PLAN, STRATEGY AND MESSAGE

Writing an effective campaign plan incorporates a coherent strategy,
a theme, and appropriate tactics to win an election. An effective
strategy can set the context for debate in a campaign. The strategy
must focus on an important personal attribute, issue, or value that
can decisively turn the debate in favor of the candidate. The
acronym KISS (Keep It Simple Stupid) helps a campaign simplify a
message that is easily memorable to voters. Distilling the message
into a pithy slogan reminds voters about a campaign's basic message. For example, Jeff Bingamann (D-NM) a candidate for U.S.
Senate in 1982 criticized his opponent, incumbent and former astro-
naut Harrison Schmidt (R-NM) for being ineffective in the Senate.
His campaign slogan—"What on earth has he done for us?"—made
the election a referendum on Schmidt's job performance. Bingamann
won the seat by a comfortable 54–46 percent margin.[30]

Campaigns develop individual strategies for the primary and general election campaign because the voting audience in each election differs. Partisan primary voters cluster around liberal populist (i.e., Democratic) or conservative (i.e., Republican) ideologies. The general election audience includes voters not affiliated with either party (independents). Most importantly, undecided or "swing" voters can represent five to 30 percent of the electorate. These voters determine who wins a close election making the fight for their support the campaign's major political battleground.

Superior campaign strategies marry the style of the candidate with the substance of the campaign. The strategy crafted for Jimmy Carter's successful 1976 presidential bid exemplifies a clear and coherent strategy. Carter was a little-known former Georgia governor with a telegenic smile who possessed an extraordinary personal drive to run for the presidency. Gerald Rafshoon, his media advisor, submitted a strategy memorandum connecting Carter's personal image with policy substance:

> He still has that Kennedy smile. . . . What he does not have is
> much depth to his image. He is not as well-known as many big-
> name politicians in the U.S. and is not known for the heavyweight
> ideas and programs that he is capable of articulating. . . . Getting
> this across should be the no.1 priority now . . . at the same time
> trying to infect all southern states . . . with the Jimmy Carter's,
> "good guy" brand of populism.[31]

Rafshoon's memo developed two tracks of strategy for Carter's primary campaign: 1) attracting policy-oriented voters from the Northeast and Midwest where early primaries and caucuses took place, while 2) maintaining his natural political base in the South with his "good guy" populism. Rafshoon demonstrates how a candidate's strengths can be adapted to different constituencies. Portraying a candidate different from their natural disposition or viewpoint makes no sense. Running Hillary Rodham Clinton as a "compassionate conservative" or George Bush as a "new progressive" would be useless. Instead, effective campaign strategies tie the substantive qualities of a candidate (character and issues) to a demographic plan targeting key voter groups for support.

General election strategy differs from party nomination strategies because expanding the political base to include "swing" voters is necessary to build a winning coalition. Karl Rove, Senior Advisor to President George W. Bush, wrote a strategy memo for Republican

REPUBLICAN STRATEGY MEMORANDUM, JUNE 4, 2002

Mid-Term Political Landscape

More favorable to Republicans control of congress will turn on handful of races decided by local issues, candidate quality, money raised, campaign performance, etc.

- Extremely Popular President
- Recovering Economy
- Increased Importance of National Security Issues
- Redistricting
- No Compelling National Issue for Referendum
- Small Number of Competitive Races

Democratic Strategy

- Support President on War
- Question President's Middle East Strategy
- Attack on Domestic Agenda—Social Security, Health Care Costs, Environment, Education
- Use Budget, Tax Cuts, and Enron for Class Warfare
- Divide President and Congressional Republicans
- Maximize Outside Resources

Republican Strategy

- Focus on War and Economy
- Promote Compassion Agenda—Education, Welfare, Faith
- Highlight Democrats' Obstructionism on Judges, Agenda
- Mobilize GOP Base, Reach Out to Hispanics, Unions, African-Americans
- Strong Teamwork between White House, Political Committees and Members
- Maximize Outside Resources and Create New Forums

2002 Bush Outreach

Maintain	Grow
Base, Coal and Steel, Farmers, Ranchers	Latinos, Suburbs (esp. Women), Catholics, Union Members, Wired Workers
Expand	**Improve**
Believers (Religious conservatives)	African Americans

Source: Karl Rove, Senior Advisor to the President, Office of Strategic Initiatives, White House, June 4, 2002.

congressional candidates for the 2002 midterm elections. The memo's contents inadvertently became public when the disk containing the document was accidentally lost on a street near Capitol Hill and picked up by a Democratic senate staffer.

The Rove memorandum written for the Republican party retained the same principles of a strategy written for an individual candidate: 1) the strategy provided an overview of the political context and environment; 2) it mapped out counterstrategies to the Democrats; and 3) the memo explained how Republicans should appeal to key demographic groups with messages of leadership and compassion. The strategy linked Republican candidates to the fortunes of President Bush. The memorandum argued that Republicans were the party of leadership and security, based on the events of 9/11, the war on terrorism, and the impending confrontation to oust Saddam Hussein from power in Iraq. Rove sought to increase Republican candidate support among key voter groups (e.g., suburban voters) who would ultimately hold the key for Republicans that autumn.

Bush conducted a whirlwind campaign trip around the country during the ten days preceding the election helping Republican candidates in southern, midwestern, and western states. Bush repeatedly drove home the message that Republicans exercised stronger leadership at a time when America became vulnerable to international terrorism. The midterm election showed Republicans increasing their majority in the U.S. House by six seats and winning two U.S. Senate seats to regain the majority in the upper chamber. Simultaneous gains in both chambers represented a feat last achieved in 1934 by the party controlling the White House. The Rove memorandum articulated the strategic plan leading to these historic Republican victories in 2002.[32]

CAMPAIGN STRATEGY TYPOLOGIES

Four popular strategies that candidates employ during a campaign are illustrated in Table 4-1. Strategies, in part, reflect the motivations why candidates run for office. The *morality/populist* strategy is exemplified by Jimmy Carter (promising never to lie), Jesse Ventura (promising to get special interests out of politics), and Jesse Jackson (fighting for the dispossessed). The strategy aims at securing the

TABLE 4-1 Strategy Typologies

Strategy	Message	Key Voter Groups	Example
Morality/ Populist	"I will not tell a lie"	Suburban women, farmers, Independents, religious voters	Carter, Pres., 1976
Incumbency	Experience, Trust, Results	Partisan base and independents	Any
Issues (e.g., slavery)	"A house divided against itself cannot stand"	Northeastern and midwestern small businesses, abolitionists,	Lincoln, Pres., 1860
Destroy the Opposition	"Too many lies for too long"	Suburban and upstate voters	Schumer, Senate, New York, 1998

support of disaffected voters through a grassroots appeal and turning them out in large numbers on election day.

The *incumbency* strategy stresses experience, reliability, and results. An overwhelming majority of congressional and senatorial incumbents wins reelection (see Chapter 3). Incumbents have name recognition and they claim credit for bringing programs, grants, and contracts back to the district or state. Senator Trent Lott (R-MS), chairman of the powerful Appropriations Committee and former majority leader, excels in procuring federally funded projects for Mississippi, the poorest state in the nation. For example, Lott secured a $4.75 million federal grant to establish dozens of "PowerUp" centers in Mississippi in 2002. "PowerUp" is a program "dedicated to helping youth succeed in the digital age." Lott's ability to secure so many grants is unique but does characterize how incumbents seek to build and secure local support among their constituents. Incumbents who deliver on services to the district or state are protecting themselves against challenger claims of unresponsiveness.[33]

Issue strategies address concerns that affect a constituency. The strategic missile defense initiative (SDI) or "Star Wars" was a wedge issue in the 1986 Colorado U.S. Senate race between Democrat Tim Wirth and Republican Ken Kramer. A wedge issue divides the electorate so that the outcome of the election may hinge on which side "wins" on the issue. The Defense Department selected Colorado Springs to deploy the missile shield system. The issue divided environmentalists and peace activists (supporting Wirth) from military dependents and defense workers in the state (supporting Kramer). Wirth prevailed by a narrow 50–48 percent margin arguing that the deployment would make Coloradoans more vulnerable to a first-strike nuclear attack by the Soviet Union.[34]

An historic example of an issue strategy was the 1858 Illinois U.S. Senate race between Republican Abraham Lincoln and Democrat Stephen Douglas. The campaign featured the famous series of debates on "the great problem." Lincoln argued that slavery was an abomination and that "the great problem" not spread into new territories or states. Lincoln's famous speech to the Republican state convention on June 16, 1858 revealed his feelings about slavery and secession. "A house divided against itself cannot stand. I believe this government cannot endure, permanently half slave and half free. . . . Either the opponents of slavery will arrest the further spread of it . . . or its advocates will push it forward, till it should become lawful in all the States, old as well as new, North as well as South." Lincoln's eloquence was not sufficient for Illinoisans to elect him to the Senate, but it did make him a national political figure. Lincoln emerged from defeat and was elected president just two years later.[35]

Negative campaign strategies seek to *destroy the opposition*. The negative approach is utilized in states or districts where the political environment is tolerant of such tactics. Senator Charles Schumer (D-NY), former Senator Alphonse D'Amato (R-NY), Congressman Tom DeLay (R-TX) and former Congressman James Trafficant (D-Ohio) have been recent practitioners of this art. The art of attacking one's opponent works under the following conditions: 1) the opponent has high personal negatives (political lingo for personal unpopularity); 2) a candidate's timing has to be impeccable and does not create a backlash of sympathy for the opponent; and, 3) the voting population is used to rough-and-tumble political campaigns (e.g., New Jersey and New York).

The New York Senate race of 1998 is a prime example of two candidates trying to destroy each other. Incumbent Alphonse D'Amato (R-NY) bragged about his propensity to bring government contracts and projects back to the state. As a no-holds-barred politician, D'Amato often intimidated or cowed his opponents in three previous Senate elections (1986, 1989, and 1992). D'Amato faced Congressman Chuck Schumer (D-NY) of Brooklyn in the 1998 election.

Schumer's hard-hitting campaign style matched D'Amato. Both candidates had aggressive personalities and there was deep animosity between them as they launched a series of attacks on one another. For example, Schumer's campaign slogan was "too many lies, for too long" implying that D'Amato was not always truthful with voters. D'Amato attacked Schumer's attendance record and then called him a "putzhead," which some interpreted as an ethnic slur. The scorched earth tactics by both candidates reflected their overall strategy to destroy one another.[36]

Merging various strategies remains a tactic to expand a candidate's voter base. The appeal can incorporate issues, moral arguments, or accusations about the opponent. The danger lies in the breadth of the strategy, which may obfuscate the campaign's central message. Ross Perot's 1992 presidential strategy exemplified how a merged strategy works. Perot argued that Washington needed an outside force to change the status quo (populism) because the political system was dominated by "special interests" that were inherently evil (morality). These special interests had hijacked the federal budget creating a tremendous deficit. The continued growth of the deficit would increase the public debt and burden the next generation of voters (issues). Perot's strategy was effective because it logically connected the candidate's populist persona with his conceptualization of the presidency. Perot's attention to the budget deficit made it a priority once Clinton assumed the presidency in 1993. The fact that Perot won 19 percent of the popular vote, the largest third party vote since 1912, was certainly not lost on Clinton.[37]

EXTERNAL SOURCES OF SUPPORT: POLITICAL PARTIES AND INTEREST GROUPS

Political parties and interest groups have played an integral and historical role helping candidates win political office. Political parties actively recruit candidates to run for U.S. House and Senate seats. Furthermore, their resources are integral to conducting statewide or national GOTV efforts. Interest groups such as the Sierra Club and the National Rifle Association have enormous memberships whom they mobilize to vote in key elections. Major interest groups can communicate their agendas via e-mail to members and advertise on television to influence public opinion before an election. These functions are comparable to traditional voter contact and mobilization roles by political parties, but on a smaller scale.[38]

Political Parties

Terry Nelson, executive director of political operations at the Republican National Committee (RNC) states that political parties play roles during two crucial phases of a campaign. First, the national party helps challengers recruit a team of operatives (consultants and staff) to run the best possible race. For example, the Republican party might advise a New Jersey congressional candidate to hire a media consultant who has experience working in the Northeast or mid-Atlantic region. Republicans and Democrats conduct training seminars for potential candidates explaining all of the necessary components of campaign management: recruiting staff and consultants, understanding the importance of a campaign plan, developing an effective message that reaches out to voters, and training candidates. (Candidate training is a series of mini-courses on how to solicit money, appear on television, and conduct press conferences).[39]

Parties play a second important role as they reemerge at the end of the campaign to mobilize the party base for a GOTV effort. Laws allow candidates and state parties to coordinate expenditures for GOTV efforts. A "coordinated campaign" means that the state party conducts a statewide GOTV effort down to the district and precinct level. National parties have the resources to coordinate massive multi-state GOTV efforts by directing resources to the state parties most in need as the election approaches. Voter registration, GOTV, and voter "education" (informing voters about issues) are legally protected rights of political parties acknowledged through a line of Supreme Court decisions including *Colorado Republican Federal Campaign Committee v. FEC* (1996).[40]

Parties, Interest Groups, Soft Money and Independent Expenditures

Voter education often takes the form of issue advocacy. Issue advocacy is any electioneering activity that does not expressly advocate the election or defeat of a candidate. The money to pay for issue advocacy was not subject to limitation under the federal law until the Bipartisan Campaign Reform Act (BCRA) went into effect on November 6, 2002. BCRA's purpose is to limit spending by parties (soft money) and interest groups (independent expenditures) to fund "sham ads" that appear on television within 45 days of a primary or 60 days before the general election that name a candidate for federal office. "Sham ads" masquerade as commercials implying the election or defeat of a candidate. The growth of soft money in campaigns to fund such advertisements grew from $262 million in 1996 to $570 million in 2000. Under the law, only "hard money" contributions (limited to $2,000 per person for each election contest) can pay for issue ads. BCRA makes it more difficult for parties and interest groups to raise large increments of money from contributors to promote "issue ads" in the waning days of a campaign. Before BCRA, parties could ask individual donors to give tens or hundreds of thousands of dollars to fund "issue ads."[41]

Opponents of BCRA claim that the law restricts free speech, which is guaranteed under the First Amendment to the Constitution. The court ruled in *Buckley v. Valeo* (1976) that money facilitates political speech. A coalition of free speech advocates including liberals and conservatives led by Senator Mitch McConnell (R-KY) challenged this law, which was argued before the Supreme Court in September 2003. The central questions the Court addressed were: 1) whether time, place, and manner restrictions are applicable to issue ads or do such restrictions violate free speech? and, 2) can political parties use "soft money" (i.e., money not subject to individual contribution limits) to "educate" voters through issue ads?[42] In a December 2003 ruling, the Supreme Court ruled that issue ads could be regulated and party soft money banned by BCRA was legal.

Interest Groups

The growth of issue advocacy enabled interest groups to become an increasingly strong "third force" in American elections, independent of both parties and candidates. Interest groups and Political Action Committees (PACs) are operators independent of the political parties; although in the past coordination of activities with Democratic and Republican leadership organizations often occurred behind the scenes. Organizations such as the National Rifle Association (NRA), Christian Coalition, the Sierra Club, and Planned Parenthood "are able to structure their campaigns similarly to those of political parties". Interest groups use their agenda to mobilize supporters for contributions, volunteering, and GOTV. Independent expenditures

---

HOW THE NATIONAL PARTIES ARE ORGANIZED

Students of politics always ask concrete question about political parties: What constitutes a political party? A congressional party? A state or national political party organization? In Washington, D.C., the locus of national parties resides in two buildings off Capitol Hill. Republican National Headquarters nearest the Capitol is home to three principal organizations: the Republican National Committee (RNC), the National Republican Senatorial Committee (NRSC), and the National Republican Congressional Committee (NRCC). Three blocks away, Democratic National Headquarters houses three counterpart organizations: the Democratic National Committee (DNC), the Democratic Senatorial Campaign Committee (DSCC), and the Democratic Congressional Campaign Committee (DCCC). Each committee is a separate organization with fundraising, communications, and political divisions.

The RNC and DNC are the national party organizations serving national and state candidates. Both organizations provide research and technical assistance (e.g., candidate training and general advice) to all party candidates. In a presidential election year, both committees serve as the organizational muscle to coordinate GOTV activities among the state parties. The RNC and DNC are also responsible for running their respective national party conventions, which nominate presidential candidates. Midterm elections feature heightened activity by House (NRCC and DCCC) and Senate (NRSC and DSCC) election committees because no presidential race takes place that year.

---

have made a great impact for issue advocacy groups enabling them to buy television time for advertising, and reach mass audiences. Interest groups associated with Democratic candidates (e.g., AFL-CIO, EMILY's List, Planned Parenthood, NAACP, Sierra Club) spent $125.5 million supporting their candidates in 2000 compared $105 million by organizations affiliated with Republican candidates (e.g., Citizens for Better Medicare, NRA, U.S. Chamber of Commerce, the Business Roundtable). Much of that money was spent on issue advertising. BCRA restricts the ability of interest groups and parties to pay for issue ads. If the Supreme Court upholds these regulations, then the communication power of interest groups will be substantially diminished.[43]

CONCLUSION

The American tradition of winning campaigns reveals a paradox about democracy and capitalism; only when a small business achieves the pinnacle of success does it disband. Modern campaigns with technological sophistication and specialization decrease the time-frame to make crucial decisions to stay on the offensive against the opposition. The essential ingredient for success according to Terry Nelson of the Republican National Committee is "teamwork." The absence of teamwork among staff and consultants imperils an incumbent's reelection chances and fatal for a challenger. The campaign has only one Michael Jordan (the candidate); everyone else is a role player helping the team win. Fundraising creates the capital needed to run essential campaign operations. Polling, advertising, and the emerging Internet are three indispensable tools providing the campaign team with the necessary information, strategy, and means to defeat an opponent. Polling provides a roadmap for how to plan the campaign. Paid advertising and the Internet are media where national candidates introduce or reintroduce themselves to voters in most cases. The Internet also serves as a fundraising and a grassroots organizational tool for candidates. In a world where citizens are bombarded with commercials playing on 100 television stations or numerous pop-up ads on web sites, capturing the attention of voters require increasing specialization and sophistication. Thus, the book's attention turns to polling, paid advertising, and campaigning on the Internet in the following three chapters.[44]

STUDY/DISCUSSION QUESTIONS

What attributes characterize a well-run campaign organization?
How do campaign strategists craft an effective message?
What strategy typologies would you argue are most effective in modern political campaigns?
How do parties and interest groups influence political campaigns?
What special problems do challengers face in raising money?

Do modern campaigns help or hinder democracy with their attention to message and strategy?

SUGGESTED READINGS

Johnson, Dennis. *No Place for Amateurs.* New York: Routledge, 2001.

Sabato, Larry. *The Rise of Political Consultants.* New York: Basic Books, 1981.

Shaw, Catherine. *The Campaign Manager: Running and Winning Local Elections.* Boulder, CO: Westview, 2000.

Shea, Daniel M., and Michael John Burton. *Campaign Craft: The Strategies, Tactics, and Art of Political Campaign Management.* Westport, CT: Praeger, 2001.

Stevens, Stuart. *The Big Enchilada: Campaign Adventures with the Cockeyed Optimists from Texas Who Won the Biggest Prize in Politics.* New York: Free Press, 2001.

Thurber, James A., and Candice J. Nelson, eds. *Campaign Warriors: Political Consultants in Elections.* Washington, DC: Brookings, 2000.

NOTES

1. David Maraniss, *When Pride Still Mattered: A Life of Vince Lombardi* (Washington, DC: Touchstone, 1999), 367–69. Maraniss discusses the origins of the quote from a film entitled *Trouble Along the Way,* then picked up by Vanderbilt and UCLA football coach Red Sanders in the late 1940s. Lombardi probably heard the Sanders quote (from where, no one is sure) and used it to motivate his own team.

2. "The War Room Drill," *Newsweek Special Election Issue,* November/December 1992, 78.

3. Ceci Connolly, "Daley to Chair Gore Campaign," *The Washington Post,* June 16, 2000, A6.

4. Mary Matalin and James Carville, with Peter Knobler, *All's Fair: Love, War and Running for President* (New York: Random House, 1992), 92 (first quote), 299 (third quote); Jack Germond and Jules Witcover, *Mad as Hell: Revolt at the Ballot Box, 1992* (New York: Warner Books, 1993), 246 (second quote).

5. Stuart Stevens, *The Big Enchilada: Campaign Adventures with the Cockeyed Optimists from Texas Who Won the Biggest Prize in Politics* (New York: Free Press, 2001), 147–49. Joe Albaugh ran the

day-to-day operations of the campaign, but Rove was clearly in charge and the final authority to make important decisions.

6. "Win-Loss Records," *Campaigns and Elections*, December/ January 2001, 59–61. The firm won six out of seven senatorial races and three out of four congressional races in the 2000 general election.

7. Charles Bierbauer, "Head Games in Virginia Senate Ad Draw Fire," *CNN.com*, October 10, 1996. Accessed June 30, 2003 at *www.cnn.com/ALLPOLITICS/1996/news/9610/10/bierbauer.warner/ index.shtml.*

8. Martin Hamburger, "Lessons from the Field: A Journey into Political Consulting," in *Campaign Warriors: Political Consultants in Elections*, ed. James A. Thurber and Candice J. Nelson (Washington, DC: Brookings, 2000), 53–64; Greener and Hook bios accessed on June 17, 2002 at *www.greenerhook.com*; James A. Thurber and Candice J. Nelson, "Introduction to the Study of Campaign Consultants," in *Campaign Warriors: Political Consultants in Elections*, ed. James A. Thurber and Candice J. Nelson (Washington, DC: Brookings, 2000), 3; Larry Sabato, *The Rise of Political Consultants* (New York: Basic Books, 1981), 14.

9. *Campaigns and Elections*, "Political Pages" 1993–1994 and 2002–2003.

10. Tony Payton, "Same Wavelength," *Campaigns and Elections*, July 2001, 24 (first quote); Joe Napolitan, "More Than They Can Handle," *Campaigns and Elections*, July 2001, 24 (second quote); see "Winners & Losers 2002: Consultant Win-Loss Records," *Campaigns and Elections*, December/January 2003, 60 (Nordlinger) and 44 (Hammond).

11. Lee Rainie, "Untuned Keyboards," PowerPoint presentation at the 2003 Politics Online Conference, March 21, 2003, Washington, DC, regarding Internet usage.

12. "Glossary," Center for Responsive Politics, Washington, DC. Accessed June 18, 2002 at *www.opensecrets.org/pubs/glossary/ Gloss13.htm* for Unruh quote.

13. "A Brief History of Money in Politics: How Americans Have Financed Elections in the Past," Center for Responsive Politics, Washington, DC. Accessed June 19, 2002 at *www.opensecrets.org/ pubs/history/history2.html* for Hanna quote; Mark Humbert, "Billionaire's Bid for New York Governor Broke Campaign Spending Record," *Associated Press*, December 2, 2002.

14. Marty Stone, "Revisions for Campaign Chapter." E-mail (May 5, 2003). Stone has served as a partner in the Democratic media firm of Laguens, Hamburger, and Stone. Stone manages his own company as well, Stone Phones, as a phone consultant. He was one of several Democratic and Republican political consultants who helped with this project.
15. Glenn R. Simpson, "The Internet Begins to Click as a Political Money Web," *Wall Street Journal*, October 19, 1999. Accessed July 17, 2003 at *www.politicsonline.com/coverage/wsj3*. According to Simpson's article, a "traditional direct-mail pitch costs 30 to 40 cents per address. . . ." Given the inflation rate since 1999, 40 cents is probably a reasonable estimate. "Direct Mail Response Rates," Direct Mail Data Solutions. Accessed June 18, 2002 at *www.directmaildata.com/id_web/DirectMailResponseRates.html* on response rates.
16. Chuck Muth, "17 Tips: How to Raise Money with Mail," *Campaigns and Elections*, May 1998, 51–53.
17. Mike Allen, "GOP Takes in $33 Million at Fundraiser." *Washington Post*, May 15, 2002, A1, A9, for all references on the Bush-GOP fundraiser.
18. Cathy Allen, "How to Ask for Money," *Campaigns and Elections* April 1998, 25.
19. "Bundling by Individuals," *FEC Record*, August 1996, 2, quote on definition of bundling; Frank J. Sorauf, *Inside Campaign Finance* (New Haven, CT: Yale University Press, 1992), 268, quote on definition of EMILY's List.
20. "How EMILY's List Works" *EMILY's List*. Accessed June 27, 2003 at *www.emilyslist.org/contribute/how_el_works.phtml*. Paraphrased quote from how the contribution system works for EMILY's List. "About Emily's List: History of EMILY's List," *EMILY's List*. Accessed June 27, 2003 at *www.emilyslist.org/about/history.phtml*, campaign contributions during the 2001–2002 election cycle.
21. Marc Humbert, "Hillary Clinton Spokesman Seeks to Downplay Tension with Gore Campaign," *Associated Press*, July 8, 2000, Wolfson quote; "Election 2000: The Players." *Pittsburgh Post-Gazette*, December 17, 2000. Accessed June 17, 2002 at *post-gazette.com/election2000/200011217pzplayers.asp*, Chris Lehane and "Soviet Commissar" quote.
22. Campaign finance official, speech to American University class, Washington, DC, September 2, 2001.

23. "The Last, Frenzied Push for Votes," *Christian Science Monitor*, November 6, 2000. Accessed June 30, 2003 at *http//search .csmonitor.com/durable/2000/11/06*, regarding Jon Corzine's GOTV plan.

24. Jonathan Karl, "Massive Christian Coalition Get-out-the-Vote Effort, *CNN/AllPolitics.com*, November 4, 1996. Accessed June 29, 2003 at *www.cnn.com/ALLPOLITICS/1996/news/9611/04/news+/ index.shtml*, on CC voter guides.

25. Will Robinson, "Organizing the Field," in *Campaigns and Elections American Style*, ed. James A. Thurber and Candice J. Nelson (Boulder, CO: Westview, 1995), 138, 144–50.

26. Jules Witcover, *Marathon: The Pursuit of the Presidency 1972–1976*. (New York: Viking Press, 1977), 230, provides a version on Voter ID and "call-lists" that is still relevant 26 years later.

27. "The War Room Drill," *Newsweek Special Election Issue*, 78.

28. "Manhattan Project; 1992," *Newsweek Special Election Issue*, 56.

29. "Dole Shakes Up Advertising Team," *USA Today*, October 15, 1996. Accessed June 20, 2002 at *www.usatoday.com/elect/ep/epr/ eprdl1225.htm*.

30. Michael Barone and Grant Ujifusa, *The Almanac of American Politics 1986* (Washington, DC: National Journal, 1985), 879.

31. Martin Schram, *Running for President: A Journal of the Carter Campaign* (New York: Pocket Books, 1977), 59.

32. Karl Rove, *The Strategic Landscape*, Office of Strategic Initiatives, White House, June 4, 2002.

33. David Mayhew, *Congress: The Electoral Connection* (New Haven, CT: Yale University Press, 1974) and Morris Fiorina, *Congress: The Keystone to the Washington Establishment* (New Haven, CT: Yale, University Press, 1989) on the power of incumbency; "PowerUp Completes $4.75M Installation of 66 Technology Centers Across Mississippi," *PowerUp*, Press Release, January 22, 2002.

34. Michael Barone and Grant Ujifusa, *Almanac of American Politics 1990* (Washington, DC: National Journal, 1989), 190.

35. Abraham Lincoln, *Abraham Lincoln's Great Speeches*. Notes by John Grafton. (New York: Dover, 1991), 25.

36. Joel Sigel, "Al, Chuck Hit Hard," *New York Daily News*. Accessed November 10, 1998 at *www.dailynews.com*; James Dao and Adam Nagourney, "D'Amato's Missteps and Self-Doubts Helped with Political Punch," *The New York Times*. Accessed November 10,

1998 at *www.nytimes.com;* and both articles summarized in Richard J. Semiatin, *1998 Mid-Term Elections Update* (New York: McGraw-Hill, 1999), 22.

37. See Wilson McCarey Williams, "The Meaning of the Election," in *The Election of 1992*, ed. Gerald M. Pomper (Washington, DC: Congressional Quarterly, 1993), 200–201, on the Perot candidacy.

38. Mark J. Rozell and Richard J. Semiatin, "Interest Groups in the 2000 Congressional Elections," in *The Interest Groups Connection: Electioneering, Lobbying and Policymaking in Washington*, ed. Paul S. Herrnson, Ronald G. Shaiko, and Clyde Wilcox (Chatham, NJ: Chatham House, in press).

39. Terry Nelson, deputy chief-of-staff, executive director of political operations, Republican National Committee. Interview at Republican National Committee (RNC) headquarters, Washington, DC, June 24, 2002.

40. Colorado Republican Federal Campaign Committee v. Federal Election Commission. (116-S.CT.) 1996.

41. Federal Election Commission. See *www.fec.gov.*

42. Buckley v. Valeo (424 U.S. 1) 1976; *McConell v. FEC* 2003.

43. Rozell and Semiatin; Mark J. Rozell and Clyde Wilcox, *Interest Groups in American Campaigns: The New Face of Electioneering* (Washington, DC: Congressional Quarterly Press, 1998); David B. Magleby, ed., 2001. (Report), *Election Advocacy: Soft Money and Issue Advocacy in the 2000 Congressional Elections* (Provo, UT: Center for the Study of Elections and Democracy, Brigham Young University, 2001), 20–21, on spending by key Democratic and Republican interest groups.

44. Nelson.

CHAPTER 5

Polling

Pollsters are like mothers and shortstops, everybody thinks they have the best.[1]

— *John R. Reilly, political consultant,*
paraphrasing an unknown source[1]

How do you run against a 20-year incumbent in a predominantly Democratic district? Republican Rob Simmons was a respected and well-known five-term state legislator in Connecticut who considered a 2000 race against incumbent Sam Gejdenson (D) in the Second Congressional District (C.D.) despite the odds against him. Simmons was a Vietnam veteran and former congressional staff member who had taught courses on "military intelligence" at Yale's Berkley College.[2]

The Second C.D. is found in the eastern third of Connecticut. Factories, nuclear power plants, and shipbuilding are the district's major industries. Gejdenson had won several close reelection races in the past, and in his most recent campaign (1998) he garnered a comfortable 61 percent of the vote. Futhermore, the incumbent had out fundraised his opponent by a massive eight-to-one margin. Rumors persisted that Gejdenson would retire in several years, providing Simmons with a better opportunity to win the seat. However, in a surprising move Simmons decided to challenge Gejdenson in 2000. To beat an entrenched incumbent, Simmons needed the expertise of a consultant to devise an effective strategy and create a winning message.[3]

Simmons hired Neil Newhouse of Public Opinion Strategies, one of the top Republican pollsters, with a proven track-record in federal and statewide races. Newhouse conducted a "benchmark" poll in the spring of 1999. Benchmark surveys provide a picture of the political environment, explaining what issues concern voters, and rate how favorable or unfavorable the survey respondents evaluate the candidates. The "horse race" between the candidates showed Gejdenson leading Simmons by a wide 53–25 percent margin. In addition, 70 percent of voters had a favorable personable impression of the incumbent Democrat. However, the poll also found only 41 percent of the district voters supporting his reelection. Newhouse said, "the dichotomy between Gejdenson's job approval rating and his reelection rate says . . . [that] Sam has worn out his welcome." Voters were well aware that Gejdenson spent most of his time living outside the district with his wife "in a gated community in Branford, in the 3rd district."[4]

Gejdenson's residence outside of the district had been an issue in two previous campaigns (1996–1998), but it resonated more strongly as the 2000 election approached. The longer he served, the more Gejdenson seemed out of touch with his constituents even though he was a Democrat in a liberal-leaning district. Newhouse's survey asked whether the Congressman "was out of touch with eastern Connecticut residents?" When 57 percent of respondents said "yes," the Simmons campaign team was sure this spelled trouble for the incumbent. As Cheryl Klock (the campaign manager) and Kevin McNeill (the research consultant) for Simmons wrote in *Campaigns and Elections* magazine: "The message of the campaign was simple: *Rob Simmons is a perfect fit for the district, Gejdenson is out of touch with the district, and it is time for a change.*" The strategy forged 18 months before the election served as the basis for Simmons' narrow 51–49 percent victory. What made his victory more remarkable was that presidential candidate Al Gore (D) won the district over George W. Bush (R) by a 55–38 percent margin. Furthermore, the presence of Connecticut Senator Joseph Lieberman (D), on the ticket as Gore's running mate, did not translate into additional Democratic votes for Gejdenson. The more important lesson learned from the Simmons-Gejdenson race is that polling reveals a candidate's political "Achilles heel." Polling provides intelligence that is indispensable to candidates in developing a winning strategy.[5]

WHY CANDIDATES NEED SURVEY RESEARCH

A campaign without polls is similar to a boat without oars. If the campaign cannot chart its way through the stiff political currents, then the undertow will submerge the campaign. Today, nearly every congressional, senatorial, gubernatorial, and presidential candidate conducts survey research as do many state legislative candidates across the country. Polls provide candidates with an understanding of the political environment and the electorate. They enable candidates to evaluate the strengths and weaknesses of their opponents and themselves. Surveys help campaigns gauge how issues affect voter choices. Polls provide "horse race" information where voters take stock of the competing candidates at any given point in time. Furthermore, trend analysis conducted throughout the campaign charts how key voter groups move in the direction of either candidate.

This chapter provides an overview of how polling works and how it benefits candidates. The ensuing discussion examines the goals, demographics, issues, personality traits, and costs found in candidate polling. Once the basics of candidate polling are established, the chapter then offers a brief primer about how polling works covering issues such as survey design, sampling, interviewing respondents, tabulating information, and analyzing results. The next section discusses the types of surveys that campaigns commonly use: benchmark surveys examine the political terrain, tracking surveys explain voter trends, and brushfire surveys briefly test prospective message strategies.

The final part of the chapter explains how qualitative research conducted through focus groups supplements the quantitative information obtained from polling. Research providing insightful information to a candidate can make the difference between winning and losing.

GOALS OF CANDIDATE POLLING

Polls have been around for nearly a hundred years. Many of the techniques used in political polling come from market research. For example, to sell soft drinks, Coca-Cola has to know the following: Who drinks cola? What brand? In what region is Coke most popular? What age group drinks more Coke than Pepsi? What is the preferred "taste" that cola should have? Do people living in the South prefer more sugar in cola, whereas people in the Northeast enjoy more carbonation? Similarly, the job of the polling consultant is to help sell the candidate to 50.1 percent of the voters by providing the research to help craft a winnable "message" by understanding the political tastes of voters.

However, the goals of candidate polling go beyond creating and testing messages. Information is used to construct profiles of voter groups to be targeted for get-out-the-vote (GOTV) operations on election day. Furthermore, polling can alert a candidate to political problems on the horizon and abrupt shifts in public opinion. This "barometric" function of polling is particularly useful to candidates when a tragedy (such as 9/11) transcends the political landscape—as it did in the 2001 Virginia gubernatorial race between Democrat Mark Warner and Republican Mark Earley (see Chapter 3).

Surveys take on a different dimension for incumbents compared with challengers. An incumbent wants voters to think back on their accomplishments during their term of office. Polling can reveal such successes and explain how an incumbent translates that information into a prospective theme of future accomplishment. Ronald Reagan's reelection campaign of 1984 against Democrat Walter Mondale produced the highly stylized "Morning in America" commercials. The "Morning in America" commercials suggested that President Reagan had restored pride to the presidency and that the nation was moving in a positive direction. The information communicated from advertisements comes from research into the demographics, preferences, and attitudes of voting groups.

Polling information can also help "inoculate" or protect a candidate from attack by the opponent during an election campaign. Surveys conducted for the 1984 Reagan campaign indicated that, "Mondale 'owned' such topics as Abortion . . . Education . . . Fairness . . . and Caring About People. . . ." Richard Wirthlin, who was Reagan campaign's director of polling reported, "the leadership box was still up for grabs." To inoculate the candidate against attack and to seize the "leadership" initiative, based on the polling data, the campaign produced the "Bear in the Woods" (a metaphor for the Soviet bear) commercial. Its somewhat cryptic message implied only a "strong defense meant peace." The lessons from the Reagan campaign are two-fold: incumbents must not only tout their achievements, but also preempt criticism by inoculating themselves against possible attack. The context of polling for an incumbent often differs dramatically from that for a challenger. The Simmons example demonstrates how polling seeks out weaknesses exploitable against a well-known incumbent.[6]

UNDERSTANDING THE POLITICAL ENVIRONMENT

Understanding the political environment represents the initial research that a pollster conducts. Polls enlighten the candidate about
cultural values, issues, and trends in public opinion that differ among
population groups. Minnesota features a population that is over-
whelmingly white (89.4 percent) with many voters of Scandinavian
or Germanic descent. On the other hand, New Mexico has the largest
percentage of Latinos of any state (42.1 percent). George W. Bush
does not campaign the same way in Minnesota as he does in New
Mexico because the cultures are different. Campaigns target appeals
to specific constituencies based on patterns of past voting behavior
and then survey those groups to find out what issues or values they
consider important.

Demographic and Voting Trends: A Case Study of Florida

Florida's regionally diverse population provides an excellent case
study about an important political environment. Florida is one of the
fastest growing states in the nation. Its population grew from 13 million in 1990 to 16 million in 2000. With 27 electoral votes, Florida has
the fourth highest number of electors of any state; only California,
Texas, and New York have more electoral votes. Florida has three
distinct regions: southern, northern, and central. The southern part
of the state features the famous vacation spots of Miami and Palm
Beach. This region tends to vote Democratic due to large numbers of
minority (i.e., Latino and African-American) and Jewish voters living there. The region also has many retirees, who are concerned
about the preservation of future Social Security benefits—a position
associated with Democrats who created the program in the 1930s.
The northern part of the state includes the panhandle, the capital
Tallahassee, and Jacksonville. This region is more representative of
the rural-white-conservative south, where Republicans are particularly strong. The residents of the panhandle are so conservative that
they call their beach region the "Redneck Riviera."[7]

Florida's central region includes Orlando, St. Petersburg, and
Tampa. The balance between Democrats and Republicans is more
even in this region than in either the northern or southern section of
the state. The influx of young middle-class voters into the central region has fueled its rapid growth. Voters are fiscally conservative, but

socially moderate. David Beattie of Hamilton-Beattie, a Democratic polling firm, which handled Insurance Commissioner Bill Nelson's (D) successful U.S. Senate race in 2000, commented on the importance of central Florida as a "swing" region of the state. Ernest Hooper, a columnist with the *St. Petersburg Times*, paraphrased Beattie's remarks before a Greater Tampa Chamber of Commerce in March 2002: "If you understand Tampa, you understand the new Florida. If you win in Tampa, you win in Florida." Beattie noted how President George W. Bush (R), Governor Jeb Bush (R), and a 2002 gubernatorial candidate, Janet Reno (D) were all campaigning in the Tampa Bay area that week, "not Miami, not Orlando." The importance of the central region reflects how closely it mirrors state voting patterns. Senate Democratic candidate Bill Nelson received 51 percent of the vote in the "I-4" corridor, which runs between Orlando and Tampa. This was identical to his overall statewide percentage of the vote in 2000. The implications are that polling enables Democrats and Republicans to allocate their resources efficiently within the state.[8]

Values

Values reflect cultural mores, religious orientation, beliefs, and ethnicity. Surveys help signal the values of a constituency. Values such as hard work, family, thrift, and honesty are important to citizens living in midwestern farm states. These states have a relatively homogenous white population and a value system guided by the Protestant ethic. Democrat Tom Vilsack, winner of Iowa's 1998 gubernatorial election, incorporated the sense of these values in his campaign slogan "working families first," a theme refined through intensive polling. Compare Iowa with New York, which has a far more heterogeneous (diverse) population. New York is a "melting pot" of ethnicity where Irish, Italian, African-American, Latino, and Jewish populations flourish. Nevertheless, many of the same values that Iowans share such as honesty, hard work, and family are important to New Yorkers as well. Framing the discourse about values in campaigns, however, may differ in Iowa compared with New York. Surveys and focus groups explain how to frame that discussion.[9]

Polling can inform candidates how to turn a cultural or religious negative into a positive. Senator John F. Kennedy (D-MA) faced the dilemma of whether or not to address voters about his Catholic faith when running for the presidency in 1960. Only one Catholic,

Governor Al Smith of New York had ever been a major political party nominee (1928), and no Catholic had ever been elected president. Insidious rumors that a Catholic presidential candidate might be an agent for the Pope or would attempt to turn the United States into a papal theocracy were a hurdle the senator would have to overcome.

The potential political liability of Kennedy's faith faced its greatest test in West Virginia where Catholics represented just five percent of the population. The state was predominantly Protestant. Pollster Louis Harris provided Kennedy with survey data suggesting that he should address the religion issue directly to West Virginians, an idea supported by his field organization in the state. Kennedy's national advisors wanted him to defer from making public statements about his Catholicism. Harris persuaded Kennedy to speak on statewide television, address the issue directly, and put it behind him. His speech to West Virginians pledged that he would uphold the separation of church and state and that failure to do so would be not only unconstitutional and an impeachable offense, but even worse, "a sin against God." The bold tactic that Harris had articulated worked and Kennedy won the primary in a landslide with more than 60 percent of the vote. The victory was so decisive that it cleared the road for Kennedy to win the Democratic presidential nomination.[10]

Issues

Issues reflect the population and its interests. Opposing Fidel Castro and communism is a highly significant issue in southern Florida where many Cuban expatriates and their offspring live. Alleged child molestation by priests became a major issue in the Massachusetts gubernatorial election of 2002, a state where one-third of the population is Catholic. Republican Mitt Romney and Democrat Shannon O'Brien were in a "bidding war" to increase the penalties for those convicted of child molestation. In Oregon, environmentalists and the logging community have gone head-to-head over whether to protect the spotted owl, clear cutting, and pollution in the last two decades. The pollster frames relevant questions about issues based on substantive background research into a constituency such as Massachusetts or Oregon.[11]

Polling can detect a "wedge" issue, which drives voters to either side of the political continuum. The 1991 U.S. Senate race in

Pennsylvania between Republican Richard Thornburgh (former governor and U.S. attorney general) and Democrat Harris Wofford (appointed to the seat on the death in a plane crash of Senator John Heinz) illustrates the effectiveness of using a "wedge" issue. Wofford was running nearly 50 points behind Thornburgh at the start of the campaign. According to James Carville, Wofford's campaign manager, the benchmark poll found three issues "that the people of Pennsylvania cared about deeply: a middle-class tax cut, more affordable education, and health care. Wofford did, too. That's what we ran on."[12]

The Wofford campaign, in fact, boiled down its message to health care. Campaign pollster Mike Donilon wrote two similar questions on the candidates' qualifications for office. When given the first question, voters surveyed favored Thornburgh by 40 percent. The difference in the second question mentioned that Wofford supported national health insurance. The results took a startling turn; Wofford had a ten-point lead over Thornburgh. By framing the context of the issue, the Wofford campaign set the tone of the debate, which led to victory.[13]

PERSONAL ASPECTS OF POLLING: NAME RECOGNITION AND PERSONALITY ATTRIBUTES

Campaigns benefit from useful intelligence about the intensity of support for their candidate and their opponent. After all, personal attributes such as trust and competence make a difference how many people vote. In 1996, Bill Clinton engendered strong feelings among supporters who believed he was a great domestic success and opponents who believed that he was a corrupt and immoral person. Almost every person surveyed has a favorable or unfavorable opinion of a president and approves or disapproves of the job they are doing. Bob Ward, senior vice president of Fabrizio-McLaughlin, a polling firm working with Republican candidates, looks at a candidate's "reelect" rate (the percentage of voters who would vote to reelect an incumbent) and their favorability ratings. When the reelect rate falls below 50 percent it is commonly a sign that an incumbent is in trouble. Furthermore, a discernable positive or negative movement in a candidate's favorable/unfavorable ratings results in gains or losses in support within three days to two weeks. Challengers, on the other hand, have to introduce themselves to voters. Challengers must determine how to increase name recognition and how to define their candidacy before their opponent defines them. Good polling provides challengers insight how to market their issues *and* their personalities to voters.[14]

Name Recognition

Improving a candidate's *name recognition* is essential to running a competitive race on any level. Consider the following hypothetical example: if only 50 percent of survey respondents recognize a candidate's name, then that candidate's potential support is only half the voting population. Earned media (news coverage) boosts the name recognition of presidential candidates. However, most candidates rely on their own means to promote themselves to voters. For example, State Representative Lisa Lutz (R) was a little-known Republican running against incumbent Tom Udall (D) in New Mexico's 3rd Congressional District (Santa Fe and environs) in 2000. Lutz spent only $39,000, versus $340,000 for Udall, and lost the election 67 to 33 percent. In the previous election, Udall then a challenger, defeated incumbent Bill Redmond by a 53–43 percent margin. Udall's family name provided the name recognition that most challengers (such as Lutz) lacked. His father, Stuart was Secretary of the Interior under John F. Kennedy, and his uncle, Morris, served in the U.S. House for 30 years from Arizona. Challengers track polling data to see how much their name recognition improves during a campaign, because poor name recognition is a challenger's first opponent. Whether that name association has positive or negative connotations is just as important.[15]

Personality Attributes

"Leadership," "trustworthiness," "intelligence," "cares about people," "understands issues," and "experience" represents personality attributes voters consider important for public officials. The positive and negative portrayal of a candidate builds upon these features providing the rationale why such questions appear in political surveys. (e.g., "Do you have a favorable or unfavorable impression of Hillary Clinton?"). Today, personality attribute questions considered so important in the candidate-centered era of politics and television appear in public as well as private candidate surveys. Reports that Gore's "trustworthiness" score fell in private polls after his first debate on October 4, 2000 with George W. Bush matched the findings in some public polls. In particular, the Vice President appeared to exaggerate some of his personal anecdotes, which generated press attention about his veracity. *Newsweek* polls conducted by Princeton Survey Associates found that the percentage of voters who found that Gore was not "honest and ethical" rose from 34 to 37 percent following the debate. Furthermore, the percentage of voters who did not find him "likeable" rose from 23 to 27 percent. These trends never reversed themselves during the latter stages of the campaign. These negative changes may have been small at first, but the shift in opinion may have been decisive in such a close election.[16]

THE COST OF INFORMATION

Ideally, pollsters provide clients with the most reliable and up-to-date information on their election contest. The expense of polling demonstrates that candidates are often constrained by their budget unless they have copious amounts of money to spend. Depending on the type of survey and the number of questions, the cost of an interview can range from $20 to $30 per respondent times 400–1000 registered voters interviewed, which works out to a cost range from $8–30,000 per survey, with the average cost between $10–20,000. The cost depends on the sample size and the number of questions asked. (The discussion on "sampling," appearing later in the chapter spells out the cost per sample size in more detail.) Decades ago, campaigns used much larger sample sizes. In 1960, the Kennedy campaign commissioned its pollster, Louis Harris to conduct a survey of 23,000 primary voters in Wisconsin. In 2004, that survey would cost $230,000 to $690,000![17]

A U.S. House campaign might spend 10 percent of its $600,000 budget ($60,000) to conducts surveys, whereas a U.S. Senate campaign might spend five to ten times that amount. In some cases, campaigns budget less or more for surveys. Campaigns take more polls as the election approaches (called "tracking polls") to see trends in voter support. RTNielson, a Republican-based polling firm in Utah works extensively on gubernatorial, senatorial, and congressional races. The company publishes its rates in the trade magazine for the profession, *Campaigns and Elections*. Nielson charges $2500 for a four-minute "brushfire" poll for 15 questions and 300 valid interviews. A three-minute "brushfire" poll with 10 questions and 300 completed interviews will cost the client $1800. RTNielson provides the phone bank and data. This no-frills survey requires the client to provide the "sample and questionnaire." In most cases, pollsters are under contract to write the survey and provide the sample. Thus, even bargain-basement polling is not cheap.[18]

Despite the cost of polling, good information is indispensable and often makes the difference between winning and losing. Irwin "Tubby" Harrison polled for Democrat Michael Dukakis' presidential campaign in 1988. Harrison found that one-third of the voters had no view on whether Dukakis was "soft" or "hard" on crime even though he was governor of Massachusetts. Harrison bluntly told Dukakis "either we fill this slate or Bush will." Harrison was nicknamed the "oracular pollster" because he seemed to anticipate issues on the horizon and his advice was uncanny. Dukakis ignored Harrison's apocryphal advice, however, and it proved to be a catastrophic error. George Bush, Sr. used the issue of gubernatorial furloughs and pardons against Governor Dukakis to portray him as weak on crime. It was a decisive factor helping Bush win the election 53–46 percent.[19]

A VERY BRIEF PRIMER ON HOW POLLING WORKS

Surveys are instruments gauging the pulse of public opinion. President Lyndon Johnson kept slips of polling data in his coat pocket just in case he wanted to impress visitors at the height of his popularity in the mid-1960s. Polls can also reveal great strengths and weaknesses about a candidate. Jesse Ventura's gubernatorial polls in 1998 showed that he had a four-to-one margin of support of men to women. The candidate realized that failure to improve his standing among women voters would result in defeat. Ventura's conclusion on reading the results appeared in his book, *I Ain't Got Time to Bleed:* "I realized it would be a good idea to bring some estrogen into the race to balance the testosterone . . . it made sense to pick a woman as a running mate." Thus, a well-designed and executed survey can provide a candidate with an understanding of how to traverse the political terrain successfully.[20]

The four main tasks of survey research entail 1) designing the questionnaire, 2) sampling a "representative" number of interviewees from the population, 3) interviewing respondents, and 4) tabulating and analyzing the results. Systematic, accurate, and unbiased data provide valid results for a client.

Questionnaire Design

Designing the questionnaire represents the first step of preparing any survey. Background research on the demographics and electoral behavior of the district or state is a necessary prerequisite. Furthermore, pollsters must research their client's and their opponent's backgrounds to understand the issues or personality factors that are important to voters. Pollsters typically peruse Lexis/Nexus for news stories, voting records (if the candidate serves in office), court records and, even records from the DMV. Years ago, the process was arduous and time-consuming. Today, T1 cable and DSL lines can deliver information in seconds, compared with the hours, days, or weeks it took to compile such information just a decade ago. The speed of obtaining information enables a campaign to adjust its strategy and redirect resources rapidly.[21]

Most opinion surveys consist of 30 to 60 questions and are completed by telephone within twenty minutes. A telephone procedure known as random digit dialing (RDD) enables the pollster to reach about 98 percent of the households in the United States for these surveys. Mail surveys have low response rates, and in-person surveys are very expensive and time-consuming. Thus, telephone polls are the predominant medium for surveying respondents because a phone bank can conduct several hundred interviews in one evening—meaning they are time and cost-effective.

Screening questions appear first on a survey and allow the survey researcher to reach the relevant population to be interviewed. For example, it would have made no sense for Public Opinion Strategies, which polled Greg Ganske (R-Iowa) to interview unregistered voters during the fall 2002 Iowa Senate race. Thus, unregistered voters would be "screened out." The *Battleground* survey, which appears on the next page provides an excellent example of how screening questions work. *Battleground* is a collaborative effort of Ed Goeas, a Republican pollster from the Tarrance Group and Celinda Lake, a Democratic pollster from the firm of Lake, Snell and Perry.

SCREENING QUESTIONS FROM THE LAKE/TARRANCE
"BATTLEGROUND" POLL, JUNE 9–11, 2002

Battleground 2002 (XXII) Final

STUDY #8970
THE TARRANCE GROUP, INC.
N = 1,000 Registered "likely" voters
Field Dates: June 9–11, 2002
Hello, I'm _____ of The Tarrance Group, a national
survey research firm. We're talking to people long distance
today about public leaders and issues facing us all.

A. Are you registered to vote in your state?
   IF "NO", ASK: Is there someone else at home who is regis-
   tered to vote?
   (IF "YES", THEN ASK: MAY I SPEAK WITH HIM/HER?)
                    Yes **(CONTINUE)**
                    No **(THANK AND TERMINATE)**

Now, thinking ahead to the election for Governor or U.S. Congress that will be held this November—

B. What is the likelihood of your voting in the upcoming election for Governor or U.S. Congress—are you extremely likely,
very likely, somewhat likely, or not very likely at all to vote?

	Extremely likely...............
(CONTINUE)	Very likely.........................
	Somewhat likely ....
(THANK AND TERMINATE)	Not very likely

UNSURE **(DNR)**

C. Are you, or is anyone in your household, employed with an
advertising agency, newspaper, television or radio station, or
political campaign?
              Yes **(THANK AND TERMINATE)**
              No **(CONTINUE)**

Source: The Tarrance Group, June 2002. Reprinted by permission of The Tarrance Group.

The first screening question asks whether the respondent lives in the state. There is no sense in interviewing a Kentuckian who answers the phone of his uncle when visiting him in Nashua, New Hampshire. The second question ("B") determines the likelihood of the respondent to vote for "Governor or U.S. Congress." Again, if the respondent says no, then they are "screened out" and the survey ends. Question "C" asks if anyone in the household works in a public affairs job (e.g., advertising, journalism, or politics). If yes, the survey is terminated because of possible bias. Some survey researchers use a battery of "likely voting" questions, asking whether the respondents had voted in the previous election or more elections to obtain a more precise sample. However, there is no conclusive evidence that a battery of "likely voting" questions will yield more accurate results.

The second set of survey items are *attitudinal/behavioral* questions. The bulk of the survey questions are comprised of issue (attitudinal), personality (attitudinal), and voter choice (behavioral) questions. Public Opinion Strategies served as Republican Bob Dole's pollster during his 1996 presidential campaign. Their survey provides the reader an excellent example of *attitudinal/behavioral* questions appearing in a survey. Two types of questions appear in the excerpt: 1) issue salience and 2) candidate favorability ratings.

Rotation of the response categories protects against bias toward one response or another. Without rotation, the likelihood is far greater that the respondent would remember the first and last choices mentioned. The data from an Arizona primary survey for Dole demonstrated that 70 percent of the respondents had a "favorable" impression of Forbes compared with 64 percent for Dole. (Add "very favorable" and "somewhat favorable" together.) The results told the Dole campaign to watch out for Forbes because a high favorability rating often predicts a strong performance in an election. In the end, Forbes did win the Arizona primary but his candidacy for the Republican presidential nomination petered out by March 1996 because of lack of support in populous states.

Behavioral questions ask the respondent whom they plan to vote for on election day. This provides "horse race" information telling the campaign who is winning and losing. For example, a horse race question from 2000 might read: "If the election for president were held today, would you vote for Al Gore, the Democrat, George W. Bush, the Republican, Ralph Nader of the Green Party or Pat Buchanan of the Reform Party." Other national surveys included the vice presidential choice. For example, the *ABC News/Washington Post*

ROBERT DOLE'S ARIZONA PRESIDENTIAL PRIMARY SURVEY
FROM JANUARY 1996

Public Opinion Strategies Survey for Dole for President '96
January 2–3, 1996
Margin of Error ±5.24%
N = 350 registered Republicans

Thinking about different issues that could be discussed in a presidential campaign, would it be more important to you that a candidate agree with your position on . . . **(ROTATE AND READ LIST)**

    15% cutting taxes
    45% balancing the budget
    11% abortion
     4% illegal immigration
     5% welfare reform
     8% getting the federal government out of Arizona's affairs
    10% DON'T KNOW **(DO NOT READ)**
     1% REFUSED **(DO NOT READ)**

Now, thinking about a different topic . . .

I would like to read you a list of names of different people active in politics. For each one, please tell me, first whether you've heard of the person; then, if so, please tell me whether you have a favorable or unfavorable impression of that person. If I name someone you don't know too much about, just tell me and we'll go on to the next one.

(IF FAVORABLE, ASK:) Would that be VERY favorable or just SOMEWHAT favorable?

The (FIRST/NEXT) name is . . . **(ROTATE NAMES)**

	VERY FAV	SMWT FAV	UNFAV	NO OPIN	NEVER HEARD	REF
Bob Dole						
1/96	23%	41%	27%	6%	3%	1%
1/95	34%	39%	17%	8%	1%	1%

	VERY FAV	SMWT FAV	UNFAV	NO OPIN	NEVER HEARD	REF
Phil Gramm						
1/96	15%	32%	21%	15%	16%	1%
1/95	17%	17%	7%	19%	36%	5%
Pat Buchanan						
1/96	12%	31%	38%	14%	5%	1%
Lamar Alexander						
1/96	3%	15%	11%	21%	47%	3%
1/95	2%	6%	3%	12%	66%	10%
Steve Forbes						
1/96	33%	37%	10%	12%	7%	*
Pete Wilson						
1/96	8%	25%	19%	23%	24%	1%

Fabrizio, McLaughlin © 1996. Reprinted by permission of Fabrizio, McLaughlin, and Associates.

poll from September 28 to October 1, 2000 asked the following question: "The candidates in November's presidential election are Al Gore and Joseph Lieberman, the Democrats, George W. Bush and Dick Cheney, the Republicans, Ralph Nader and Winona LaDuke of the Green Party, and Pat Buchanan and Ezola Foster of the Reform Party. If the election were being held today, who would you vote for Gore, Bush, Nader, or Buchanan?" Pollsters agonize over the proper wording of questions to reflect voter preferences. Media surveys not including vice presidential choices in their questions (e.g., *MSNBC/ Reuters/Zogby* and *CBS News/NY Times*) came closest to approximating the results on election day. The anecdotal evidence suggests that surveys requiring less recall from respondents produce results yielding greater accuracy. In other words, pollsters should keep the questions simple.[22]

Demographic questions completing the survey provide information concerning respondents' gender, age, race, income, marital status, employment status, ideology, regularity of church attendance, and education level, for example. Pollsters can construct a candidate "profile" by finding out which groups support a candidate and their policies. For example, Al Gore and Bill Clinton both did exceptionally well among working women, but among women who work at home, their support was less strong in Voter News Service surveys from 1996 and 2000.[23]

Sampling

How does a pollster attain accurate survey results with 400–1000 interviews? It's based on the laws of probability. Imagine you are flipping a quarter 100 times. The results produce around 50 percent heads and 50 percent tails. However, flipping the same quarter 500 times would bring you a lot closer to 50-50 than with only 100 tosses. Flipping a quarter 1000 times would approximate 50-50 even more closely. However, the difference between 500 and 1000 tosses is not as great as between 100 and 500 tosses (as statisticians have shown). This is the principle upon which *sampling* is based—the larger the sample size, the more accurate it reflects the population as a whole about 95 out of 100 times.

However, the improvement in accuracy diminishes as the sample size increases. A sample of 100 completed interviews has an error margin of 11 percent, meaning that the results can be 11 percent higher or lower than the tabulated results. Therefore, Candidate "X" who receives 50 percent of voter support in a poll could actually be receiving as high as 61 percent or as low as 39 percent of the vote. Therefore, 100 is not a good sample size to yield accurate results. A sample size of 200 would still leave an error margin of 8 percent. Most surveys have between 400–600 completed interviews—meaning that the error ranges between 5 percent (a sample of 400) to a slightly lower 4 percent (a sample of 600). The cost for a survey of 30–40 questions and 400 completed interviews is approximately $10–12,000. The same survey with a sample size of 600 would cost approximately between $16–18,000. Increasing the total number of questions in the survey to yield detailed information might be necessary to help the campaign plan its message or detect weaknesses in the opposition. The same survey with 50 to 60 questions increases the cost by $3–5000.[24]

Polling companies buy their samples from market research firms such as Survey Sampling or Donnelly's known to produce high-quality survey lists for Fortune 500 companies, as well as political clients. High quality means that there is little chance that the samples are "corrupted" with business phone numbers or non-working home numbers.

Tracking surveys are daily or weekly surveys that repeat the same questions to determine changes in candidate support. Consider a survey that will ultimately have a sample size of 600 "likely voters" (i.e., registered voters who say they are likely to turn out and vote). Two hundred completed interviews each night, over a three-day period, will yield these 600 "likely voters." A three-day sample protects against bias or artifice appearing from a single day's results. Bias includes representation issues (one demographic group under- or overrepresented); the effect of a public event or crisis (e.g., 9/11, Wall Street scandals of 2002); or lower response rates on a given day. Thus, a "rolling" sample should smooth out any inconsistencies over a three-day time-period, although nothing is perfect. The "rolling" sample has become staple of all tracking surveys.

Interviewing

Most political survey outfits contract their interviewing to phone bank companies, which actually do the interviewing. The phone bank conducts the interviews according to the instructions given by the pollster. Instructions include the number of interviews to complete in a specified location. Most polling companies hire phone banks to do the actual interviewing by phone. Companies such as the Communications Center, Inc. of Washington, DC, Meyer Associates Teleservices of Minneapolis, MN, and New England Interviewing, Inc. of Manchester, NH provide phone bank services to pollsters around the country. A few large polling companies maintain their own phone bank operations, especially if much of their work is non-political market research for business clients. For example, Market Opinion Research (MOR) and Wirthlin Worldwide conduct surveys for Republican candidates and for corporations.[25]

Most polling organizations conduct interviews at night, and during weekend days. One public opinion and candidate polling company that is highly respected, Zogby International, conducts polling during the mid-day hours during the week to reach a higher proportion of women working in the home. The firm interviews only "likely voters" because they have the highest probability of voting. Zogby was very accurate in predicting the popular vote in the 2000 presidential election.[26]

Interviewing is becoming more difficult because the response rate to telephone polls is declining dramatically. The Council of Marketing and Opinion Research found that in 2000, 60 percent of respondents hung up "or decline[d] to complete the survey. That's up from 41 percent in 1980. The widespread use of Caller ID, answering machines and computers that tie up phone lines" often requires a phone bank to make more than ten calls to the same location before yielding a successful response. A study by the Pew Research Center for the People and the Press found that upper middle-class and affluent voters refused more often. Nevertheless, the survey also found little gender, racial or educational differences in the demographic makeup of respondents versus non-respondents. Furthermore, the widespread use of cell phones also contributes to fewer voters being reached at home, if at all. Modern technology has yet to overcome this problem, implying that the accuracy of telephone surveys may be waning.[27]

Tabulation of Results and Analysis

Technology and computerization have dramatically changed the process of tabulating results and analyzing data from surveys. Today, survey information is input onto an interactive screen by the interviewer through Computer Assisted Telephone Interviewing (CATI). Statistical Package for the Social Sciences (SPSS) and similar statistical programs permit pollsters to analyze percentage results and run cross-tabulations of different questions (two or more questions compared with each other) to analyze data. Pollsters seeking more sophisticated and precise information use complex statistical tests such as regression analysis or logit models to tease out the data.

Weighting survey results is a common practice utilized by pollsters. Despite the artificiality created by weighting results, pollsters have found that it more accurately reflects the voting population's actual candidate preferences. Weighting results by a mathematical formula more accurately reflects the actual population. For example, let us take a survey of 600 "likely" voters in a potential statewide senate race in Mississippi where 34 percent of the adult voting population is African-American. The completed survey yields results showing that only 22 percent of the respondents are African-American. The results would then have to be "weighted-up" to give a more accurate picture of the voting population in Mississippi.

TYPES OF SURVEYS: BENCHMARK, TRACKING, AND BRUSHFIRE POLLS

Not every survey is the same. Pollsters use different types of surveys to elicit the information helpful to their clients, because the terrain changes over the course of a campaign season. Benchmark, tracking, and brushfire polls represent the array of surveys commonly used in national political campaigns. More polling conducted at the outset of a campaign facilitates the creation of a coherent strategy and message, according to pollster Bob Ward. However, polling is expensive and not all candidates can hire a pollster to provide services. Congressional elections expert Paul Herrnson says: "15 percent of all challengers are forced to depend on volunteers for their polling, and 24 percent take no polls." Since many challengers lack the financial resources to hire consultants and conduct in-depth surveys, they are at a strategic disadvantage against incumbents. For challengers with financial resources, the competitive gap is less difficult to overcome.[28]

Benchmark Surveys

The benchmark survey is the first commissioned poll by a candidate for public office. The benchmark poll provides an overview of the political landscape, and the insight needed to market a successful candidacy. Since a benchmark survey takes place 12 to 18 months before an election, the horse race numbers are less important than understanding the issue and political context of the jurisdiction. Former Los Angeles Mayor Richard Riorden held a 60-point lead in the polls over businessman William Simon less than a year before the 2002 California Republican gubernatorial primary; however, Riorden's lead over Simon evaporated by the March 2002 primary. Simon was able to drive up Riorden's unfavorable ratings through negative advertising while keeping his own unfavorables low. Horse race figures at an early stage of a political race are of minimal value and often reflect name recognition.[29]

Benchmark polls benefit challengers trying to emerge from a pack of candidates. Political scientists Barbara and Stephen Salmore explain that benchmark polling tell the campaign "how and where to schedule the candidate, what issues to stress and how to convey them." Colorado Senator Gary Hart, a long-shot candidate for the Democratic presidential nomination commissioned a 1983 benchmark poll to gauge his chances to defeating frontrunner and former Vice President Walter Mondale. The benchmark poll found that serious problems plagued Mondale's candidacy. "(H)is linkage to the Carter legacy . . . that he had no fiscal discipline . . . [and] the public saw him as too tied to special interest groups." Hart exploited Mondale's weaknesses in the primary campaign, claiming that *he* was the candidate of new ideas and devoid of special interest ties. Although Mondale won the nomination, the same weakness concerning his ties to special interests appeared in surveys conducted by Richard Wirthlin for President Reagan's 1984 reelection campaign. The Reagan campaign promoted the president as a leader who rose above special interests, implying that Mondale lacked that ability. Reagan defeated Mondale by 59–40 percent with the former Vice President carrying only Washington, D.C., and his home state of Minnesota.[30]

Benchmark surveys can be quite extensive featuring 100 questions and a sample size of "500–1200 likely voters in statewide races to 400–500 in congressional races, depending on the size and heterogeneity of the constituency." The late and respected pollster William Hamilton, conducted surveys in two phases, which he called Future trend 1 and 2. Future trend 1 is a mini-benchmark poll, conducted 12–18 months before the election. Future trend 1 lacks a component for testing various campaign-advertising messages. This saves money in the early stages of the race. Future trend 2 asks respondents a series of open-ended questions (with no specific response categories). The open-ended responses enable the pollster to perform a "content analysis" to provide a qualitative measure of what issues resonate with the respondents. The next stage of Future trend 2 categorizes responses by typology to analyze trends. Hamilton reported that content analysis was a major development in benchmark surveys in recent years. Content analysis through benchmark surveys allows pollsters to find out what "buzzwords" or messages work with voters. For example, the 2002 congressional strategy memo by President Bush's chief political operative, Karl Rove, stated that "compassion" and "trust" were two key elements Republicans wanted to stress with voters.[31]

Tracking Polls

Effective tracking surveys "will tell a campaign if its strategy is working." According to Republican pollster Bruce Blakeman, "if, for instance, you need 38 percent of Hispanics to reach 52 percent on election day, your tracking program should monitor how the campaign is progressing among Hispanics. . . ." Tracking polls explain how prospective "target groups are performing according to strategy and which are not." Surveys conducted on a regular basis reveals trends in how a candidate and their opponent perform among core constituencies and swing voters. "Swing" (i.e., undecided) voters may constitute five percent of the electorate, or 30 percent of the electorate, depending on who is running for office, what the issues are, and where the election takes place.

The frequency of taking tracking polls depends on how much money the campaign can allot to survey research, how close the race is, and how often valuable information is being rendered from the tracking survey. In presidential races, tracking polls are taken daily throughout the election year for major candidates, although it is very expensive. Campaigns take tracking polls on a weekly or bi-weekly basis during September, but poll every night during the closing weeks of the campaign. Finally, most congressional candidates take tracking polls on a monthly or bi-weekly basis (and, in rare cases weekly) because of the prohibitive expense of taking them daily.

The horse race component of the tracking survey becomes more important when election day approaches and support solidifies for the candidates. The "rolling" averages of a three-day track, on a day-by-day basis, appear on a chart to study positive and negative trends of support for both candidates. The *ABC News/Washington Post poll* and *CNN/USA Today*/Gallup poll from the 2000 election that appear in figure 5-1 use "trend lines" to follow candidate performance. Media tracking polls employ the same methodology as campaign surveys. (Since tracking polls from campaigns are proprietary information, media polls often serve as a surrogate source of information reporting the same basic data.)

Both charts in figure 5-1 report trend lines drawn from the daily performance of the Bush-Gore 2000 presidential race. The *ABC News/Washington Post* poll on the left shows greater stability and less change than does the *CNN/USA Today*/Gallup poll on the right. The *ABC News/Washington Post* poll, for example, more closely resembled the stability found in the tracking polls conducted by the Bush and Gore campaigns. The methodology used by *ABC News* and Gallup accounts for the difference. For example, the Gallup poll made a concerted effort to "push" undecided voters to declare a preference in the horse race. Frank Newport, editor-in-chief of the Gallup organization, stated, "When you go into the polling booth,

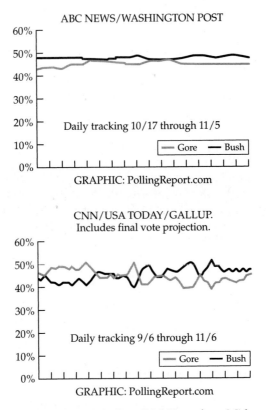

FIGURE 5-1 Bush-Gore Trial Heats from Mid-October to November 2000, Presidential Race.

Source: Pollingreport.com. Reprinted by permission of Pollingreport.com.

you can't lean." *ABC News* did not push as hard for a preference commitment. Nevertheless, tracking polls by presidential campaigns are primarily interested in the fifty separate state contests on election day since the Electoral College vote in each state is a winner-take-all system. Bill McInturff, a Republican pollster, found that, although "Bush was dead even in national polls, he was 5 points behind, on average, in the key swing states." Therefore, the utility of national tracking polls is less advantageous than state-by-state tracking polls for presidential campaigns. Recent evidence seems to indicate that tracking polls have greater utility on the state and congressional district levels, than on the national level.[32]

Brushfire Polls

Brushfire polls are short surveys, focusing on a specific message, that are conducted just prior to the "media push" in late summer or early fall. Brushfire polls typically ask eight to 12 questions compared to 30–60 questions found in a standard tracking survey. (Some tracking surveys have fewer questions when polling nightly during the final phase of the campaign.) Furthermore, the sample size of a brushfire survey is small—ranging from 200 to 300 interviews. "The brushfire study should be used to refine the message and test the effectiveness of the effort to this point." The polls should take no more than four minutes to complete by phone interview compared with five to 12 minutes for a standard tracking survey. Brushfire polls are sometimes mistaken for tracking polls. Brushfire polls, unlike tracking polls, do not track daily or weekly trends, rather they appear episodically and focus on a specific message rather than on trends in voter preferences over time.[33]

FOCUS GROUPS

A focus group is a qualitative interview conducted by a moderator sitting with a group of individuals around an oval table or in a semi-circle. Focus groups normally contain eight to 12 persons who fit a particular demographic criterion. The group could be composed of white women over 55 years of age or rural male farmers between the ages of 35–54 and, so forth. Thus, focus group participants are scientifically selected, and not pulled off the street at random.

Focus groups can provide a campaign insight into how messages or themes appeal to voters. This is a tactic borrowed from market research, where testing product items through focus groups is the norm of business practices. Procter and Gamble, General Foods, Ford Motor Company, and Nike do extensive product testing through marketing surveys, but also through focus groups. Focus groups provide an essential qualitative element of product testing to find out *why* respondents feel a certain way. For example, a survey can tell a pollster who is a Democrat, a Republican, or an Independent, as well as the strength of their party identification. However, a focus group participant can explain to the moderator *why* they identify with a political party. Focus groups in conjunction with telephone surveys provide pollsters a more holistic view of voter attitudes.

The Manhattan Project

The best-documented use of political focus group research was the "The Manhattan Project." Media consultant Mandy Grunwald and pollster Stanley Greenberg dreamed up "The Manhattan Project," given the same name as the secret plan to develop the atom bomb. The plan reintroduced Bill Clinton to the electorate as a populist after securing the 1992 Democratic nomination. Greenberg conducted focus groups and fed them information about Clinton's background. Most focus group participants were not aware of Clinton's "humble origins," growing up in lower-middle-class and rural Arkansas. Clinton was also the child of a single parent. His mother was a nurse who spent much of her time and money gambling.[34]

Greenberg convened two focus groups in the San Fernando Valley of California and in Allentown, Pennsylvania:

> Each participant was presented with a one-page listing of facts about Bill Clinton, including . . . "born in a small town called Hope, Arkansas," "worked his way through Georgetown," "makes $35,000 a year—never had a pay raise in 11 years". . . . The result was breathtaking . . . voters began to speak of Clinton in radically different terms: "down to earth," "a middle-class boy," "self-made" . . . . "the opposite of Bush."[35]

Since Clinton was not from a patrician background and struggled to achieve the American dream, introducing elements of his background changed the dynamic of the campaign. Focus groups enabled the campaign to test market the populist theme of "A Man from Hope (Arkansas)" before launching a paid advertising campaign and using public events and forums to sell the "new" Clinton to voters. The plan worked as Clinton emerged from last place to win the November election.

Dial Groups

Dial groups enable a pollster to observe how a focus group reacts to a television presentation by a candidate. A target demographic group watches the presentation on television. "Viewers chart their reaction to a TV presentation by moving an electronic needle along a calibrated scale: 0–50 indicates frigid to cool, 50–100 registers cool to warm, warm to hot, hot, hot." Richard Wirthlin made extensive use of dial groups to test the effect of messages from Ronald Reagan's speeches. Stanley Greenberg used dial groups extensively to test commercials for his top U.S. Senate and House clients in 2002. The use of simple words or messages can send the trajectory of the needle dramatically up or down. For example, candidates using hot-button terms such as "gay marriage," "affirmative action," and "weapons of mass destruction" evoke strongly emotive responses from dial group participants. Subtle generic messages such as compassion, courage, and leadership, taken together, can create a positive image that gently nudges the needle upward.[36]

USE OF POLLING FOR GOTV OPERATIONS

A campaign measures the intensity of its support among core constituent groups through polling. The degree of intensity ascertains the likelihood of different constituent groups to get out and vote. This information helps the field coordinator and campaign manager allocate strategic resources on election day.

The intensity of support among key voter groups is the most important variable that surveys can identify for candidates. For example, in the 2002 midterm elections suburban white women played a key role in swinging the election to either party. Ann Wagner, co-chair of the Republican National Committee (RNC), alluded to this key demographic group when speaking to a reporter (who paraphrased her remarks): "Women voters, particularly those in the independent-minded suburbs, are a key constituency that cannot be ignored or alienated by harsh rhetoric and campaigns that aren't based on issues they care about." Wagner was concerned that suburban white women would turn out in large numbers to vote Democratic, helping Democrats win control of the U.S. House. Only polling data could have enabled Wagner to make such inferences. Similar to the law of physics, a bad message can have an opposite but equal reaction for voter turnout.[37]

CONCLUSION

The pollster provides a campaign critical intelligence regarding the public mood, values, beliefs, and voter preferences. A campaign without polling is akin to hiking in the desert without a map. Without a map, a hiker cannot find the landmarks necessary to find their destination. Similarly, without polling a candidate can have only a perfunctory understanding of the political environment. This lack of understanding handicaps the candidate's ability to win votes. Therefore, the 24 percent of U.S. House challengers who rely on volunteers to do their polling, as described earlier, are at a distinct disadvantage.

Polling provides a critical function to develop and test campaign messages that are integral elements building candidate support. Modern polling operations utilize focus groups to supplement benchmark and tracking polls, techniques that were unheard of forty years ago when Louis Harris was polling for John F. Kennedy. These techniques enable campaign strategists to study the intensity of voter attitudes and preferences in greater depth than in the past.

The longitudinal trends of attitudes and opinions remain the important focus for a campaign. David W. Moore in his book *The Super Pollsters* discusses the findings of public opinion analysts Howard Schuman and Eleanor Singer: "What is needed . . . is less reliance on the results of one question and more efforts to probe the various shades of opinion by using many different questions with different formats." In other words, an effective survey captures more than what appears at first glance. Only a well-written, sampled, and analyzed survey provides a pollster the necessary insight to produce or alter strategies and tactics. Furthermore, polling coupled with focus groups enabled the Clinton campaign to recreate Bill Clinton's personal image to voters at a time when his candidacy was wallowing in last place behind an increasingly unpopular president (Bush) and an upstart third party candidate (Perot).[38]

Technology not only provides real-time results through the CATI system but also provides the pollster greater flexibility in preparing and analyzing the data. Today's Pentium computers run at 2 to 5 gigahertz compared to 8 megahertz a decade ago. Thus, campaigns receive data, develop, and execute strategic decisions within hours. As a result, the tools that are available to candidates from pollsters are increasingly diverse, sophisticated, and valuable. However, a candidate and campaign manager can receive too much information, creating confusion and resulting in a loss of confidence in their pollster. Given the availability of information, self-restraint by the pollster can enable a campaign to remain focused.

The events of a campaign season are unpredictable. The best strategy crafted by pollsters, media advisors, and other campaign strategists can be upended by events, such as impeachment, or mistakes made by the candidate themselves. Al Gore's first debate with

George W. Bush in October 2000 hurt his credibility when several anecdotes he used stretched the truth. Gore's credibility suffered from that debate, as his unfavorable rating climbed. Gore never regained the initiative he possessed before the first debate, damaging his chances for election. As Cassius tells Brutus in Shakespeare's *Julius Caesar*: "the fault, dear Brutus, is not in our stars, but in ourselves."[39]

STUDY/DISCUSSION QUESTIONS

How does polling aid a challenger against an incumbent?

How can a pollster help a campaign craft a message to voters?

Why do pollsters use focus groups? What information do they provide that telephone polls cannot provide?

What is the difference between benchmark and tracking surveys? What role does each survey play in a campaign?

Why does polling using scientific methods to select a sample of voters?

What responsibility does a pollster have to a client? to voters?

What ethical issues does political polling pose for society?

SUGGESTED READINGS

Asher, Herbert B. *Polling and the Public: What Every Citizen Should Know*. Washington, DC: CQ Press, 2001.

Mann, Thomas E., and Gary R. Orren. *Media Polls in American Politics*. Washington, DC: Brookings, 1992.

Moore, David W. *The Superpollsters*. New York: Four Walls Eight Windows, 1992.

Roll, Charles W., and Albert H. Cantril. *Polls: Their Use and Misuse in Politics*. Cabin John, MD: Seven Locks Press, 1972.

Traugott, Michael W., and Paul J. Lavrakas. *The Voter's Guide to Election Polls*. New York: Chatham House, 2000.

NOTES

1. Jonathan Moore, ed. *Campaign for President: The Managers Look at '84* (Dover, MA: Auburn, 1986), 252.

2. Michael Barone with Richard Cohen, *Almanac of American Politics 2002* (Washington, DC: National Journal, 2001), 333.

3. Kevin McNeill and Cheryl Klock, "Connecticut Upset," *Campaigns and Elections,* May 2001, 38; Michael Barone and Grant Ujifusa, *Almanac of American Politics 2000* (Washington, DC: National Journal, 1999), 353–55.
4. McNeill and Klock, 38.
5. McNeill and Klock, 38–39, 42; Barone with Cohen, 333–34 on Gore performance in the district.
6. Leo Bogart, (Book Review) "The Superpollsters" by David Moore. *Columbia Journalism Review,* July/August 1992. Accessed June 27, 2002 at *www.cjr.org/year/92/4/books-pols.asp.*
7. Barone with Cohen, 374, quote on "Redneck Riviera."
8. Barone with Cohen, 369, 371; Ernest Hooper, "Florida, simply is us; a military salute; the best eats." *St. Petersburg Times.* Accessed July 1, 2002 at *www.sptimes.com/2002/03/09/Columns/Florida_simply_is_u.shtml.*
9. John Kupper, "Anatomy of an Upset," *Campaigns and Elections,* April 1999, 39, quote on Vilsack slogan.
10. Theodore H. White, *The Making of the President 1960* (New York: Pocket Books, 128–29 for the quote) 120–31, in passim.
11. "Spotted Owl Declines at Four Times the Expected Rate," *Associated Press,* July 10, 2000.
12. Mary Matalin and James Carville, with Peter Knobler, *All's Fair: Love, War, and Running for President* (New York: Touchstone, 1994), 74; Phil Duncan, ed. *Politics in America 1994* (Washington, DC: Congressional Quarterly Press, 1993), 1288.
13. Jacob S. Hacker, *The Road to Nowhere: The Genesis of President Clinton's Plan for Health Security.* (Princeton, NJ: Princeton University Press, 1997), chap. 1, "The Rise of Reform." Accessed July 2, 2002 at *http://pup.princeton.edu/chapters/s5921.html,* for all references found in the chapter 1 summary.
14. PollingReport.com. Accessed July 2, 2000 at *www.pollingreport.com/clinton1.htm,* on Clinton polling evaluations by voters; Bob Ward, Senior Vice President, Fabrizio-McLaughlin, interview, Alexandria, VA, July 2, 2002.
15. Barone with Cohen, 1029; "New Mexico Freedom to Carry," constituent news alert, Gun Owners of America, February 10, 1998.
16. "White House 2000: Comparing the Candidates," Princeton Survey Research Associates tracking polls for *Newsweek* magazine taken on a weekly basis from July 27 through October 20, 2000. Accessed January 1, 2003 at *www.pollingreport.com/wh2.cand.htm.*

17. Theodore H. White, 110–11.
18. "Political Polling," (Advertisement), RTNielson Company, *Campaigns and Elections,* August 2000. No page number.
19. Ibid.; David Moore, *The Super Pollsters* (New York: Four Walls Eight Windows, 1992), 188, 184.
20. Jesse Ventura, *I Ain't Got Time to Bleed: Reworking the Body Politic from the Bottom Up* (New York: Villard, 1999), 159.
21. Bob Ward. Ward mentioned that technology has made a vast and appreciable difference in survey research. When he started in the business, in 1990, it was still a "paper and pencil" business. Today, his firm delivering results online from surveys within seconds.
22. The version of the poll not using vice presidential candidates is similar to the wording by *CBS/NY Times* in their 2000 presidential surveys. For vice presidential choices included in the survey, see the *ABC News/Washington Post* poll, September 28–October 1, 2000. Accessed July 3, 2002 at *www.washingtonpost.com/wp-serve/politics/vault/stories/data/100300.htm;* the two most accurate surveys in the final pre-election poll were the *MSNBC/Reuters/Zogby* survey, which had the popular vote, Gore 48, Bush 46, Nader 5, and Buchanan 1, and the *CBS News/NY Times* poll, which had the race, Gore 45, Bush 44, Nader 4, and Buchanan 1. The information can be found at pollingreport.com. Accessed July 3, 2002 at *www.pollingreport.com/election.htm#latest.*
23. See VNS surveys from 1996 and 2000 from national data and states. The VNS was a consortium of the national television networks to do exit polling together VNS was disbanded after the 2000 election.
24. Estimated costs are taken from the price sheet of Fabrizio-McLaughlin, Alexandria, VA, price sheet, 2002.
25. "The Political Pages 2002–2003," *Campaigns and Elections,* 2002, 76.
26. Go to *www.zogby.com* to find out about client list. E-mail from John Zogby about polling techniques, February 2002.
27. Rick Montgomery, "Telephone polls' days may be numbered," *Kansas City Star,* September 22, 2000. Accessed July 3, 2002 at *www.kcstar.com/item/pages/printer.pat,local/3774c826.922,.html.*
28. Ward; Paul Herrnson, "Campaign Professionals in House Elections," ed. James A. Thurber and Candice J. Nelson in *Campaign Warriors: Political Consultants in Elections* (Washington, DC: Brookings, 2000), 73, quote.

29. Mitch Frank, "How Riorden Lost California's Primary," Time.com. March 8, 2002. Accessed July 4, 2002 at *www.time.com/ time/columnist/frank/article/0,0565,216170,00.html;* Public Opinion Strategies Poll conducted for Republican William Simon, February 17–18, 2002, of six hundred "likely" Republican primary voters in California, released February 22, 2002.

30. Barbara G. Salmore and Stephen A. Salmore, *Candidates, Parties and Campaigns* (Washington, DC: Congressional Quarterly Press, 1989), 115; on the Hart strategy, see Moore, 176, quote and information.

31. William R. Hamilton, "Political Polling," in *Campaigns and Elections American Style,* ed. James A. Thurber and Candice J. Nelson (Boulder, CO: Westview, 1995), 173; Karl Rove, "The Strategic Landscape," Office of Strategic Initiatives, White House, June 4, 2002; Bob Ward. Ward discussed how he can collect qualitative information online by corresponding with hundreds of interviewees to test messages issue strategies.

32. Craig Gilbert, "Who leads, Bush or Gore? Polls give mixed message," *Milwaukee Journal-Sentinel,* October 10, 2000. Accessed July 5, 2002 at *www.jsonline.com/news/nat/oct00/polls11101000.asp,* all references.

33. Chris Wilson and Bill Cullo, "When should you take a poll," *Campaigns and Elections,* 1998 February, 56; Dennis W. Johnson, *No Place for Amateurs* (New York: Routledge, 2001), 93.

34. Stanley B. Greenberg, *Middle Class Dreams: The Politics and Power of the New American Majority* (New Haven, CT: Yale University Press, 1995), 222–25.

35. Greenberg, 224–25.

36. "Manhattan Project; 1992," *Newsweek,* 1992, 42; Greenberg Quinlan Rosner, website accessed July 5, 2002 at *www.greenbergresearch.com/ campaigns_us.*

37. David Ammons, "GOP targets women voters for winning edge," *Associated Press,* May 31, 2002; Richard Semiatin, *1998 Mid-Term Elections Update* (Boston: McGraw-Hill, 1999), 19, quote.

38. Moore, 352.

39. Robert Novak, "Worries About Gore," *The Washington Post,* July 4, 2002, A23; William Shakespeare, *Julius Caesar,* Act I, Scene II, quote.

CHAPTER 6

Paid Advertising

*"Ads seem to work on the very advanced principle that a small
pellet or pattern in a noisy, redundant barrage of repetition will
gradually assert itself."*[1]
—Famed media commentator Marshall McLuhan

"It's the hot TV series you cannot escape," wrote *Philadelphia Inquirer*
reporters Josh Goldstein and Tom Infield about the 2002 Pennsylvania
Democratic gubernatorial primary. Candidates Edward Rendell and
Bob Casey, Jr. ran "campaign ads more than 30,000 times" from
January until the primary in late May. Rendell, the former mayor of
Philadelphia, and Bob Casey, Jr., state auditor and son of a former
governor, spent nearly $30 million in a state with one-third the
population of California. Two hundred fifty hours of advertising
consumed half of all campaign expenditures. The ads targeted undecided voters in a closely contested race. One Rendell spot stressed his
success in revitalizing the city and school system in the late 1990s.
Casey countered with an ad blaming Rendell for doing a poor job
managing Philadelphia's schools because the state had to provide an
extra $75 million to fund the school system in 2002. "Rendell's failure
is costing you, because today all of Pennsylvania's taxpayers will
have to pay for Philadelphia schools," the Casey ad said. Ads appeared dozens of times in the closing days of the campaign to push
undecided voters to support Rendell or Casey. In a tightly contested
primary or election, this type of "redundant barrage" targets a small
group of swing voters constituting five or 10 percent of likely voters.
The advertising blitz of the Rendell-Casey race is a perfect example
of how high-profile elections are fought today—less on the ground
and more on the air.[2]

The air war demonstrates how political advertising provides
a cost and time-effective means to reach mass audiences through

television, radio, newspaper, and direct mail. Understanding how paid advertising works in campaigns serves as the purpose of this chapter. The chapter begins with an assessment of television advertising and its growing sophistication to reach discerning audiences. The second section examines television advertising strategy. Here the chapter explores how modern campaigns target their audiences with precision, how the marketplace of advertising has diversified, why campaigns "source" their advertising claims, and why opposition research provides invaluable help to refute or support claims in commercials. The next part focuses on the components that make television ads work. Symbols, sounds, and music can be as important as the script. The subsequent section turns to a discussion of the types of television ads that campaigns produce. Biographical, enhancement/issue, and negative/comparative advertisements provide an overview how advertisements work to influence voters and then the next part explores the art of buying advertising time.

The chapter proceeds to examine how radio, newspaper, and direct mail are advertising modalities that supplement or appear in lieu of television advertising. Radio, newspaper, and direct mail are particularly important for low-budget campaigns given the cost of television advertising. Furthermore, political parties and interest groups represent outside forces (aside from the competing campaigns) that advertise hoping to influence the outcome of an election. Political parties have an agenda to elect their own candidates, whereas interest groups may have their own agenda. The chapter then examines campaign advertising's effect on the political process.

TELEVISION AS AN ADVERTISING MEDIUM

Television as the major medium for advertising in American elections is a phenomenon of the past half-century. Prior to television advertising in the 20th century, campaign advertising or communications techniques consisted of radio, newspaper advertising, signs, billboards, bumper stickers, and lapel pins. Television first came into the homes of Americans following the Second World War. From 1950 to 1959, the aggregate number of television sets bought grew from 9.7 million to 67.1 million. The impact of television on political campaigns emerged most forcefully during the 1960 presidential campaign because John F. Kennedy was the first "telegenic" candidate. In other words, he looked good on television. John F. Kennedy transformed the medium of television through his famous debates with Vice President Nixon, his personal appearances, and his television-friendly news conferences in the 1960 presidential race. Kennedy's cool demeanor, handsome looks, confidence, youth, vigor, ability to articulate ideas, and humor have been the model for many candidates for public office since his victory in 1960. Presidents Jimmy Carter and Bill Clinton have been among the many candidates featuring a "blow dry" hairdo emulating a Kennedyesque image.[3]

Television advertising is not the sole medium for communicating with voters in the 21st century. Direct mail is quite effective in metropolitan areas such as New York, Los Angeles and Chicago where congressional television commercials are often obscured by more prominent gubernatorial and senatorial races. Furthermore, the expense of paid advertising can be prohibitive. Radio is a reliable source of advertising for low-budget campaigns that need to reach a specific demographic audience. Newspaper advertising is less popular as an advertising choice, but it remains part of the ad mix for some campaigns, as explained later in the chapter.

THE CHANGING WORLD OF TELEVISION AND ADVERTISING

Effective political ads are much more sophisticated than slogans and content; visual symbols, colors, music, and sound connecting emotively with voters send a powerful message. Television stands as the most potent medium because information is passively received through two senses (sight and sound) while other media involve only sight (print) or sound (radio).[4]

Campaign commercials have matured in refinement, technical complexity, and effectiveness over the years. Early campaign television ads such as the "I Like Ike" ads (touting General Dwight Eisenhower's 1952 presidential bid) look rather amateurish by today's standards. Today, campaign commercials are as sophisticated as Madison Avenue advertising with superior audio and video production values. These ads either directly or passively "cue" viewers about how they should vote. The colors, sounds, and visual dynamics also help to entice viewers.

Paid political advertising differs from Madison Avenue advertising in two major ways: First, information is sourced at the bottom of the advertisement to provide veracity for the claims made in the commercial. Second, the repetition of campaign ads in the closing weeks is far more prevalent than any single industry produces at one point in time, driving home a message to uncommitted voters. Given that the stakes for choosing candidates are greater than those for the choices of laundry detergent, the accuracy of campaign advertising must adhere to a higher standard. *The New York Times* and *The Washington Post* are the most prominent ad watchers in the media reviewing campaign commercials for factual accuracy.

Television Advertising Strategy

Presidential campaigns from the 1950s through the 1980s used a nationwide advertising strategy to target voters. Purchasing commercial advertising time to show ads during the network's daytime soap operas or the early evening hours was commonplace.

The widespread introduction of cable television to homes across America in the 1980s helped campaigns change their perception of advertising. Advertising strategy changed when the 1988 George Bush, Sr. campaign tactically targeted advertising resources to key states. In fact, Bush, Sr. spent "76 percent of his advertising money in key battleground states." Furthermore, an analysis of Bush's opponent, Democratic Governor Michael Dukakis of Massachusetts, found that the latter had "spread out" his money in states "he could not possibly win." The Clinton campaign of 1992 not only targeted such messages to battleground states, but also developed and produced ads aimed at specific constituencies in competitive states. "By September, Clinton was so far ahead in so many states, his campaign team gambled they could skip advertising in most of them." Among the ten remaining target states were Colorado, Michigan, Ohio, Georgia, Louisiana, and North Carolina. (North Carolina was the only state that Clinton lost among these selected states.) The Clinton issue ads were full of statistics and facts focusing on such subjects as the economy, jobs and welfare reform, which appealed to white- and blue-collar workers who were concerned about becoming unemployed. Ads developed from the work of "The Manhattan Project" discussed in Chapter 5 targeted suburban women, a key voter group in the Midwestern battleground states. These ads focused on Clinton's character and humble beginnings as "The Man from Hope."[5]

Advertising strategies are more complex now, given the expand-ing number of cable televisions, satellite television, declining view-ership, and increased use of the Internet. The viewing audience has fragmented from 20 years ago when ABC, NBC, and CBS dominated television. Campaigns are less concerned about the growth of inde-pendent networks such as FOX, WB (Warner Brothers), and Para-mount because their audience is comprised of adolescent and young adult viewers representing a high proportion of non-voters.

A fragmented viewing audience suggests that all advertisers are reaching fewer viewers. According to a Media Dynamics Report in 2002, the percentage of all advertising dollars that went to the three major networks declined from 80 percent in 1988 to 49 percent in 2000. The growth of personal Internet use may account for a substan-tial portion of the reduction. A 2002 study from the U.S. Department of Commerce reported that 143 million Americans (52 percent of the population) use the Internet, including 64 percent of adults be-tween the ages of 18–49. The U.S. Department of Commerce report augments an earlier study by the UCLA Center for Communication Policy (2001), which found that Internet users watch 4.5 hours less television per week than non-users. This fragmented environment makes it far more difficult and expensive to reach target audiences such as suburban women from 30–39 years old or southern white-collar males from 40–54 years old, via campaign advertising. The implications are that television advertising now has to "grab" audi-ences more effectively than in the past.[6]

Sourcing campaign advertisements with facts and disclaimers has become a mainstay in political campaigns because of the bom-bardment of various advertising claims on television. Sources are par-ticularly important when running a negative ad because the attack has to be credible to convince a skeptical viewer. One excellent exam-ple was Dennis Moore's (D) "Concealed Gun" ad against incumbent Vince Snowbarger (R) in the Third Congressional District of Kansas in 1998. Snowbarger accused Moore of being soft on crime. In response, the Moore campaign released a commercial it had "in the can" wait-ing for Snowbarger. The voiceover in the ad said: "Vince Snowbarger supports legalizing military-style assault weapons." The video featured a still-shot of Snowbarger underscored with the message, "Supports military-style assault weapons." The source appeared on the screen: "Kansas City Star 7/30/96 & 8/7/96." The subsequent claim provided another banner listing the source. Banner: "Voted to Allow Concealed Weapons Source: House Journal, 1996, HB 2885."[7]

The purpose of "factual" messages is to provide an independent source of confirmation for claims made by the campaign. The message is "if you don't believe us, check the source yourself." The Moore ad proved highly effective against Snowbarger, portraying the congressman as out-of-step with mainstream values on gun violence. Moore, a former criminal defense lawyer, successfully turned a liability into an asset. Moore was one of five House challengers to unseat an incumbent in the 1998 congressional elections by deftly turning an issue against his opponent. The utilization of credible sources gave Moore's advertising clout against Snowbarger.[8]

Opposition Research

Opposition research plays a critical role in deconstructing an opponent as it did in the Snowbarger-Moore race. To save costs, U.S. House campaigns often conduct opposition research within the campaign rather than hire a consultant. However, big budget campaigns hire political consultants to research the opponent. Opposition research is not new; the Federalist party "dug up information that Thomas Jefferson had children by a slave mistress," and Grover Cleveland admitted that he fathered an illegitimate child in his 1884 presidential campaign. The difference today is that the techniques of finding out information about the public record and private lives of candidates are far more sophisticated and invasive. Campaigns peruse the Internet, examine Lexis-Nexus for periodical and newspaper articles, scrutinize voting records, review opponent press releases, and investigate court and driving records. The "oppo" consultant analyzes the information and then presents it to the candidate, pollster, and the media consultant.[9]

Oppo research investigates not only the opposition, but the client as well. For example, Jack Palladino was an investigator hired by the 1992 Clinton campaign to look into allegations of Clinton's womanizing. Palladino investigated at least two dozen different women. The material he collected enabled the campaign to prepare for any exigencies. The results of his investigation enabled the Clinton campaign to move forward with its advertising focusing on women's issues without any immediate causes for alarm. Several Clinton campaign commercials for the general election such as "Journey," "Morning," and "Milwaukee" were aimed specifically at working women.[10]

Counterpunching the opposition rapidly and effectively is often correlated with the successful use of opposition research.

Representative Tim Johnson (D-SD) was a well-funded challenger ($2.9 million budget) who upset incumbent Senator Larry Pressler (R-SD) because of his extensive use of opposition research to build a media campaign. Karl Struble, who served as Johnson's media consultant in his 1996 bid said: "We documented Larry's arrogance and abuse of office. We made his conduct and indulgence in the perks and privileges of incumbency 'the issue' in the race." The Johnson campaign documented how Pressler had received meals, free hotel stays, and overseas junkets from cable television and telecommunication lobbyists. Pressler sat on the powerful Senate Commerce Committee, which oversees the telecommunications and broadcast industries. Pressler's junket to Hong Kong highlighted his abuse of office. Johnson's campaign used this information in an advertisement that proved to be very effective. Johnson's offensive on Pressler's ethics enabled the South Dakotan Democrat to be the only Senate challenger to upset a Republican incumbent in 1996.[11]

Technology and research tools enable campaigns to respond within hours to attacks from opponents. Major senatorial, gubernatorial, and presidential campaigns utilize existing research in their files to refute such claims. An "oppo" research consultant organizes the newly discovered material and forwards it to the media consultant. The consultant uses the research to help write and produce a final cut of the commercial within hours. The media consultant, in most cases, then buys the air-time and transmits the commercial by satellite to a television station to be aired later that day. Technology now facilitates the ability where media consulting firms with satellite dishes can intercept an opponent's commercials when beamed to a television station; this enables the intercepting campaign to get a head start in responding to attacks.

MAKING ADS THAT WORK

The primary focus of campaign advertising is to develop a simple "hook" or message that emotionally or intellectually connects with viewers. Media consultant Adam Goodman tells a folksy story about the late governor of Florida, Lawton Chiles (D-FL) alluding to raccoons ("he-coons") in a campaign advertisement. "Lawton Chiles whose once sagging [poll] numbers for reelection were bolstered by home-spun allusions to 'he-coons.' Translation: the wisdom and judgment of age and maturity still count for a helluva lot." The

FIGURE 6-1 The 1964 Johnson Campaign's "Daisy" Girl Commercial

pedestrian use of language by a politician "hooks" the audience to pay closer attention to the ad's substance. The hook may entail something dramatic, subtle, folksy or humorous.[12]

Campaign media consultants are always striving to create an ad or a series of ads that will define a campaign; either through shock value or through constant repetition on the air. The most famous and dramatic commercial produced for a candidate aired only once—the "Daisy" ad made for President Lyndon Johnson in 1964. The ad starts with a little girl counting the petals of a daisy as she plucks them and counts towards ten. When she reaches the "nine" the picture freezes with the little girl staring innocently at the camera. Instantly, a missile countdown begins, "10, 9, 8, 7 . . . 2, 1" and boom! A mushroom cloud from a nuclear explosion emerges. In the background President Johnson says, "These are the stakes—to make a world in which all God's children can live. . . ." The banner asks viewers to vote for President Johnson, with a concluding voice-over: "Vote for President Johnson on November 3. The stakes are too high for you to stay home." The symbolism of peace represented by the little girl contrasts with the reality of nuclear war.[13]

Tony Schwartz, an advertising executive who rarely left his brownstone in Manhattan because he suffered from agoraphobia (the fear of open spaces) produced "Daisy" for Lyndon Johnson's campaign. Schwartz had been responsible for writing and producing commercials for corporate giants such as Ivory soap and Post cereals. His unique advertising philosophy was succinctly stated in his book *Media: The Second God*. The purpose of advertising is to "build confidence among shareholders." In other words, to apply this principle to a political campaign, the idea of advertising is two-fold: to build confidence in your candidate among supporters (i.e., shareholders) and conversely, cast doubt upon the credulity of your opponent. The brilliant "Daisy" ad undermined confidence in the opponent (without naming Arizona Republican Senator Barry Goldwater). "Daisy" implied that Goldwater was reckless and might start a nuclear war. Furthermore, the ad implied that the incumbent (Johnson) was the safer choice. Goldwater's statement that "extremism in the pursuit of liberty is no vice; moderation in the pursuit of justice is no virtue" at the Republican convention the previous summer enabled the Johnson campaign to use the motif of extremism to paint the Republican nominee as a man who would risk nuclear war if elected president.[14]

September 7, 1964 marked the single appearance of "Daisy" on CBS's *Monday Night at the Movies*. The switchboard at CBS lit up with protests. The next day and for days afterward, the ad became a major focus of stories on the evening news. The ad garnered so much attention that it never ran again.[15]

The "Daisy" ad broke conventional techniques in political advertising. First, the network did for the campaign, what the campaign could not do for itself—provide free advertising. Second, Daisy was the first major *comparative* television ad in presidential politics. A comparative ad contrasts the negative attributes or positions of an opponent to the advertising candidate's positive self-portrait. Third, the ad, by inference, depicted Goldwater as a threat to world peace, but the ad never mentioned his name. Fourth, the Daisy ad provided two stories—one of the little girl and the second of a nuclear bomb exploding, to great effect. Schwartz's skill in creating this advertisement demonstrates that a simple commercial is actually quite complex. Daisy's success has been mimicked a number of times. More recently, an anti-Gore group produced "Daisy II," appearing in media markets in the Midwest during the 2000 presidential campaign.[16]

Symbols connote important messages to voters through visuals and music. The "Bear in the Woods" commercial produced by Hal Riney for the Reagan reelection campaign in 1984 symbolized the threat of the "Russian bear" to American interests. The purpose of the ad was to inoculate (i.e., protect) Reagan against charges that the United States had overspent on military defense. The commercial features a menacing bear prowling the woods. The narrator concludes the commercial with a rhetorical question: "Isn't it smart to be strong as the bear—if there is a bear?" The bear resonated with many voters' unspoken fears concerning real or imaginary threats to American security and implied Reagan would protect the nation from such fears.[17]

Flags became the most prominent visual symbol in campaign advertising since the Reagan era of the 1980s, as the nation emerged out of the post-Vietnam era riding a wave of patriotism. After attacks on the World Trade Center and Pentagon on September 11, 2002 the intensity of patriotic sentiment rose even higher. Democrat Tom Harkin (Iowa) faced a tough senate reelection campaign in 2002. Early in June, the U.S. Ninth Circuit Court in California struck down the Pledge of Allegiance as a violation of the separation of church and state because of the phrase "under God." The massive public outcry in favor of protecting the flag created problems for Tom Harkin's reelection campaign because he had voted against a flag burning constitutional amendment in March 2000. To make sure that Harkin's patriotism was not called into question, his ad showed the former Navy officer surrounded by veterans saluting the flag.[18]

Music can profoundly affect how a viewer identifies with a candidate. The tone can arouse patriotism, soften the image of a candidate (e.g., Bob Dole), or make the candidate seem more human (e.g., Al Gore). "The Story" created for Bob Dole's presidential bid in 1996 by Mike Murphy and Don Sipple makes extensive use of soft brass that plays inspirationally and sentimentally in the background. The tone of the music is reminiscent of soft patriotic brass heard in "Saving Private Ryan," which debuted the previous year. While the music plays in the background, "The Story" tells a voter who Bob Dole is through the words of his wife Elizabeth, his own words, and a list of his accomplishments throughout his career. The theme of this main-street biographical ad appears in the tagline: "The Better Man for a Better America." The ad subtly suggests that Dole's opponent, President Bill Clinton, lacked the moral character to serve another term in office.[19]

Sound can capture the attention of a passive viewer. Shudder-ing noises, screaming, and laughter represent attention-getting techniques. Vice President Hubert Humphrey, the Democratic presi-dential nominee in 1968, running 20 points behind Richard Nixon heading into the fall election campaign, led a party badly splintered by the Vietnam War. Nixon's choice of Governor Spiro Agnew of Maryland to be his running mate provided the Humphrey campaign with an opportunity. Agnew was regarded as a political lightweight and an "attack dog," selected by Nixon to appease conservatives in the Republican party. A poll of voters told the Humphrey campaign that Nixon was vulnerable on the Agnew selection. The Humphrey campaign hired Tony Schwartz to produce an "attack" ad belittling Agnew. He produced an ad in which the voiceover is simply con-tagious hysterical laughter. The first banner says, "Agnew for Vice-President?" The second banner then flashes on the screen, "This would be funny if it weren't so serious." The first reaction of the viewer is to laugh, and then to respond "ooo" or "gotcha" when the second banner appears. The ad is distinct because no words are spo-ken. The emotional reaction and reasoning powers of the viewer come together differently than in other political advertisements— the audio, not the visual, provides drama and emotion. Doubts about Agnew, reinforced by this advertisement did contribute to Humphrey's closing the gap with Nixon, but no evidence suggests that the ad was a singular factor making the race more competitive.[20]

TYPES OF CAMPAIGN ADS

Consultants use different types of ads to build a narrative about their candidate. Often the first ad features a description of candidate accom-plishments (biographical ad). Another kind of commercial may ex-plain the candidate's values or issue positions (enhancement/ issue ad). A third type of ad draws a contrast between the candidate and op-ponent (negative/comparative ad). All advertising elements should fit together in a comprehensive framework. For example, Mitt Romney's successful campaign for Massachusetts governor in 2002 incorporated each of these elements in his advertising campaign. Romney, a Repub-lican businessman, had run unsuccessfully for the Senate against Ted Kennedy in 1994 and five years later agreed to serve as president of the Winter Olympic Committee in Salt Lake City after corruption forced the previous president to resign. One ad entitled "Independence" weaves biographical, issue, and comparative elements together. "Independence" addressed the scandal-plagued "Big Dig" in Boston. The "Big Dig" was a $15 billion construction program to reroute traffic in downtown Boston. Romney's message was that he would "clean-up" state government and corruption associated with cost overruns from the "Big Dig." The ad suggested that Romney would help restore "independence" to the people of Massachusetts by ending the cycle of patronage and corruption. The ad had three messages: 1) the "Big Dig" was an issue about corruption (issues/ values), 2) the state government was tainted by corruption (negative), and 3) Romney's background showed that he was capable of cleaning up a mess (biographical). Romney would bring independent leadership back to state government, similar to a cowboy in a white hat riding into town to rid Boston of the bad guys.[21]

The race determines what tactics are most effective in advertising strategy. Campaign strategists may decide that highlighting the positive attributes of a candidate who has an appealing personality is advantageous (e.g., Democrat John Edwards' election to the U.S. Senate from North Carolina in 1998 or Republican Orrin Hatch's re-election to the U.S. Senate from Utah in 2000). Campaigns look at their candidate's "favorable" or "unfavorable" ratings versus those of their opponent. Parris Glendening's (D) reelection race for governor of Maryland against Ellen Sauerbrey (R) in 1998 featured an incumbent with a high unfavorable rating. The Glendening campaign went negative almost from the start painting Sauerbrey as an extremist pro-gun and anti-environment candidate. The effective tactic drove Sauerbrey's personal unfavorable ratings upward, diminished her support, and resulted in her defeat.[22]

The target audience for a successful advertising campaign is relatively small. An advertising campaign's goal aims at building a candidate's political base, shoring up political support, or persuading undecided voters. Five to 30 percent of undecided or weakly committed voters in a close election contest can swing the race to either candidate. However, for the other 70 percent or more who have decided ads are relatively unimportant.

Biographical Ads

The purpose of the biographical ("bio") ad is to introduce or reintroduce a candidate to voters. Bio ads are longer advertising spots than

issue or negative ads because they seek to condense someone's entire life into one minute. Bio ads illustrate the character traits and
values of the candidate, which resonate with the constituency. Family members sometimes appear in bio ads extolling the virtues of
their spouse's candidacy. Elizabeth Dole passionately described her
husband's courage, experience, and integrity to voters in advertising
in 1996 when Bob Dole ran unsuccessfully for the presidency against
Bill Clinton. Bob Dole returned the favor with more success when his
wife Elizabeth ran successfully for the U.S. Senate from North
Carolina in 2002 by appearing in ads that praised his wife.

The bio ad produced for Ben Nighthorse Campbell's 1992 U.S.
Senate victory in Colorado in 1992 remains one of the best advertisements created in the last 20 years. Campbell's life appears as a short
documentary, portrayed through black and white still pictures and is
unusually long (two minutes) for a campaign advertisement. The
compelling story traces Campbell's life from his impoverished
native-American childhood as a high school dropout, to his job as
a truck driver as he earned his way through college, to the Olympic
judo team in 1964, to successful rancher, to election to the United
States House of Representatives. The Campbell ad creates an
authentic American hero—the triumph of an individual over
adversity—with a black-and-white head shot of the candidate at the
end showing him as an American hero and a western icon.

Candidates with high name recognition often do not run biographical ads because their personal character is well-known. Ted
Kennedy did not run any bio ads in his 1994 reelection contest. Consultants Tad Devine and Bob Shrum produced issue ads augment-
ing Kennedy's political character rather than his personal character.
The commercials stressed that the Massachusetts senator had the
right political values for the state. Incumbent presidents rarely produce bio ads since they have universal name recognition. Ronald
Reagan (1984) and Bill Clinton (1996), for instance, did not run biographical ads in their reelection bids. Richard Nixon's reelection
campaign ran a biographical ad entitled, "The Man" in 1972 to
humanize his image and counter the perception that he was a cal-
culating and manipulative politician. The ad shows a pensive
Nixon quietly working at his desk and an extroverted Nixon playing the piano at a black-tie dinner. Why the ad appeared in September 1972 was not clear since Nixon had a 34-point lead over his opponent Democrat George McGovern. Biographical ads introduce or

reintroduce voters to a candidate. Enhancement ads, which often follow, develop themes about the candidate and broaden that discussion to include values and issues.[23]

Enhancement and Issue Ads

Enhancement and issue ads play an integral role linking the candidate's personal characteristics to specific policy positions and messages. These ads frequently represent the second phase of campaign
advertising. The enhancement ad may simply develop character
themes from a biographical ad. The issue ad may transition the campaign from the candidate's individual story to issues that concern
voters. The approach and content of the ad may differ for challengers and incumbents. Challengers often use an enhancement ad
to build on the foundation and reference the introductory biographical ad since they usually have low name recognition. Incumbents
tend to use enhancement ads during any phase of the campaign
when it serves a purpose to remind voters who they are, what they
have accomplished, and how they will build on their record if
reelected.

Russ Feingold's (D-WI) successful 1992 campaign for the U.S.
Senate is illustrative how *enhancement* advertising can benefit a
challenger. Feingold's unusual commercial reminds voters of his previous ad, filmed as a home movie, and uses humor. Feingold's campaign ran the ad in the Democratic primary against his opponents:
wealthy businessman Joe Checota and Congressman Jim Moody.

The ad begins with a question: "Hi, Russ Feingold, the candidate
for senator?" This is an unusual technique because the candidate
reminds voters of his earlier advertisement. Feingold personally visits the homes of his Democratic primary opponents. Feingold's first
visit is to the estate of Joe Checota. When he rings the doorbell, there
is no answer, but you hear a barking dog. Feingold recoils slightly
and says, "I guess no one is at home." Next, Feingold stands in front
of the home of Jim Moody, but again no one is present. Feingold
shows a picture of Moody's townhouse in Washington, D.C. and
suggests that Moody spends most of his time there. Both visits imply
that Feingold's opponents are out of touch with voters. The next
scene moves to Feingold's modest suburban ranch home. On the
garage door he has hand-painted his campaign promises. Feingold
takes the viewer on a tour of the house. He opens a closet door and
says in mock horror, "no skeletons." Feingold reemphasizes to

voters throughout the ad that he is an ordinary person; that he can best represent Wisconsin because he lives in the real world unlike Checota ensconced in a protected personal fortress or Moody who seems to spend more time in Washington, D.C. than in Wisconsin. Modesty, populism, and humor characterize Feingold and the ad underscores Wisconsin's tradition of populist senators such as Robert LaFollette, Sr. (R), Robert LaFollette, Jr. (R), and William Proxmire (D) railing against big money campaigns and special interests. Feingold easily defeated his primary opposition (receiving 70 percent of the vote) and beat incumbent Republican Bob Kasten (53–46 percent) in the general election.[24]

Enhancement and issue ads positively demonstrate a candidate's position on issues, substantive legislative accomplishments, and the ads tie these personal perspectives to personal values and achievements. They provide a preview of what a candidate hopes to accomplish if elected. Greater credibility is lent to the ads when the candidate is featured talking about programs or issues that concern constituents. Congressman John Thune (R-SD) narrated his own enhancement/issue ad called "Fairness" when he ran for the U.S. Senate against incumbent Tim Johnson (D-SD) in 2002. Thune called for "lower taxes for middle class families" and said that he represented "South Dakota values" of thrift and smaller government. The commercial shows Thune interacting with farmers, women, and children in various scenes as he discusses lowering the tax-burden for middle-class voters in the state. The ad closes with a soft-filter sunset shot of Thune walking hand-in-hand with his wife through a farm field. Thune's portrayal is of an ordinary man who understands the concerns of the rural middle class in South Dakota. The ad is entirely positive. While Thune was defeated in the closest U.S. Senate contest in 2002, the ad effectively connected Thune's character to specific issues and values. Enhancement and issue ads are essential elements of a campaign that develop a strategic character or issue story of a campaign, explain the candidate's skill in addressing voter concerns, and lay the future groundwork for a comparison with the opposition.[25]

Negative/Comparative Ads

Negative ads attack the opponent's character, stance on issues, or link both disapprovingly together. Negative ads engender controversy, yet research demonstrates their effectiveness in shifting preferences of non-committed voters. "Non-partisans . . . by contrast usually tune out political advertising . . . Only negative messages resonate with such attitudes." The *comparative* ad features an attack on the opponent followed by material that extols the virtues of the candidate running the ad. Many comparative ads use black-and-white stills or film footage in the negative portion. Saturated color film is then used to emphasize the warmth, connectedness, and thoughtfulness of the advertising candidate. The sudden shift in tone, film, and substance suggests a stark choice between evil (black-and-white) and good (warm colors).[26]

"Willie Horton" produced by independent consultant Floyd Brown in the 1988 presidential race helped change the course of the campaign. Surveys indicated that crime was the pivotal issue of the presidential campaign and the competence of how each candidate addressed it—Republican Vice President George Bush and Democratic Governor Michael Dukakis—was the seminal factor affecting the outcome of the race. Prior to Dukakis' service as Massachusetts governor, the state legislature had passed and former governor had signed into law a bill making possible the weekend furlough of prisoners, including convicted murderers, who were model inmates, serving life terms. Republican and Democratic governors had routinely granted furlough requests from the state parole board. In 1974, Willie Horton was convicted of murder for stabbing a woman 19 times. Horton was released on a weekend furlough in April 1987. He traveled down to suburban Washington, D.C. "where he broke into a house, beat and stabbed a man, and raped a woman." The Horton episode raised the question of whether Massachusetts' furlough laws were too lenient. The course black-and-white footage in the "Willie Horton" ad drove home the point that Dukakis was soft on crime. The ad was so effective that the Bush campaign followed up with a separate commercial entitled "Revolving Door." (The official Bush campaign was independent and not connected to Floyd Brown's group "Americans for Bush"). The ad shows the Massachusetts penal system as a revolving door of prisoners going in and out of jail. The tag line of the ad was "Weekend prison passes: Dukakis on crime." Dukakis' inability or unwillingness to respond to such attacks made him appear weak and ineffective. The attacks contrasted with the Dukakis' Democratic nomination speech in August 1988, where he spoke about his governing competence.[27]

USING HUMOR TO PORTRAY AN OPPONENT:
THE "JABBERWOCKY" AD

———

Humor can disarm the opposition by ridiculing it more effectively than a heavy-handed negative advertisement. In 1991, the state of Louisiana held a gubernatorial contest between former governor, Democrat Edwin Edwards (who had run up enormous gambling debts) and Republican state legislator David Duke (former Grand Wizard of the Ku Klux Klan). Duke was so unpopular among Republicans outside of Louisiana that the Republican National Committee refused to lend support to his candidacy. Edwards' media consultants Dino Seder and Dawn Laguens knew that they had to attack Duke but also feared a backlash and did not want to drum up sympathy for the former KKK leader. After all, Duke had run a surprisingly strong U.S. Senate race against incumbent Democrat J. Bennett Johnston in 1990, garnering 44 percent of the vote. Seder and Laguens produced an ad that was a "Jeopardy" type of game show with a host and three white contestants, two men and a woman, called "Jabberwocky."

Audio	Video

Game-show host, Paul:
    Debbie, you first.
	Host Paul Anthony
	    stands by a game board
	    before a panel of three
	    contestants as on Jeopardy.

Debbie: I'll try "False
    Patriots" for $300.
Paul: He was kicked out
    of ROTC, lied about serving
    his country and never spent
    a day in the military.
(Buzzer) Debbie.
Debbie: Who is David Duke?
Paul: Correct!
Debbie: "Good Buddies" for $300.
Paul: He hired ex-Nazis to work
    on his political campaigns.	

(Buzzer) Bill!
Bill: (Enthusiastically) Who
   is David Duke?
Paul: Yes!
Bill: I'll try "Tax Cheats" for $200.
Paul: He failed to file state income
   taxes from 1984–1987.
(Buzzer) Alan!
Alan: (Nonchalantly) Who is
   David Duke?
Paul: That's right!
Alan: "Racist Ideas" for $300.
Paul: He has advocated that the
   United States be separated into
   separate race nations.
(Buzzer) Debbie.
Debbie: (Very enthusiastically)
   Who is David Duke?!!

. . . etc.	Video
Paul: And that's the end of Round two. Stay tuned, folks; we'll be right back.	Banner headline imposed on game show as Anthony finishes: "Who is David Duke?"[28]

Reprinted by permission of Laguens, Hamburger and Stone.

Analysis
   "Jabberwocky" worked because it made deadly serious
subjects, bigotry and fraud, accessible to white voters in
Louisiana. "Jabberwocky" was effective for the following
reasons: 1) the contestants are all white, middle-class and con-
servatively dressed appearing like the state's swing voting
population, 2) the ad belittled Duke's ideas, humorously implying that a vote for this man would reflect poorly on the
state, and 3) the ad asked, "Who is David Duke?" The rhetorical question suggests that Duke is still a racist and a liar.

Increasingly, comparative ads have emerged as the choice of negative advertising in comparison with explicit negative attacks such as the "Willie Horton" or "Daisy" ads of earlier years. The popularity of the comparative ad emerged in the 1980s as advertising became more prevalent and consumers became more discerning about choices, according to a study by the Anderson School of Graduate Management at UCLA. Nutritional labels, safety warnings, and product information became more important to consumers. For example, Shoppers Food Warehouse, a national grocery store chain asked viewers to shop, compare prices, and save. Political advertising campaigns have followed the same marketing trends as business exhorting voters to make qualitative comparisons in choosing elected officials.[29]

"The Choice" provides an excellent illustration of a short but direct comparative ad. Shrum, Devine, and Donilon prepared the ad for Jon Corzine (D-NJ) in his 2000 New Jersey U.S. Senate bid. Corzine, a former chairman of the Goldman Sachs investment house, spent $63 million in his Senate bid, mostly on television advertising. Bob Franks, a moderate Republican congressman, was his opponent. "The Choice" compares Jon Corzine and Bob Franks on the issue of abortion, affirmed as a federal right by the United States Supreme Court in the case of *Roe v. Wade* (1973).

> Announcer: "The Supreme Court is divided on whether *Roe v. Wade* will remain the law of the land. A woman's right to choose hangs in the balance. Jon Corzine has made it clear that he will support judges who will protect a woman's right to choose. Bob Franks has made it clear he will support judges . . . most determined to overturn *Roe v. Wade*. The choice? Putting a woman's right to choose at risk with Bob Franks, or protecting a woman's right to choose with Jon Corzine."[30]

Sourcing is a key feature of Corzine's abortion ad giving enhanced credibility to the claims made in the commercial. The ad is "sourced" from both the *Newark Star-Ledger* debate and a Franks campaign press release. Second, the thematic message of the ad is that the choice on abortion embodies the essence of the choice voters will make in the Senate race. "The Choice" carefully avoids attacking Bob Franks' personal character while saying that his political character is out of step with New Jersey voters. In other words, Jon Corzine shares the same values as New Jersey residents whereas Bob Franks' values are out of the political mainstream. Comparative advertising at its best defines a creditable and clearly articulated choice between "our" political values and the opponents' wrong-minded political values.

BUYING ADVERTISING TIME

Few people outside the advertising industry know that a savvy media buyer can be more important at times than the ad production company. For example, if commercial time is purchased during the "Late Fringe" time-period (after 11:00 PM in the Eastern time zone) and the target audience is women over the age of 55, then the buy is almost worthless. Purchasing time during the "Day" stretching from 9 AM–3 PM would be highly effective since this demographic dominates the time-period watching soaps, talk shows and the noon news.[31]

Most advertising consultants charge a flat fee or retainer ($100,000 for a Senate race is typical) plus 18 percent of the cost of buying television time. Federal Trade Commission rules stipulate that campaigns must be charged the lowest unit rate of cost when purchasing air-time in an attempt to drive down the cost of campaigns. Advertising costs are measured in gross ratings point (GRP) units estimating the viewership at any particular time. GRPs are sold in batches such as 100 units, which buys about 30 seconds of air-time for one viewing of a campaign ad at a particular time of day. The repetitive showing of commercials enhances a voter's recall of a specific message; thus, the same commercial needs to be shown 10 times (or cost 1000 GRP) units to resonate. If "Day" unit advertising (9 AM–3 PM) in Kansas City, MO were valued at approximately $110 per GRP unit, then the cost for showing the ad would be 100 GRP units or $11,000. Showing the ad the desired 10 times yields a total purchase of $110,000 for the "Day" time period. Another ten showings of the same ad during prime time in Kansas City might cost approximately $165,000. Given this scenario, purchasing the same ad time in New York City would cost about seven times the Kansas City price due to the size of the market. It is easy to see how candidates can spend millions of dollars on advertising during a primary or general election campaign.[32]

Advertising on cable television has become more attractive for campaigns managing resources on a tight budget. Cable reaches more than 75 percent of the homes in the United States and is less expensive than advertising on network television (ABC, NBC, CBS, and FOX). The cost of a 30-second spot for a premium cable show such as *Sex in the City* may be substantially less than a spot on television's highest rated show, *CSI*. More importantly, cable advertising may reach niche audiences better than the networks. For example, if Jesse Ventura were to run for the U.S. Senate, then he would advertise locally on ESPN because his strongest cohort of voters (18–30 year old men) watches the sports network in large numbers. Therefore, if Ventura's media buyer purchased a local spot on ESPN's *Sportscenter* at 11 PM, he would likely reach his target demographic group. Increasing segmentation of the viewing audience has made cable advertising more attractive to candidates.[33]

RADIO AND NEWSPAPER ADVERTISING

Fifty years ago, radio broadcasts, newspapers, bumper stickers, lapel pins, and signs represented the scope of campaign advertising. The technological revolution transforming media operations does not obviate the need for radio and newspaper advertising. Radio and newspaper advertising is part of the "media mix" that candidates use to reach different types of audiences. The strategic purpose of such advertising placement is to extend the reach and frequency of a candidate's message from television to radio and print. Tight budgets might impede a candidate's ability to advertise on television. Instead, a candidate may opt for radio or print media as a cost-effective choice.

Radio

Campaigns with a small budget find that radio advertising can be highly effective. Modern technology through digital generation systems (DGS) enables an ad produced in the morning to air on radio by afternoon. The effect of DGS has driven down the prohibitive costs of production and transmission that campaigns faced in the past. Baker Sound Studios of Philadelphia boasts: "with DGS we can transmit digital copy of your radio spot to most major radio stations faster than Kenneth Starr can issue a subpoena." (Starr was the independent counsel for the Clinton-Lewinsky investigation). The cost of sending the ad runs about the same as a Federal Express package.[34]

Radio advertising can be particularly effective for congressional races in large media markets. Major metropolitan areas such as

New York (30 plus congressional districts), Los Angeles (25 plus congressional districts), and Chicago (15 plus congressional districts) have television stations with large viewing audiences. Local television advertising for major metropolitan areas encompasses a radius of numerous congressional districts. The impact of such advertising may be negligible for a congressional candidate compared with radio's offering a more targeted demographic audience in this situation. For example, Representative Carolyn Maloney (D-NY) of the Upper East Side of Manhattan may derive little benefit from advertising on local television (WNBC, WCBS, or WABC) covering the tri-state area, including western Connecticut, northern New Jersey, the city, Long Island and the northern New York suburbs, in addition to her district. Maloney's "Silk Stocking" district from 14th to 96th Street on the East Side is wealthy, highly educated, and sophisticated. Her advertisements may have greater impact running on WQXR, a classical music radio station reaching many of the affluent constituents of her district. While radio has the disadvantage of reaching a smaller audience than television, it is still a potent medium for congressional advertising in major metropolitan areas.[35]

Newspapers

Newspaper advertisements promoting major candidates running for national office are akin to finding moon rocks on earth; they are few and far between. Modern technology enhances the speed and reduces the cost of an ad placement. The optimal use of newspaper advertising appears during the closing days of a campaign showing candidate endorsements by respected citizens, organizations, or office-holders. Such ads are geared to encouraging readers to vote on election day. Working against print ads are the high standards and lengthy time frame that print media require for ad approval. John Stewart of National Media, Inc., a prominent Republican media firm, believes that less lag time in the approval process would make newspaper advertising a stronger candidate-advertising vehicle to compete with television, cable, radio, and the Internet.[36]

The print media most effectively influencing voters comes straight to voters' mailboxes—"direct mail." Direct mail provides a targeted approach to advertising that is second to television in importance. Direct mail has become the most potent force of advertising outside of television for candidates on limited budgets or for candidates using various media to communicate their message to voters.

DIRECT MAIL

"Tom Downey's limousine liberal guide to surviving the recession"
—Republican Rick Lazio's direct mail piece from 1992 depicting
incumbent Congressman Tom Downey (D) of Long Island.[37]
Direct mail can be very hard-hitting as a communications medium.
In 1992, Rick Lazio, a 34 year-old Republican Suffolk County legisla-
tor, ran an uphill race against long-term congressional incumbent
Democrat Tom Downey in Long Island's Second Congressional
District. Lazio had less than $300,000 in his war chest compared with
$1.4 million for Downey. Downey served on the powerful House
Ways and Means Committee dealing with all revenue issues including taxes. Downey's career sailed along until scandal plagued the
House of Representatives when reports revealed that many members overdrafted checks at the House "bank." The investigation
found that Downey had 151 overdrafts. The Republican legislator
used direct mail to communicate with voters arguing that Downey
was a "limousine liberal" a euphemism for arrogance symbolized by
his many overdrafts. Lazio painted Downey as out of touch with
constituents, a tool of lobbyists, and unable to represent the middle-
class interests of Suffolk County because of his arrogance. Downey
was a popular and effective member of the House of Representatives, but the cost-effectiveness of direct mail enabled Lazio to win
a 53–47 percent victory even though he was outspent nearly five-
to-one.[38]

Direct mail is a staple in modern campaigns for congress and the
senate. The 114 national direct mail consulting firms advertised in
the 2002–2003 listing of consultants in *Campaigns and Elections* magazine demonstrates the demand for this service. Most direct mail consultants do not double as media consultants, with few exceptions,
such as Republican Jamestown Associates and Democratic Muenster
and Robinson. Direct mail firms specialize in designing, writing,
editing, and producing advertisements to catch the eye of the con-
sumer at home.[39]

The most sophisticated and effective direct mail, called the "self-
mailer," no longer comes in an envelope or a package. The outside
cover (called a "teaser") visually piques the reader's curiosity to
open the mailer. Eliminating the obstacle of opening an envelope
means that virtually every addressee sees a portion of the candidate's message and saves the time and expense of envelope stuffing.
The typical four-sided brochure comes unstapled with a cover and

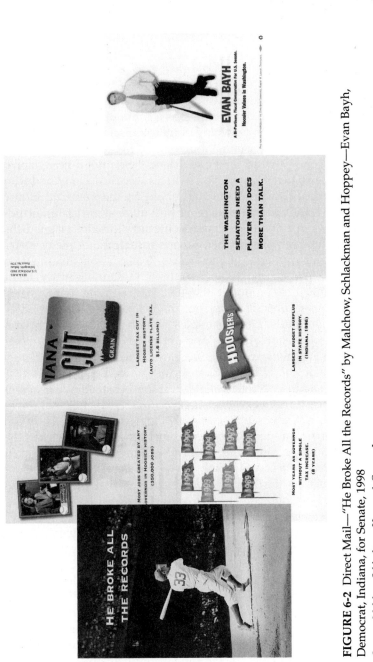

FIGURE 6-2 Direct Mail—"He Broke All the Records" by Malchow, Schlackman and Hoppey—Evan Bayh, Democrat, Indiana, for Senate, 1998

Courtesy: Malchow Schlackman Hoppey & Cooper, Inc.

backside with an affixed or a computer-printed address of the recipient. Self-mailers work when they communicate a powerful message with great simplicity.

Evan Bayh's (D-IN) self-mailer entitled "He Broke All the Records" won a *Pollie* award (the political consultant's equivalent of an Oscar) for the best direct mail piece of 1998. "He Broke All the Records," produced by Malchow, Shlackman and Hoppey, is a combination bio/enhancement advertisement for Bayh, a Senate candidate from Indiana (see Figure 6-2). The "teaser" cover page with number 33 swinging the bat intrigues the reader to open the brochure. The ad lacks a "hard sell" instead focusing on the accomplishments of Bayh's eight years as Indiana governor. Flags advertise the record of eight consecutive years as governor without a tax increase. An auto license plate represents a $1.6 billion tax cut, the largest in Indiana history. The ad implies that, if voters elect Bayh to the U.S. Senate, he will continue to set records for his team, the state of Indiana. Bayh's portrayal as an All-American candidate with fiscally conservative values had veracity because he was a fiscally conservative governor (1989–1997). Bayh's television advertising articulated the same values of fiscal conservatism and competence, which were a winning combination.

Issue ads are a critical component of the direct mail strategy, and are designed to fit a demographic profile of a jurisdiction or state. Pittsburgh, PA "is highly Democrat, although conservative on the issues of guns and abortion." The strong economy of 2000 meant that the election would focus more intently on social issues. Melissa Hart was a Republican state senator from Pittsburgh with a reputation for her legislative work fighting pornography. Hart's campaign functioned on two tracks: the economic track was pro-labor and the social track (abortion, guns, and pornography) was conservative. The effective direct mailer in Figure 6-3 is an issue/comparative ad entitled "Reason" produced by Arena Communications. Most comparative advertisements on television start with a negative premise. Hart's ad begins with a positive premise: a happy infant swaddled in a blanket is "Reason #1" to vote for the Republican in this pro-life advertisement. Even the arrow's color for "Reason #1" is baby blue. Inside the mailer Hart appears on the right side featured in soft colors. Her opponent, Democrat Terry Van Horne, is featured in a black-and-white photo on the left side. Note the similarities to the use of black-and-white versus color in comparative television

FIGURE 6-3 Direct Mail—"Reason," Arena Communications. Melissa Hart, Republican, U.S. Congress, Pittsburgh, Pennsylvania, 2000

Courtesy: Arena Communications

advertising. Furthermore, Van Horne's profile occupies only one-third of the page. In a subtle way, the old Western motif of the "good guys" prevailing over the "bad guys" applies here because Hart argues that she shares the values of Pittsburghers, not Van Horne.

Campaigns use different models for the teaser: humor (one teaser featured the game "Operation" to parody the opponent on health care); news (a news magazine cover for a sophisticated audience); striking visuals (such as crime or drugs); or a warm and fuzzy cover (such as a father and son fishing). Direct mail has become an increasingly important tool to reinforce messages appearing on television. Al Gore's discussion of putting Social Security in a "lockbox" to protect retirees' funds appeared in direct mail advertising during his 2000 presidential campaign. The direct mail ad reinforced the same message appearing in other media.[40]

The coordination of television with direct mail advertising can drive a message home to a targeted demographic group. The campaign first runs an attack ad claiming that a position the opponent holds is "risky" (such as privatizing Social Security for Republicans or being soft on defense for Democrats). The campaign follows the television advertisement with a direct mail piece emphasizing a "safe" plan to protect the program protecting the interests of constituents. The sophistication that characterizes campaigns in the 21st century means that a mix of media to engage and attract voter support is common.

OUTSIDES FORCES: ADVERTISING BY PARTIES AND INTEREST GROUPS

Parties and interest groups played an increasing role in competitive House and Senate campaigns late in the 1990s and early in the 2000s. The soft money loophole created by the Federal Election Commission (FEC) to strengthen party activities enabled political parties and interest groups to collect contributions not subject to limits if the purpose was "voter education" or issue advocacy (as discussed in Chapter 4). The only caveat was that issue advocacy could never use the magic electoral words such as "vote for," "vote against," "elect" or "defeat." The Supreme Court had ruled in two decisions, *Buckley v. Valeo* 425 U.S. 1 (1976) and *Colorado Republican Federal Campaign Committee v. FEC* 116 S.Ct. (1996), that issue advocacy was not subject to speech limitations as guaranteed by the First Amendment to the Constitution. The Bipartisan Campaign Reform Act (BCRA) of 2002 attempted to narrow the scope of issue advocacy by claiming that soft money contributions to parties were a form of electoral promotion. The constitutionality of BCRA was upheld by the U.S. Supreme Court in December 2003.

Soft Money and Parties

The soft money explosion that funded issue advocacy ads by political parties began shortly after the *Colorado* decision in 1996. Data from

the Center for Responsive Politics, the watchdog of campaign finance, show that soft money contributions to the Democratic and Republican national parties increased six-fold from $86 million in 1992
to $500 million in 2000 and 2002. The primary purpose of the money
was to create issue ads, attacking opposition candidates. BCRA out-
laws parties from collecting soft money. Thus, in the 2004 election
cycle, neither the Democratic nor Republican parties could collect or
spend soft money on federal races (see Chapter 4).[41]

Issue Advocacy Ads

Independent expenditures by interest groups not coordinating their
activities with candidates allowed them to raise unlimited contributions in the past, until the Supreme Court upheld BCRA. The new
provisions limit an interest group's ability to run issue advocacy ads
within 60 days of an election and 30 days of a primary that name
federal candidates. All ads that name federal candidates are now
subject to federal contribution limits.

One ad run by the AFL-CIO in California's 27th Congressional
District race in 2000 demonstrates how issue advocacy commercials
appeared in congressional elections. The ad features a pharmacist,
named Michael Weisman, stating that Medicare is inadequate to
cover the costs of prescription drugs to seniors. "I know [senior citi-
zens] skipping their medication to pay for food." The ad blames incumbent Republican James Rogan for opposing prescription drug
reform. The ad concludes by asking viewers to call Rogan at 202-225-
1476, tell him to stop supporting the drug companies, and instead to
support working-class families and seniors. The AFL-CIO spent
$65,000 on ads in the district. A Republican group, Citizens for Better
Medicare spent $165,000 on advertising in the district. Estimates find
that independent groups spent $2 million, and the Democratic and
Republican parties spent a total of $4.5 million on this congressional
district race alone; with the bulk of expenditures on advertising. In
comparison, the two candidates (Rogan and Democrat Adam Schiff)
spent a total of $4.5 million. The extraordinary spending by interest
groups and parties enabled them to set the agenda for discussion on
the Medicare issue, not the candidates. Medicare was one of the two
major issues (the other being Rogan's role as a Republican impeachment manager in the Senate trial) in the race. Schiff ultimately
prevailed over Rogan but this race was not atypical for highly

competitive house races in 2000 and 2002. In 2004, fewer "issue" ads, such as those run by the AFL-CIO described before, will appear given the new campaign law restrictions.[42]

CAMPAIGN ADVERTISING AND THE POLITICAL PROCESS

Campaign communications impart different kinds of information to persuade voters through campaign advertising. Samuel Popkin argues in his book, *The Reasoning Voter*, that more information better equips a voter to choose a candidate. Popkin argues that quantity of information matters, because voters have the ability to sort out the quality of the information they seek. In essence, voters are rational actors able to discern the utility of the information they receive. Popkin contends that his information-seeking model of voting demonstrates that an informed citizen makes better decisions, which benefit democracy. Candidates and parties, in particular, should further communicate to voters to engage them civically in the political process. Advertising is one of those information modes, although Popkin prefers a return to more traditional campaigning. Popkin is less interested in the affective orientation (positive or negative) of campaign information and more concerned with its availability.[43]

Alternatively, psychological studies of campaign commercials suggest that negative ads may drive down voter turnout. Researchers Ansolabehere, Behr, and Iyengar contend that this effect may be substantial. In their study, participants were shown an ad produced on behalf of gubernatorial hopeful Pete Wilson (R) of California from 1990. Ansolabehere, Behr, and Iyengar found that individuals shown the ads "were less likely to vote than those who viewed self-promotion ads." (Self-promotion means bio or enhancement ads). Turnout would only be one percent lower for those viewing the negative ad, but viewers were shown the negative ad only once. The researchers imply that a voter's tenuous attachment to a candidate weakens when repeatedly exposed to negative ads about them. Researchers can point to highly negative races such as the 1998 New York Senate race between Alphonse D'Amato and Chuck Schumer where voter turnout decreased compared with the previous midterm senate election in 1994. Anecdotal evidence may also suggest that negative advertising can drive up voter turnout. Maryland's close and divisive governor's race between Ellen Sauerbrey and Parris Glendening in 1998 was a rematch from 1994 when Glendening, the Democrat, won by 5,000 votes. Glendening ran an almost entirely negative ad campaign against Sauerbrey in 1998; nevertheless voter turnout increased by 125,000, in comparison with 1994. Contrary to conventional wisdom, the evidence is far from conclusive and requires additional study before coming to a definitive conclusion.[44]

CONCLUSION

Paid advertising plays a crucial role in campaigns because it represents the primary way that candidates can transmit unfiltered messages to large blocs of voters. Television ads have matured from the simplicity of the "I Like Ike" ads of the 1950s (concerning Dwight D. Eisenhower) to the complexity of modern comparative ads that juxtapose messages (negative to positive) and color schemes (black-and-white to color) to influence the opinions of undecided voters. The market for advertising is becoming increasingly diffuse because of cable and satellite television resulting in smaller audiences for network affiliates. The repetition of messages on the airwaves tries to create an impression that resonates with targeted constituencies to support the campaign's candidate. Campaigns also diversify their "media mix" to include cable television, radio, newspaper, and direct mail. These other media serve as a supplemental or a primary source of advertisement, depending on the size of the campaign's budget. Campaign managers and consultants know that a visible presence on the air is the most cost-effective way to reach large numbers of voters. Today, campaigns must adapt to the information age quickly, factually, and directly, given the sophistication of a media-savvy public. Furthermore, campaigns have to contend with the political parties and interest groups that have a stake in the outcome of a particular race. Disseminating that information requires greater skill and planning than ever before. The new century also finds national campaigns looking toward the Internet, which integrates advertising, organization, and fundraising into one interactive medium. The implications demonstrate that communication between advertiser and viewer, reflect the range of emotions or ideas necessary to build political persuasion.

STUDY/DISCUSSION QUESTIONS

In what ways have political advertising techniques changed from the 1950s to the present?

What makes a good campaign advertisement, whether it is a biographical, an enhancement/issue, or a negative/comparative ad?

How does sound, music, and color enhance moods or images in political advertising?

How does a campaign integrate its message into advertising?

Why has opposition research been important to political campaigns from the 1800s to the present?

Why is radio and newspaper advertising essential to low-budget campaigns?

What makes direct mail such a powerful advertising medium?

Does campaign advertising have a positive or a negative effect on political participation?

SUGGESTED READINGS

Ansolabehere, Stephen, Roy Behr, and Shanto Iyengar. *The Media Game: American Politics in the Television Media Age*. New York: Macmillan, 1993.

Ansolabehere, Stephen, and Shanto Iyengar. *Going Negative: How Political Advertisements Shrink and Polarize the Electorate*. New York: Free Press, 1997.

Diamond, Edwin, and Stephen Bates. *The Spot*. Cambridge, MA: MIT Press, 1992.

Jamieson, Kathleen Hall. *Dirty Politics: Deception, Distraction and Democracy*. New York: Oxford University Press, 1993.

Kaid, Lynda Lee, and Anne Johnston. *Videostyle in Presidential Campaigns: Style and Content of Televised Political Advertising*. Westport, CT: Praeger, 2000.

Schwartz, Tony. *Media: The Second God*. Garden City, NY: Anchor Books, 1981.

Thurber, James A., Candice Nelson, and David Dulio. *Crowded Airwaves: Campaign Advertising in Elections*. Washington, DC: Brookings, 2000.

The American Museum of the Moving Image (AMMI). The museum features an online collection of presidential campaign ads from 1952 to 2000. Go to *www.ammi.org* and click on "Online Exhibitions." Then click on "The Living Room Candidate" and choose an election year to view campaign commercials.

NOTES

1. Marshall McLuhan, "Quotes." Accessed July 8, 2002 at *www.brainyquote.com/quotes/quotes/m/q103287.html*.
2. Josh Goldstein and Tom Infield, "There is no escape from Casey, Rendell," *Philadelphia Inquirer*, May 17, 2002. Accessed July 8, 2002 at *www.philly.com/mld/philly/news/politics/3281361.htm*, quote; "Casey Ad Blames Rendell for School Problems," *Pittsburgh Channel*, March 22, 2002. Accessed July 8, 2002 at *www.thepittsburghchannel.com/politics/1318732/detail.html*.
3. For figures on the sale of television set, go to the tvhistory website, *www.tvhistory.tv/Annual_TV_Sales_39-59.JPG*.
4. Tony Schwartz, *Media: The Second God* (Garden City, NY: Anchor Books, 1981), 11.
5. Tom Rosenstiel, *Strange Bedfellows: How Television And The Presidential Candidates Changed American Politics, 1992* (New York: Hyperion Books, 1993), first two quotes, 279; third quote, 278–79.
6. *TV Dimensions 2002—Exerpts*. Media Dynamics, Inc. New York. Accessed July 9, 2002 at *www.mediadynamics.com/tvexerpt.htm*. *A Nation Online: How Americans Are Expanding Their Use of the Internet*. National Telecommunications and Information Administration (NTIA), Department of Commerce, Washington, DC. February 2002. See the "Executive Summary" for data on the total number of users. Find the demographic breakdown by age on page 26 of the report. Jeffrey Cole, Director. *Surveying the Digital Future: Year Two*. UCLA Internet Report., (Los Angeles: UCLA Center for Communication Policy, 2001), 6.
7. "Concealed Gun," produced by Laguens, Hamburger and Stone, of Washington, DC, for Dennis Moore for Congress 1998.
8. Ibid.
9. See John F. Persinos, "GOTCHA!" *Campaigns and Elections*, August 1994, 21 for the Jefferson quote. See Dennis W. Johnson, *No Place for Amateurs* (New York: Routledge, 2001), 71–73, on techniques of opposition research, such as search public records.

10. Johnson, 79 (on Jack Palladino); "Journey," "Morning," and "Milwaukee" produced for Bill Clinton, 1992. Accessed from the American Museum of the Moving Image, July 11, 2002 at *www.ammi.org/cgi-bin/years.cgi?1992,,56,,,*. Go to the Online Exhibitions section of the website and click on "The Living Room Candidate" for commercials from U.S. presidential elections 1952–2000.
11. Karl Struble, "How to Beat an Incumbent: The Inside Story of the Hard-Fought Johnson v. Pressler U.S. Senate Race in South Dakota," *Campaigns and Elections*, June 1997, 24, quote; "SD: Democrats Slay Incumbent Pressler," November 5, 1996. Accessed July 11, 2002 at *www.cgi.cnn.com/ALLPOLITICS/1996/11/05/senate/sd* regarding Pressler's travel junkets.
12. Adam Goodman, "Producing TV: A Survival Guide," *Campaigns and Elections*, July 1995, 22, quote.
13. Edwin Diamond and Stephen Bates, *The Spot* (Cambridge, MA: MIT Press, 1992), 126–27, on the "Daisy" ad. This remains the finest book written on campaign advertising.
14. Tony Schwartz, 59, quote on building support among shareholders. See Theodore H. White, *The Making of the President 1964* (New York: Signet, 1965), 261, for the quotation from Goldwater's speech.
15. Diamond and Bates.
16. Carter M. Yang, "Down and Dirty," ABCNews.com. Accessed July 10, 2002 at *www.abcnews.go.com/sections/politics/Daily/News/Bush_Gore_ads001027.html*, on anti-Gore "Daisy."
17. "Bear" produced by Hal Riney, Reagan for President 1984, from the American Museum of the Moving Image. Accessed July 9, 2002 at *www.ammi.org/cgi-bin/years.cgi?1984,11,56,R,,#*.
18. "Pledge," produced by Shrum, Devine and Donilon of Washington, DC, for Senator Tom Harkin, debuted statewide July 4–7, 2002, Iowa.
19. "The Story," produced for Bob Dole 1996. American Museum of the Moving Image. Accessed July 9, 2002 at *www.ammi.org/cgi-bin/years.cgi?1996,,56,,R,,*.
20. Diamond and Bates, 169.
21. See Diamond and Bates on construct of evaluation for advertising campaigns, 297–341. They use four phases: identification, argument, attack, and "I see an America"; ad for Mitt Romney for governor of Massachusetts, 2002. "Independence," produced by

Murphy, Gautier, Pintak and Hudome of Alexandria, VA. The ad went on the air late June 2002 in the Boston metropolitan area. Accessed July 11, 2002 at *www.romney2002.com.*

22. Charles Babington, "Glendening Leads Democrats to Victory," *Washington Post,* November 4, 1998, A1, on the effectiveness of the Glendening campaign portraying Sauerbrey as negative.

23. American Museum of the Moving Image. "The Man," produced for Richard Nixon, 1972. Accessed at *www.ammi.org/cgi-bin/video/years.cgi?1972,,56,,,.*

24. "Russ Feingold for U.S. Senate," 1992. (Video) "The 25 Funniest Political Campaign Commercials," *Campaigns and Elections.*

25. "Fairness," (Video) produced by McAuliffe Message, for John Thune for Senate. The ad debuted in July 2002. See *www.johnthune.com* for further details.

26. Stephen Ansolabehere and Shanto Iyengar, *Going Negative: How Attack Ads Shrink and Polarize the Electorate* (New York: Free Press, 1993), 2–3, quote.

27. Diamond and Bates, 227, on the Brown ad, and 229, on the "Revolving Door" ad.

28. Laguens, Hamburger and Stone. (Video). "Jabberwocky" from *Laguens, Hamburger and Stone Demo Reel 1999–2000,* Washington, DC.

29. Szi Zhang, Frank F. Kardes, and Maria L. Cronley. "Comparative Advertising: Effects of Structural Alignability on Target Brand Evaluation." (Paper). Anderson Graduate School of Management, UCLA, 3. Accessed July 12, 2002 at *www.anderson.cula.edu/faculty/szi.zhang/pdf_files/comparative_advertising.pdf.*

30. David Beiler, "Jon Corzine and the Power of Money," *Campaigns and Elections,* April 2001, 31. Corzine ad quote from "The Choice," produced by Shrum, Devine, and Donilon of Washington, DC, for Jon Corzine for Senate 2000. Reprinted by permission of Shrum, Devine, and Donilon.

31. Tobe Berkowitz, "Political Media Buying Guide," Boston University. Accessed July 12, 2002 at *www.ksg.harvard.edu/case/3pt/berkowitz.html.*

32. Ibid.

33. Ibid; Ray Reggie, "Buying TV Spots on Cable," *Campaigns and Elections,* October/November 1997, 37–39.

34. "Get your radio spot faster there with Digital Generation Systems," Baker Sound Studios, Philadelphia, PA. Accessed July 13, 2002 at *www.bakersound.com/dgs/htm.*

35. Michael Barone and Richard Cohen, *The Almanac of American Politics 2002* (Washington, DC: National Journal, 2001), 1080–81.
36. Peter Wendel, "Stretching Ad Dollars," *Campaigns and Elections,* June 1998, 38, quote.
37. Keith Moore, "Rick Lazio: Is he or isn't he? And who the heck is he?" Salon.com. Accessed July 14, 2002 at *www.salon.com/ people/feature/1999/08/13/lazio/print.html.*
38. Phil Duncan, ed., *Politics in America 1994* (Washington, DC: Congressional Quarterly Press, 1993), 1028.
39. *Campaigns and Elections Political Pages 2002–2003.*
40. "Nobody Hits Harder Except . . . the Baughman Company" (advertisement), *Campaigns and Elections Political Pages 2001– 2002,* 35. All advertisements discussed in the paragraph were produced by Baughman.
41. Center for Responsive Politics. Accessed March 13, 2003 at *www.open-secrets.org,* regarding soft money and parties.
42. "Rogan," AFL-CIO commercial debuted July 26–27, 2000, Los Angeles, CA; "AFL-CIO begins TV ads," *Associated Press,* July 21, 2000, ad quote; Drew Linzer and David Menefee-Libbey, "The 2000 California Twenty-Seventh Congressional District Race," in *Election Advocacy: Soft Money and Issue Advocacy in the 2000 Congressional Elections,* ed. David B. Magleby (Provo, UT: Center for the Study of Elections and Democracy, 2001), 145, on spending from the Rogan-Schiff race.
43. Samuel Popkin, *The Reasoning Voter* (Chicago: University of Chicago Press, 1991); Anthony Downs, *An Economic Theory of Democracy* (New York: Harper & Row, 1957).
44. Stephen Ansolabehere, Roy Behr, and Shanto Iyengar, *The Media Game: American Politics in the Television Media Age* (New York: Macmillan, 1993), 180, quote on Pete Wilson ads.

CHAPTER 7

Campaigning on the Internet

The future ain't what it used to be.[1]
—Hall of Fame catcher, Yogi Berra

Imagine reading an e-mail written in the handwriting style of a candidate giving it a personal touch. Imagine raising millions of dollars online without having to spend 40 cents out of each dollar to solicit each donor. Imagine using your remote to choose what campaign commercials you wish to see. You need not imagine this because each of these new technologies is in use today. Campaigns are on the verge of an information revolution that is taking politics into a new domain and literally puts more control into the hands of citizens. Campaigns will adapt and change far more rapidly than in the past as information exchanges occur almost instantaneously. If campaigns do not adapt, they will fail to survive. Welcome to the campaign world of the 21st century.[2]

The Internet is changing the face of modern campaigns. According to Lee Rainie, Director of the Pew Internet and American Life Project, 46 million Americans now use the Internet to get political information and news. Those Internet users represent approximately one-fourth of the voting age population in the United States. This chapter explains how the Internet helps candidates: who the Internet audience is, what the dynamics of the Internet market are, how to attract interest to a website, and how to build and manage an effective online campaign. Campaigns use the Internet to attract volunteers, raise money, and advertise. According to Republican Internet consultant Becky Donatelli: "Today, they [campaigns] are using the Internet as an integral component of all aspects of the campaign—from distributing press releases to coordinating volunteers' efforts, fundraising and online GOTV efforts." Internet consultants help shape the strategy of campaigns even if the Internet does not yet overshadow or dominate the traditional campaign functions of fundraising, polling, and media; however, as the power of the Internet grows so does its impact on campaigns. The future of convergence technology as television and the Internet are integrated into one medium completes the discussion of the chapter.[3]

THE INTERNET AUDIENCE

Unlike television, the Internet audience is not passive but active. Internet users are information seekers. A 2002 survey by the Pew Internet and American Life Project found that 42 million Americans used the Internet to research policy issues and nearly 20 million stated that the Internet helped them get information about elections. Campaign activities included seeking information about candidate voting records (45 percent), voting online (32 percent), participating in online discussions (10 percent), and contributing to political candidates (6 percent). Multi-functional designs of websites, address and anticipate audience interests.[4]

The bottom line for managing a successful candidate website is to keep the viewer interested. Campaigns face the initial task of competing in an enormous digital universe. There are over 120 million active websites for American users according to Nielson/NetRatings Inc. in a study released on February 2003 usage. Campaigns measure success, in part, by tracking the length of time a visitor remains on a website at a given point in time. Longer visits increase the probability that a visitor will agree to volunteer or contribute money to a campaign. RealNetwork, an entertainment website, reported that 31.6 million viewers spent an average 26 minutes and 47 seconds per visit in November 2002. (RealNetwork provides entertainment for viewers through streaming media and music.) One cannot expect that most candidates can compete with that kind of time. However, Max Fose, an Internet fundraising guru for John McCain's 2000 presidential bid, reported that the average amount of time spent at the portal was 20 minutes per visit, which was remarkable for a political website. Long visits contributed to the millions that McCain raised online (see the box, "Planning Ahead: The McCain Campaign Website" on page 169).[5]

ATTRACTING INTEREST TO A CAMPAIGN WEBSITE

Attracting an audience, means that a website must be visually appealing, easy to navigate and informative because the Internet user
can surf away at the click of a mouse. Candidates must compete with
websites offering products, promotions, news, weather, sports, and
entertainment. Websites should be refined, vetted, and completed
for online usage when first available to visitors. Emilienne Ireland
and Phil Nash, Internet architects for Richard Gephardt's 2004 presidential campaign, point out that "if voters . . . find empty pages that
say 'under construction' or 'come back soon' your unspoken message is, 'this candidate is not ready.'" According to Ireland and Nash
an alternative to launching a full-fledged website is to debut with an
announcement site. Senator John Warner (R-VA) utilized a simple
but clear announcement site advertising his reelection bid in 2002.
Warner's announcement site featured a home page with five links
for the petition drive, the campaign schedule, campaign contributions, and an e-mail sign-up for updates.[6]

Humor can attract a wide audience to your website and encourage people to return. Steve Kelley, a Democratic state senate incumbent from the Minneapolis suburbs running for reelection in 2000,
used self-deprecation to promote himself on his Internet site. Kelley's
bio on the site featured the "Short Version" or the "Long Boring Version." The following excerpt is from the "Long Boring Version"
demonstrates the value of humor.

> Just before he started law school at Columbia University, Steve
> married Sophie Bell, a member of the unofficial New Jersey
> aristocracy. Steve graduated from law school and persuaded
> Sophie to move to Minnesota which he repeatedly referred to as
> "God's country." Sophie acquiesced after Steve agreed to quit
> talking like that. Upon arriving in Hopkins, Steve got some sort of
> lawyer job. On the home front, Steve and Sophie proceeded to "be
> fruitful and multiply" and soon added Son Paul and Daughter
> Eleanor to the Kelley clan.[7]

Kelley's website exemplifies how humor amplifies the interest of a
visitor, encourages them to return (to read more), and provides a
great link to send to friends via e-mail. Keeping an audience enter-
tained is essential because the competition from other political and
non-political websites means that a visitor can leave with one click of
the mouse. Candidates with limited resources benefit most from

PLANNING AHEAD: THE MCCAIN CAMPAIGN WEBSITE

Superior planning enabled the 2000 McCain presidential primary campaign to use the Internet for tremendous organizational and fundraising advantage. Max Fose and Wes Gullett,
the campaign's Internet architects, convinced senior campaign
aides that an online presence paid large dividends. Fose and
Gullett "devoted six weeks to planning, one month to programming, and then four to six hours a day to maintaining the online
operation." The McCain campaign received a burst of Internet
activity following the Arizona senator's 19-point victory over
George W. Bush in the 2000 New Hampshire primary (the first
presidential primary every four years). Through the McCain
2000 website, the campaign raised a remarkable $21,000 per
hour for the first four days following the primary. Furthermore,
the campaign's e-mail list grew from 60,000 to 142,000 in a very
short time period. The e-mail list provided a ready source of
campaign volunteers to work for the Arizona senator in upcoming primaries. If navigating the system had been difficult or if the
Internet architects had not designed methods to handle the traffic, the website could have easily crashed for 24 to 48 hours leaving a void when momentum was building. The payoff kept the
McCain campaign a viable force for the next seven weeks of the
primary campaign. McCain's campaign might have grounded
to a halt soon after the New Hampshire primary, if it were not for
the Internet.[8]

creativity to attract visitors to their websites, since their capacity to
advertise on television is limited.

Incumbents have an established base of support, but for challengers the launch of a website may be more critical. Steve Schneider,
a professor at the SUNY Institute of Technology, reported that 74 percent of senatorial, gubernatorial, and congressional incumbents had
websites in 2002 compared with 60 percent for challengers. Websites
are relatively cheap to build and provide a new candidate with credibility to advertise themselves to constituents. Today, 65 percent of
voters expect information online, and that number is growing. The
expectation is no less for a challenger than for an incumbent.[9]

BUILDING A SUCCESSFUL WEBSITE

Emilienne Ireland and Phil Nash state in their book *Winning Campaigns Online* that successful websites are built through good structure ("ease of use", the choice of a "good domain name", "regular maintenance," "top quality graphics," and "speedy download times"). Effective websites provide personal information about the candidate (biography, personal statements, speeches, issue discussions, and endorsements) and the campaign (methods for volunteering, e-mail sign-ups, donations, and upcoming campaign events). Design, simplicity, and personalization are three key aspects of building a successful candidate site.[10]

Good Design

Design is critical to attracting visitors to a website and induce them to return. Simple graphics, well-organized web pages, distinctive links, and easy navigation are the attributes of effective website design. Good designs feature a lead story on the home page, which provides current and important information about a candidate. The lead may discuss a new poll showing the candidate doing well, a successful campaign event, an important endorsement, or an upcoming speech of import. For example, Governor George Pataki's (R-NY) website featured an endorsement for his 2002 reelection prominently on its home page from popular New York Yankees baseball manager Joe Torre. Torre's endorsement was released during the baseball playoffs (October 6) and appeared simultaneously on the website and on a campaign commercial.[11]

The home page, in particular, should be immaculate. Ireland and Nash discuss one federal candidate who was loath to have his picture taken. He did not care about the picture quality or his appearance. The web layout designer showed the picture to her 11-year old son before it appeared on the home page. Her son said, "Mommy, he looks like a criminal."[12]

Keep It Simple Stupid (KISS)

The adage "Keep it simple stupid (KISS)" is important for website developers to keep in mind to help Internet neophytes navigate through a website. Home pages, in particular, should be inviting, simple and clear so that a visitor is not confused and frustrated when coming to the portal.

Lamar Alexander's website "Come On Along" was nominated for a Golden Dot Award (a political website Oscar) for the best senatorial-candidate website in 2002. Alexander was the Republican senatorial candidate from Tennessee. He had served as a former governor and U.S. secretary of education. The home page featured two adjoining sidebars, "Campaign Headlines" (focusing on upcoming events) and "The Big Idea" (addressing important issues). The home page was relatively short and simple to navigate. At the bottom of the home page was a section called "Alexander Interactive" which featured pictures and links including: "Biography," "Calendar," "Susie's Campaign [Manager's] Notebook," "Come on Along" (to invite friends to join), and "Multimedia" (featuring campaign commercials). Appearing on a short lefthand sidebar was "E-leader" which enabled visitors to sign up for an e-mail newsletter. The top bar of the home page provided smaller links, which included "How You Can Help," a subtle way of asking for a campaign donation. The home page's design was user friendly and not overwhelming for visitors. The graphics were not difficult to load, and navigating through the system was simple. Contacting the campaign or interacting with other "volunteers" was encouraged and facilitated by the design of the website. The folksiness of "Come on Along" complemented the impressive political resume of Alexander. "Come on Along" provided a warm grassroots invitation to get involved with the Alexander campaign. The professionalism of the web design was representative of the entire Alexander campaign organization. He won election to the Senate by a comfortable 10-point margin.[13]

Personalize the Website

The rationale of running for office should appear in a candidate's personal statement. Earlier in the book, we discussed motivations and decisions to run for office. Websites typically feature a personal statement about the candidate. The personal statement may appear on the home page or through a distinctive link from the home page. Phil Bredesen, the Democratic nominee for governor in Tennessee for 2002, provided a brief but effective rationale for his candidacy. Bredesen emphasized his experience as Nashville mayor to provide

FIGURE 7-1 "Letter to Constituents: Phil Bredesen for Governor of Tennessee, 2002." Used with permission.

"leadership" and "common sense" solutions, which indicated a pragmatic approach to address policy issues. A picture of Bredesen, which accompanied his personal statement, showed him interacting with children. The photograph and statement implied that his "common sense" solutions would provide a better future for the children of Tennessee (see figure 7-1). Bredesen won the election by a narrow 51–48 percent margin over Republican Congressman Van Hilleary. Bredesen's personal statement characterized the message of his campaign, that he was a leader with compassion who understood the problems of average Tennesseeans.

Campaign journals help personalize websites and demonstrate that a candidate is in touch with constituents. Emily Pataki, the daughter of Governor George Pataki (R-NY) running for a third term in 2002, wrote a weekly campaign journal, which was published on her father's website. The journal related personal ruminations about campaigning and how her father felt about campaigning in 2002 (he did not feel comfortable given the events and aftermath of 9/11). Emily's journal was a very popular feature generating tremendous interest from visitors looking for her weekly installment. The following is part of one entry (August 12, 2002) from Emily's journal:[14]

> My father loves New York, and he is having so much fun on the campaign trail. Everywhere he goes, the response from people is overwhelmingly positive. They can't wait to meet 'the Gov,'—to shake his hand and talk to him about his proud and proven record of cutting taxes, creating jobs, investing in education, protecting our environment and health care.[15]

Accompanying the journal were daily pictures from campaign events giving it greater immediacy and impact. Emily Pataki's journal helped solidify support among moderate women in the state, an important swing vote in the suburbs of New York City and in upstate rural jurisdictions.

MANAGING A SUCCESSFUL ONLINE CAMPAIGN

Managing a successful online campaign does not guarantee victory. A successful online campaign complements the public relations and fundraising aspects of a campaign. Jesse Ventura was the first candidate to use the Internet to advertise and recruit volunteers for a grassroots campaign. John McCain used the Internet to raise $6.4 million online for his 2000 presidential bid. Success means first engaging and activating supporters. Internet users have a different demographic profile from the general voting population, according to Eric Loeb, Chief Internet Architect of the Democratic National Committee. Data from the Pew Internet & American Life Project shows that Net users tend to be younger, white, and middle-to-upper income. Managing a successful Internet website requires understanding the demographic profile of users, rather than targeting who the website manager wants users to be. Good sites are content driven, informative, positive (promoting the candidate) and negative (attacking the opponent). Content takes the form of position papers, issue briefs, candidate statements, and press releases.

Promotion means creating an exciting virtual online environment through daily updates. Attacking the opposition enables a candidate to go negative online while conducting a positive television advertising campaign. The final and most important component of an online campaign is e-mail, which serves as the primary vehicle for contacting and activating supporters.[16]

Content and Promotion

"On the Web, content is king." Websites must not only look good but they must be good substantively. Promoting a candidate means that the content of a website or an e-mail alert is very important. Internet consultants often use resources such as HitBox to "help determine what's working and what's not." Tools such as HitBox serve as a diagnostic to determine the effective means of reaching target audiences when developing and test marketing a new candidate website. Companies such as HitBox can evaluate whether the home page, links, content, and message match the target audience. Statewide and national campaigns have the resources to use consultants such as HitBox for content analysis while smaller congressional campaigns must rely on internal analysis. Campaigns also receive supplemental help from the national party committees to provide general consulting services and advice.[17]

Constant promotion and communication is essential for the Internet part of the campaign to function effectively. E-advocates President Pam Fielding and author David Bennett argue that continuous and daily promotion interacting supporters with the campaign organization is a necessity. Promotion includes news, other links, and fostering interactive communication among supporters. Fielding and Bennett state that campaigns should "post alert messages to relevant Websites, news groups, chat rooms, forums. . . . Recruit your friends and online supporters to volunteer for other campaign efforts. Write a simple press release about your cyberspace campaign" and release it to the press. The approach should be multifaceted to take advantage of all the opportunities to target and recruit supporters.[18]

The daily volume of news material such as press releases, policy papers, or speeches, now appears on the websites and (or) released through e-mail. The George W. Bush campaign was putting out mounds of information every day. Professor Michael Cornfield writes, "The George W. Bush site was a news machine: 5–10 releases a day, and 100 pages in one day. . . ." The Bush campaign also released a Spanish language edition every day. The Bush campaign was conveying a message that the governor was a serious and substantive politician. A campaign with a large research staff (such as those for presidential candidates) can produce and respond with information to the press in a few minutes. Only a decade ago, a "rapid response" or an initiative would have taken hours to prepare and sent one-by-one via fax to news outlets.[19]

Attacking the Opposition

Candidates choosing to run a positive paid advertising campaign may opt to use their Internet site to attack the opposition. The purpose of the strategy is to communicate positively with undecided voters (on television), and to energize the candidate's political base (online) by criticizing the opponent. The attack proposition appears on the home page if it is time-sensitive material. If not time-sensitive, then it might appear through a link on the home page. Democratic businessman Mark Warner's successful gubernatorial race in Virginia in 2001 was an example of using the Internet to attack his opponent. Warner's website posted attacks and counterattacks on his opponent, Republican Attorney General Mark Earley, through a link entitled "Newsroom." For example, the Warner website reprinted a story from *The New Republic* magazine of October 18, 2001, which was entitled "Earley Peddles Fear—and Fails." Earley used his platform as Virginia's attorney general to argue that after September 11, 2001, it was more important than ever to have an experienced politician as the chief law-enforcement official in the state. The official message from the Earley campaign was that voters should not "change horses in midstream." The article implied there was little else to Earley's campaign than fear. Using a reputable news source enables a campaign to attack the opposition through a third party, which is effective because the critique appears to be objective.[20]

Using E-mail to Contact and Activate Supporters

E-mail provides a campaign with the opportunity to connect to voters on a continuous basis. The successful recruitment of e-mail addresses requires a lot of imagination. For example, the Republican National Committee sent out an e-mail to its subscribers in 2000: "You Could Win a Free Palm Pilot! Simply enter just two e-mail addresses of GOP friends!" If marketing websites are analogous to newspapers, e-mail is similar to direct mail. The object is to attain as many addresses as possible to interest, recruit, and activate supporters. The cost of sending bulk e-mails is about one to five percent of the cost of mailing a direct mail advertisement. The downside is that campaigns have to compete with spam e-mail to attract attention.[21]

Katherine Harris' (R) successful e-mail letter to supporters in her bid to win Florida's 13th Congressional District in 2002 illustrates how a personal touch can garner generous support. Harris was the Florida secretary of state at the center of the Bush-Gore recount controversy in 2000. As a result, her bid to win a U.S. House seat attracted substantial attention outside of the district and state from Republicans and Democrats. Consultant Becky Donatelli noted that Harris' flowing handwriting looked like calligraphy. The campaign developed a font based on Ms. Harris' handwriting and wrote a personal appeal for donations via e-mail. The donor response was overwhelming to Harris' appeal, making it the second most profitable venture online next to her official campaign announcement.[22]

Internet consultants recognize that campaigns must be proactive when soliciting volunteer or donor support through e-mail. Phil Noble, publisher of *PoliticsOnline*, the web bible on campaigns and the Internet, has stated that insurgency campaigns benefit most from grassroots campaigns. Candidates such as Jesse Ventura, John McCain, and Howard Dean run against the status quo. Jesse Ventura's campaign successfully used voter contact through e-mail to promote his candidacy for Minnesota governor in 1998. Ventura's campaign signed up 5,000 people at the State Fair; and then entered their names online with the help of his volunteers known as the D-team (Database team). The D-team worked to expand the initial data base, which eventually included volunteers throughout the state. The D-team expanded to address the education issue through e-mails to volunteers in each of the state's 300 school districts. The D-team also conducted a "72-hour" online campaign tour across the state, and operated an online campaign paraphernalia store full of Ventura t-shirts. One t-shirt said "Retaliate in '98" echoing Ventura's gubernatorial campaign theme in Minnesota to replace status quo politicians with outsiders.[23]

Campaigns should be cautious and plan their approach to using e-mail. Internet users receiving unsolicited e-mail often consider it spam, says Larry Pupuro, the founder of RightClick Strategies. Anti-spam advocates effectively shut down the gubernatorial primary campaign of Republican Bill Jones in 2002. Jones was California's secretary of state, but faced two well-funded opponents: millionaire businessman William Simon and former Los Angeles mayor Richard Riorden. Anti-spam advocates lobbied Internet Service Providers (ISP) to shut down Jones' e-mail campaign when his campaign sent a million unsolicited e-mails to California's Republican voters in a desperate attempt to win support as the gubernatorial primary neared. Jones' campaign attracted negative publicity in the press and among state Republicans. "In the waning days of the campaign, Jones' contracted ISP refused to send any more e-mails and shut down his Web site. His online campaign ground to a halt." This marked the effective end of Jones' entire campaign because he lacked the financial resources to compete with his opponents.[24]

The cost-effectiveness of e-mail, which can reach hundreds of thousands of recipients at a cost of $5–25,000, enables a campaign to mobilize an army of supporters to support its GOTV operation. The cost for demographic targeted audiences may be a bit higher. For example in 2000, the Sierra Club (the largest environmental organization in the country) "paid Aristotle International, a voter database company, $5,000 for the e-mail addresses of 10,000 independent-registered women ages 25–55 in Pennsylvania and Ohio." On the other hand, "the U.S. Chamber of Commerce, which is backing pro-business candidates, is buying lists of e-mail addresses of high school and college graduates who subscribe to business publications such as Fortune or Inc." Greater precision in selecting a particular audience (such as with the Sierra Club) will drive up the cost. Most political campaigns have to rely on a broader-based approach as used by the U.S. Chamber of Commerce because it is more cost-effective.[25]

Campaigns are using "eNewsletters" and egroups to help build volunteer support through e-mail contact. "eNewsletters, when written and delivered properly, establish campaign momentum while driving repeat traffic to your web site." Traffic and response increase from user groups that "chat" and meet on the website building enthusiasm and activities both on and offline. New Media Communications, one of the leading political website design firms created "Groopz" for Lamar Alexander's 2002 Senate campaign in Tennessee. The site "allowed visitors ... to have live chats with campaign staffers and volunteers identified based on what page of the site the visitor was viewing." The personal touch of "Groopz" gave the campaign a more populist feeling. *PoliticsOnline* believes that the approach of "chat groups" is the wave of the future. Candidates sometimes get into the action by answering e-mails. Congressman Tom Campbell (R-CA) running for the California's senate seat in 2000 answered five e-mails a day from visitors to his website. The public relations benefits from an online grassroots communication are becoming an important feature of a growing number of statewide campaigns. In this way, the Internet and e-mail make campaigning more egalitarian because citizens can interact directly with candidates, even in a limited format.[26]

FUNDRAISING ONLINE

Campaigns are seeking to harness the Internet as a tool to raise money for campaigns. Unlike direct mail solicitations or fundraising events, where each additional dollar of revenue that is sought will cost the campaign money each time (in economics, they call this the marginal cost), the cost through the Internet is far cheaper. Direct mail costs 40 cents for each dollar raised compared to one cent per dollar on the Internet. Furthermore, the fixed costs of establishing a campaign website are relatively cheap. The total cost for the design and launch of a professional site for a statewide campaign is about $15,000 and for House campaigns $7,500. Campaigns spend up to $50,000 for more sophisticated website designs that may include photo galleries, pop-up windows, and voice-text interactive features.[27]

The Internet fundraising team should "be in the loop" and coordinate with offline fundraising consultants. Similar to direct mail, online appeals must communicate a sense of urgency and provide a deadline, according to Max Fose. According to Vince Wishrad, the Internet fundraising guru for the largest pro-choice interest group National Abortion Rights Action League (NARAL), a successful

online appeal is both passionate and urgent. The average contribution received over the Internet is $43.73 compared with $32 by direct
mail for NARAL. Republican Doug Forrester's (R-NJ) 2002 U.S.
Senate campaign in New Jersey raised an average of $54 online. The
online fundraising story of the 2002 elections was that the size of
contributions from the Internet was almost the same as it was from
direct mail. The implications are that the Internet is not full of big
donors and is becoming a broader-based medium for contributors
like traditional fundraising.[28]

Facilitating the donation process is key to online fundraising
because potential donors should feel welcome. Every web page
should feature a link called "contribution" or "donate." Imagination
and personalization of the contribution link can be very helpful.
Senator John Edwards' (D-NC) donation link on his 2004 presidential
campaign home page had a photograph of mountains accompanied
by a banner headline saying, "You can help me: Donate today." Another 2004 presidential hopeful, Senator Joseph Lieberman (D-CT)
used a virtual campaign button that read "Go Joe!" for his contribution link. Thus, the design and placement of the contribution link on
each page are carefully determined. Most contribution links are easily located near the top of the page because it is the best place to lo-
cate a page item for a visitor. Websites have the goal of making the
contribution process as effortless as possible.[29]

Internet users and donors tend to be content-oriented. More content drives traffic back to the site, which in turn increases interest
and the propensity to contribute. Content includes issue papers, biographical information, voting records, legislation supported, volunteer information, upcoming campaign events, and online campaign
events (such as chats with the candidate). Direct mail or paid television advertising providing the Internet address also drives traffic to
the website and increases the propensity for a contribution because
potential donors are relieved of the responsibility of how to contact
the campaign.[30]

Privacy remains the greatest source of concern for any contributor. A campaign's website should use a secure server and *never*
release or sell the information without specific permission from
the visitor. A survey of 9,705 Microsoft Network (MSN) users
found that 31 percent hesitated to provide their e-mail address or
credit card number to a political website. Among those who hesitated, the largest proportion (41.3 percent) were turned off because

the website did not provide a privacy statement and another 18.8 percent were concerned about providing credit card information online. A study by Jonah Singer of the Institute of Policy, Democracy and the Internet (IPDI) found that 56.5 percent of all interviewees pay "a lot" or "some" attention to privacy statements on political websites. Standard language that is in the process of adoption by the Internet industry will help protect users' privacy from spam, credit card fraud, and personal identification with particular political organizations or candidates. Both America Online (AOL) and MSN are taking steps to increase privacy for their clients in response to complaints. Privacy ensures that the contributor or volunteer is protected when personal information is collected.[31]

ADVERTISING ON POPULAR WEBSITES

Banner advertising on popular websites became far more pervasive in the 2002 elections according to Internet consultant Becky Donatelli. Republicans pioneered many of the efforts by running campaign banner ads for AOL users checking in-boxes, and even on sports websites. She reports that 13 million impressions of candidate comparison ads from the National Republican Senatorial Committee (NRSC) appeared on AOL. Stock car racing's parent organization, NASCAR.com featured "ads in the North Carolina senate race comparing Elizabeth Dole (R) and Erskine Bowles (D). The website experienced one of the highest click-through rates" running for the senate seat. The click-through rate is the rate at which viewers actually go through the ad. Thus, the ads do have an effect. News websites feature the highest proportion of candidate banner ads and click-through rates. Even as far back as 1998, "Sen. Barbara Boxer scattered ads on California news sites. Peter Vallone, who ran for governor in New York, found that banners on *The New York Times* site actually increased opponent George Pataki's negative polls," says campaign Internet analyst Jonah Singer. Careful attention to the demographics of an advertiser can determine whether placing a banner ad is worth the effort. "It would make little sense for a candidate running for the 7th district of Virginia to advertise to Web surfers in Nevada" says Singer. The right message for the wrong audience does not payoff.[32]

2004 DEMOCRATIC PRESIDENTIAL CANDIDATE WEBSITES

The Internet is the new grassroots organization for political candidates. Presidential candidates need grassroots support to build an effective campaign because primary voters in each party tend to be activists. As demonstrated earlier, the Internet has become a medium to activate a volunteer organization. By early 2003, nine Democratic candidates had announced they would seek their party's nomination in 2004 to challenge the incumbent, Republican George W. Bush. Public opinion polls in September 2003 showed that the six leading candidates were Senator John Edwards (D-NC), Senator John Kerry (D-MA), Senator Joseph Lieberman (D-CT), Congressman Richard Gephardt (D-MO), and former Governor Howard Dean (D-VT) and former General Wesley Clark (D-AR).

The home pages of the six leading candidates demonstrated three different strategic approaches: character, issues, and ideology. The Edwards, Kerry, Lieberman, and Clark websites focused on character. The John Edwards website promoted the candidate as a positive-future oriented candidate full of ideas and vigor. Edwards, the youngest candidate in the field at age 49, was portrayed as energetic, positive, and charismatic. The righthand corner featured a snapshot of the earth from outer space commemorating "Earth Day." The website provided news such as "Fueling America's Future," which is Edwards' new energy program. John Kerry's home page shows him as a man of substance, talent, and experience who could beat President Bush. The headline at the top of the page featured a news story: "N.H. (New Hampshire) Democrats Think Kerry Can Beat Bush" (based on a report for National Public Radio's *Morning Edition*). Kerry drew off his experiences as a decorated Naval Officer during the Vietnam War, and his two decades of experience in the Senate. Choosing Senator Joseph Lieberman meant selecting a man who has lived the American dream and wants to provide the same opportunity for other Americans. The banner on his home page stated: "The American Dream isn't just a story . . ." Lieberman's ethnicity (Jewish) and middle-class roots illustrated his independence and compassion. Wesley Clark's website calls for a "New American Patriotism." The website builds on Clark's military background and leadership.[33]

Congressman Richard Gephardt's website focused almost exclusively on policy issues such as health care, small business, social security, pensions, the economy, and the environment mean for middle class families. The congressman's website argued that the election was a choice between the haves (the rich) represented by President Bush and everyone else (the have nots) best represented by Gephardt.[34]

Former Governor Howard Dean's home page illustrated the populist, insurgency strategy of his campaign. Dean, the first candidate to announce, advertised his liberalism calling for a government-run prescription drug plan, announced his opposition to the U.S.-Iraq war, and condemned Senator Rick Santorum (R-PA) for comparing gay Americans to bigamists. The slogan "Dean for America" (featured on the banner running on the top of the home page) articulated that he was the candidate who best represented people "regardless of race, gender, class or sexual orientation."[35]

Campaign advertising on commercial websites has one drawback—if candidates seek to use "pop-up" advertising to attract visitors. Pop-up ads can be dramatic but also annoying to the Internet user. Software that blocks pop-up ads is becoming increasingly prevalent on home computers; that is why Internet consultants urge candidates to use banner ads instead. Banner ads do not interfere with website navigation by the viewer and avoid turning off potential visitors.

The proliferation of websites means that advertising has far more promotional avenues than television and cable. Targeting websites to purchase banner ads requires researching and finding a specialized audience that meets the strengths of the candidate. For instance, Governor Arnold Schwarzenegger (R-CA), the former action-hero movie star, would be better suited advertising on ESPN's website than on *Home and Garden* magazine's website to reach his target audience of men between the ages of 18–35. On the other hand, advertising Senator Hillary Clinton (D-NY) on *Home and Garden* magazine's website would make far more sense than advertising her on ESPN's home page to reach a target audience of women 35–54 years old. Matching the candidate's demographics to the audience also requires that the campaign's Internet advertising buyer find a website with a sufficient number of visitors to make the purchase of a banner ad payoff. Otherwise, the investment is wasted.

THE FUTURE: THE INTERNET, TELEVISION, AND TECHNOLOGY IN CAMPAIGNS

Convergence or the integration of the computer and television into one medium is now commercially available. While in a nascent stage, it represents the future of multi-media because the technology is demand-driven. The emergence of TiVo (given the name because it rhymes with TV) has created a stir in the communications industry. TiVo advances convergence technology by using Digital Video Recorder (DVR) technology. DVR enables the viewer to record "more than 13 videotapes worth of programs, without the clutter" (meaning commercials) on a hard drive. "It automatically records your favorite shows, all season long even if the timeslot changes." Watching *American Idol* at 3:00 PM or 3:00 AM or any time the viewer prefers is the type of choice TiVo offers. Consequently, viewers have the option of recording nearly 30 hours of programming and watching it on demand.[36]

Demand-driven viewership had a decisively negative impact on the utility of campaign advertising in the 2002 campaign. "The way video killed the radio star, TiVo killed the campaign commercial," said Steve Schmidt, former communications director for the National Republican Congressional Committee at a New York University Conference following the 2002 elections. "People don't want to watch these ads and they're finding ways to get around it." Although the claim may be premature, it could become a reality in the near future.[37]

The fragmentation of the viewing audience is of great concern to the advertising industry. Cable and satellite, emerging media in the

past two decades offer hundreds of choices to viewers. TiVo technology can expand that to thousands of choices. Collective pressure from
private industry on TiVo to provide advertising through its DVR
technology has spurred new efforts to achieve a happier medium. *Advertainment*, introduced by TiVo and its distributor Best Buy, works
like accessing a website through television. TiVo subscribers "simply
click their remote control while the ads are on their television screen"
transporting them to a "Video Showcase," "where they can view Best
Buy" products. For example, the Video Showcase at one time offered
a Sheryl Crow jam session or "Go Mobile" (cell phone) products to attract viewers to shop at Best Buy. The advertising is akin to a home
page that links viewers to the subject of their interest.[38]

Political campaigns given access to this medium could use static
(web page links to issue papers, event listings, newspaper clips) or
live action (video links) technologies to *advertain* voters. Viewers
would choose advertainment options by clicking-through with their
remote. The political campaign industry would need to test-market
the cost-effectiveness in reaching audiences through this technology.
Initial resistance to expanding TiVo technology is likely until advertainment proves to be cost-effective in reaching mass markets. Given
the pace of technological development in the video industry, coupled
with a greater demand for viewing choices by the public, campaigns
and private industry must adapt because convergence technology
represents the future of televised communications media to citizens.

INTERNET VOTING AND ITS NORMATIVE
IMPLICATIONS FOR CAMPAIGNS AND GOVERNING

Internet voting has yielded mixed results by increasing political participation, yet diminishing the role of political parties. Internet voting has yielded higher turnout in some cases, but the cost for the
vendor can be substantial. The 2000 Arizona Democratic Presidential
Primary of the week of March 6 more than doubled the turnout from
39,000 to 86,000. There were minor glitches in the performance of
the system but the elongation of the voting process over a week's
time provided enough cushion to ameliorate any problems.
Election.com provided the technology to administer the Internet
portion of the primary (yielding about 45 percent of the primary
voters). The cost, however, may have been prohibitive for the company. "[Election.com] spent like mad to ensure that this election

worked. . . . They hired an expensive PR firm, flew a dozen or so staffers to Arizona—some of whom stayed there for weeks . . ."[39]

In Internet voting, campaigns lose some control over the get-out-the-vote (GOTV) process. Phone banks and e-mails can alert voters to cast their ballots for a preferred candidate; however, the organizational muscle of unions, powerful interest groups, campaign organizations, and parties diminishes because an online voter no longer needs a ride to the polls. Candidates and parties lose control of GOTV in exchange for the potential of higher voter participation. Expanded implementation of Internet voting throughout the United States will only become more prevalent when issues of security, privacy, and voter authenticity are resolved to the satisfaction of state and national officials of both political parties.[40]

The normative implications of the Internet for democracy are immense. The Internet is a forum for grassroots, responsive political activity. The massive populist citizen organization *MoveOn.org* (1.7 million members) conducted its first presidential primary in June 2003 to endorse a progressive Democratic candidate. *MoveOn* started as an online organization opposing President Clinton's impeachment (1998) and later became the leading online organization opposing war with Iraq (2002–2003). Over 317,000 votes were cast to endorse a prospective candidate with former Governor Howard Dean (D-VT) getting the most votes (44 percent), although not receiving the required 50 percent to receive MoveOn's endorsement. Dean has been the most active candidate using the Internet by creating "Meet-Ups" or meeting rooms to promote his populist presidential candidacy in 2004. It helped Dean raise over $4 million on the Internet from April through June 2003 (see Chapter 1). Dean's approach was similar to Jesse Ventura's (1998) and John McCain's (2000) grassroots efforts, by building support and organization through the Internet. The purpose was to make Dean competitive in the nation's first primary, New Hampshire, right next door to his home state of Vermont. By July 2003, Dean had signed up over 202,000 volunteers.[41]

Grassroots activities make politicking through the Internet increasingly responsive. Participation of activists or interested persons may substantially increase. The issue is whether the Internet heightens candidate- or ideological-centered politics. Campaigns conducted across the Internet have greater participation and an immediate impact, but the deliberative job of governing may become more difficult if the expectations are in "real time."

CONCLUSION

The Internet is revolutionizing campaigns by tailoring messages even more precisely to voter groups. Websites integrate organizational, advertising, and fundraising functions into one domain. They provide campaigns the opportunity to go on the offensive by releasing press statements, working papers, and speeches each day to keep the opposition on the defensive. Campaign can "blast" e-mail information to hundreds of press sources instantaneously and no longer have to rely on paper fax machines. Campaigns now integrate their web designs into their entire marketing and advertising strategy—that means that the net consultant has to work closely with the media and polling consultants to ensure that the campaign's message remains consistent through all media utilized. The construction of a website is essential for success. Visitors must be able to navigate the site with ease and feel welcome to return. The Internet complements traditional organizational tools important to campaigns such as fund raising, polling, paid advertising, and GOTV operations. The future of campaigns however, lies within electronic technology as the approach to targeting voters, raising money, and promoting candidates diversifies. Campaigns will be challenged to adapt every election cycle to new technologies in the foreseeable future. Failure to adapt to such changes means that the opposition could be one-step ahead; that step could mean the difference between defeat and victory. The daily ground war of a campaign builds on the tools that a campaign uses to achieve victory: fundraising, polling, advertising, and the Internet. Events, speeches, debates, and personal appearances designed for news coverage provide information that citizens need to make their voting decisions.

STUDY/DISCUSSION QUESTIONS

How do Internet campaigns complement traditional campaign functions, such as fundraising and advertising?

Why are more candidates spending time and effort to develop campaign websites?

What are the attributes of an effective campaign website? What pitfalls should campaigns avoid?

How would you design one of the presidential candidates' websites for 2004? What elements would you include?

What impact does the Internet have on future democratic participation?

SUGGESTED WEBSITES

loc.gov/minerva   The Library of Congress' archive of campaign websites for House, Senate, and governor races beginning in 2002

www.politicsonline.com   The weekly Bible of the Internet and campaigns; sends a free e-newsletter

www.campaignline.com   The website for *Campaigns and Elections* magazine

www.dnc.org, www.dscc.org, www.dccc.org, www.rnc.org, www.nrsc.org, www.nrcc.org   Websites for the national party (dnc, rnc), senatorial (dscc, nrsc), and congressional campaign committees (dccc, nrsc) of Democrats and Republicans, respectively

www.pollingreport.com   Updated daily polling information on politics and issues

www.politics1.com   Daily online campaign news

NOTES

1. "Quotations Page," accessed April 19, 2003 at *www.quotationspage .com/the+future*.
2. Glenn R. Simpson, "The Internet Begins to Click as a Political Money Web," *Wall Street Journal*, October 19, 1999. Accessed July 17, 2003 at *www.politicsonline.com/coverage/wsj3*. Also cited in Chapter 4 regarding direct-mail costs.
3. Lee Rainie, "Untuned Keyboards," from a PowerPoint presentation at the 2003 Politics Online Conference, March 21, 2003, Washington, DC, regarding Internet usage; "Consultant Q&A: Campaigning on the Internet," *Campaigns and Elections*, September 2002, 51, quoting Becky Donatelli.
4. Rainie.
5. "More Than 72 Percent Of The U.S. Online Population Uses Internet Applications, According to Nielsen/NetRatings." Accessed April 19, 2003 at *www.nielsen-netratings.com;* Max Fose,

panelist, "Raising Money Effectively and Profusely," at the 2003 Politics Online Conference, March 21, 2003, Washington, DC, on Internet fundraising.

6. Emilene Ireland and Phil Nash, "Announcement Sites: A Simple Way to Launch Your Web Campaign," *Campaigns and Elections,* July 2002, 50–51, all quotes and examples.

7. Steve Kelley, for Minnesota State Senate, 2000 website. Accessed January 12, 2002 at *www.kelley.com.* Written by Steve Fillbrandt on behalf of Steve Kelley. Reprinted by permission of Steve Kelley.

8. Michael Cornfield and Jonah Singer, "The Net and the Nomination Spring 2003," from the forthcoming book *The Making of the Presidential Candidates 2004,* ed. William G. Mayer (Washington, DC: Rowman & Littlefield, publication date not known), 10, quotation regarding Fose and Gullett's activities; Max Fose and Becky Donatelli, panelists, "Raising Money Effectively and Profusely," at the 2003 Politics Online Conference, March 21, 2003, Washington, DC, on Internet fundraising.

9. Steve Schneider, presentation at the 2003 Politics Online Conference, March 21, 2003, Washington, DC, regarding how national political candidates structure websites; the 65 percent figure comes from Rainie.

10. Emilienne Ireland and Phil Tajitsu Nash, *Winning Campaigns Online: Strategies for Candidates and Campaigns,* 2d ed. (Bethesda, MD: Science Writers Press, 2001), chap. six, 86–100, describing the techniques of building a good website.

11. "Joe Torre Endorses Pataki," from George Pataki for Governor 2002 website. Accessed May 2, 2003 at *www.georgepataki.com* (web page edition, October 6, 2002).

12. *Winning Campaigns Online,* 99.

13. United States Library of Congress' MINERVA project, which archives national campaign websites starting with the 2002 elections. Accessed April 19, 2003 at *www.web.archive.org/e02/20021001070329/http://lamaralexander.com* (web page edition, October 1, 2002).

14. Donatelli.

15. "Emily's Summer Journal, August 12, 2002. George Pataki for Governor 2002. Accessed May 2, 2003 at *www.georgepataki .com/cgi-data/journal/files/21.shtml.* Reprinted by permission.

16. Eric Loeb, panelist, "Fool's Gold? . . . Targeting Your Message Beyond Voter Files," at the 2003 Politics Online Conference,

March 21, 2003, Washington, DC, on voter targeting; Robyn Greenspan, "Internet Not for Everyone" at *www.cyberatlas.com*, April 16, 2003. The article reports a study by Lee Rainie of the Pew Internet and American Life Project on "Truly Unconnected" groups such as minorities; Fose, on the discussion of content.

17. Reid Goldsborough. "Creating Political Web Sites . . . with Substance!" *Campaigns and Elections*, August 2000, 48, all references. Also go to *www.hitbox.com* and see the webside story site.

18. David Bennett and Pam Fielding, "10 Steps To Building A Successful Online Campaign." Accessed April 19, 2003 at *www.e-advocates.com*.

19. Michael Cornfield, "The Final Four Sites," *Campaigns and Elections*, February 2000, 53.

20. Mark Warner for Governor 2001 website. Accessed December 29, 2001 at *www.markwarner2001.org/newsroom/101801.htm*.

21. John Mintz, "Political Groups Scramble to Find E-Mail Addresses of Likely Backers," *The Washington Post,* September 22, 2000, A21.

22. Donatelli, panelist, March 21, 2003.

23. "Why they could not have won without the Internet," Jesse Ventura as Candidate, PoliticsOnline. Accessed April 23, 2003 at *www.politicsonline.com/jv/internet.html*.

24. Larry Purpuro, "The Big Push: The Case for Political E-Mailing," *Campaigns and Elections*, October/November 2002, 47.

25. Mintz, both quotes.

26. Rand Ragusa, "Publishing Campaign eNewsletters Gets Results," bayoubuzz.com. Accessed April 22, 2003 at *www .bayoubuzz.com;* Ireland and Nash, *Winning Campaigns Online,* regarding Tom Campbell's senatorial campaign in California, 208.

27. See chap. 4 for the cost of direct mail. "Consultant Q&A: Campaigning on the Internet," *Campaigns and Elections*, September 2002, 53; Becky Donatelli interviewed by Mary Clare Jalonick. The interview provided the cost information.

28. Fose; panelist, March 21, 2003, Vince Wishrad, panelist, "Raising Money Effectively and Profusely," at the 2003 Politics Online Conference, March 21, 2003, Washington, DC, on Internet fundraising.

29. Edwards for President 2004 website. Accessed April 25, 2003 at *www.johnedwards2004.com;* Joe Lieberman for President 2004 website. Accessed April 25, 2003 at *www.joe2004.com/index.jsp*.

30. Fose.
31. Jonah Singer, "Privacy, Trust and Security on the Political Web," IPDI, paper presented to the Politics Online conference, March 21, 2003. See pages 8 (the percentage of those who hesitate), 9 (hesitate to provide e-mail address because of the lack of a privacy statement and credit card information), and 11 (the percentage of users who pay attention to privacy statements).
32. Becky Donatelli, "Hunting Where the Ducks Are: How Banner Ads Were Used in the Last Election," *Campaigns and Elections*, April 2003, data and quotes from pages 38–39 on Dole and click-through rates; quote on Boxer campaign from Jonah Singer, "Internet Banners: Better than 30-Second Spots," *The Political Standard*, May/June 1999. Accessed May 3, 2003 at *www .bettercampaigns.org/standard/display.php?StoryID=166*.
33. *www.johnedwards2004.com*. All candidate websites were accessed on the same day to draw valid comparisons; John Kerry for President 2004 website. Accessed April 25, 2003 at *www.johnkerry .com/site/PageServer*; *www.joe2004.com/index.jsp*; *www.clark04.com*, accessed December 17, 2003.
34. Gephardt for President 2004 website. Accessed April 25, 2003 at *www.dickgephardt2004.com*.
35. Dean for President 2004 website. Accessed April 25, 2003 at *www.deanforamerica.com*.
36. TiVo Inc. home page accessed April 26, 2003 at *www.tivo .com/1.0.asp*.
37. Steve Schmidt, "Back and Forth: Looking Back at the 2002 Midterm Elections and Ahead to 2004 (sic)," post-mortem panel, December 10, 2002. Accessed April 26, 2003 at *www.nyu.edu/ gsas/dept/politics/pcm/conference/2002elect_recap.html*.
38. Dawn Anfuso, "TiVo Introduces New Ad Format: Measurement," imedia.com, May 20, 2002. Accessed April 26, 2003 at *www.imediaconnection.com/content/news/052002.asp*.
39. James Ledbetter, "'Virtual Voting' Faces Real-World Concerns," *The Industry Standard*. Accessed April 23, 2003 at *www.thestandard .com/article/display/0,1151,12981,00.html*, quote on election.com spending. Also reference the "Historic Online primary in Arizona," March 13, 2000. *Associated Press*.
40. For a discussion of security, privacy, and authenticity issues, see Kevin Coleman and Richard M. Nunno, "RS20639: Internet

Voting: Issues and Legislation," *CRS Report for Congress* (Washington, DC: Congressional Research Service, January 26, 2001).

41. Zack Exley, panelist, "Analyze This, Analyze That—Real Time Usage of the Internet," at the 2003 Politics Online Conference, March 21, 2003, Washington, DC, on campaigning through the Internet; Lois Romano, "Internet Becoming Candidates' Domain," June 29, 2003, A4 on the MoveOn.org primary. See MoveOn.org "About Us" at *www.MoveOn.org* providing background on the organization's history. Go to *www.deanforamerica.org*, which reports on its home page the number of Dean supporters. Both websites accessed July 18, 2003.

CHAPTER 8

Campaigning for Office

The play's the thing wherein I'll capture the conscience of the King.
  —*Hamlet stages a play about murder to embarrass his uncle the King, whom he believes killed his father to assume the crown and marry his mother. (Hamlet, Act II, Scene ii)*

Capturing the conscience of voters by politicians is the essence of campaigning. Capturing that conscience does not always depend on money but rather on organization, the skillful implementation of a message, the showcasing of a candidate's personal story, or the highlighting of an issue of integrity. Jesse Ventura's (I-MN) grassroots online campaign organization for governor (1998), Russ Feingold's (D-WI) senate campaign explaining his support of campaign reform (1992), Ben Nighthorse Campbell's (R-CO) senate campaign illustrating his rise from poverty to Olympian (1992), and Shelley Moore Capito's (R-WV) anti-corruption campaign for congress (2000) illustrate how candidates win elections despite being outspent by opponents. Each campaign above successfully demonstrates different ways campaigns win elections by earning attention through the press and alternative media.

Campaigns for public office demonstrate how important the daily strategy is to mobilize support and maximize news coverage as discussed in this chapter. Each day campaigns seek to manipulate the schedule, events, symbols, speeches, or debates to garner news coverage. *Earned media* are public events designed by the campaign for press coverage to deliver the one or two focus messages that will resonate with voters. *Earned media* complements *paid media* (i.e., direct mail, radio, newspaper, and television advertising) and the Internet to constitute the campaign's entire media strategy. Campaigns expend tremendous efforts to maximize earned media. In the worst cases, news coverage brings to light a potentially destructive crisis or scandal. Effective crisis management enables the campaign to minimize its losses and recover quickly. Campaign manager James Carville, consultant Paul Begala, and communications director George Stephanopoulos expertly handled allegations of an extramarital affair and draft dodging against Bill Clinton in the weeks preceding the 1992 New Hampshire primary. Clinton miraculously finished second in the primary and dubbed himself the "Comeback Kid." Direct and immediate responses prepared by Clinton's strategists enabled the campaign to put the issues behind them much faster than his opponents would have preferred. The Clinton example illustrates how circumstances dictate the proper way for a campaign to respond in light of a personal crisis or political event that can reshape the campaign landscape.

Finally, the chapter discusses how common it is for candidates to adjust their tactics during the final days of a campaign, if losing or locked in a tight battle, to win crucial swing votes and mobilize partisan turnout. The adrenaline rush that candidates experience during the final days of a grueling election campaign to sustain themselves is remarkable. Many of the elements described in previous chapters, such as candidate adaptation to events (Chapter 3), the role of campaign organization and message (Chapter 4), polling (Chapter 5), and media techniques (Chapter 6) coalesce as the campaign for public office gets into full swing.

GOAL: WINNING EACH DAY

Campaigns try to "win" each day of an election contest to build a pyramid of success. Winning a day on the campaign trail means that the candidate is on the offensive and puts the opponent on the defensive. Candidates wage their general election campaign once they win their party's nomination (usually, but not always in late spring). Campaigns adjust their tactics daily to promote the candidate's message through press coverage, trying to stay on the offensive. The paid advertising portion of a campaign may not begin until the fall, but the earned media campaign is an ongoing effort. Challengers with momentum are particular beneficiaries. Political consultant Anita Dunn calls this her "pet rock" (i.e., favorite) theory of news

coverage: "A challenger who gets 'hot' suddenly becomes the bene-
ficiary of celebrity coverage." Dunn described how *The Today Show*
ran a glowing five-minute bio story on Pete Dawkins, the Republican senatorial candidate from New Jersey in 1988. He went to West
Point, won the Heisman Trophy as college football's best player, and
became a war hero. His personal story was riveting and *The Today
Show* piece served as free campaign advertising. However, incumbent Democrat Frank Lautenberg defeated Dawkins that fall because
the glow from the story did not last. Early publicity is helpful but
campaigns must find ways to build on positive exposure to keep
their candidate in the news.[1]

Focus

The key to maintaining daily momentum on the campaign trail is
focus. Candidates repeat themes or messages continually to the
press that have been test-marketed through public opinion surveys
and focus groups. George Nethercutt (R-WA) defeated Speaker of
the House Tom Foley (D-WA) by running on the issue of term limits,
which the state of Washington tried to pass on its congressional representatives. Foley challenged the issue in court, which provided
even more fuel for Nethercutt's efforts. Nethercutt argued that
Foley's 30 years in Congress put him out of touch with his eastern
Washington constituents and that his interests concerned the aggre-
gation of personal power rather than the agricultural community in
his district. Nethercutt repeated a daily mantra on the campaign trail
that the district needed "a listener not a speaker" as he campaigned
from factories to wheat fields. Foley was the first U.S. Speaker of the
House defeated since Galusha Gow of Pennsylvania (1862). Ironically, Nethercutt who took a pledge to serve only three terms broke
that pledge in 2000, yet won reelection with 57 percent of the vote.[2]

Nethercutt's discipline of staying "on message" explains how
persistence helped a long-shot win the most significant congressional upset of the 1990s. Campaign managers often find that candidates think they know best and wander off-message. For challengers
in particular, having a message that resonates, and staying disciplined by repeating that message to voters (such as Bill Clinton and
Ronald Reagan did), enhances their opportunity to win an election.
An incumbent's message reflects what political scientist David Mayhew calls "credit claiming" for accomplishments and (or) position-

taking on key issues while in office. High reelection rates for senatorial, gubernatorial, and congressional races indicate relative satisfaction with the performance of most incumbents because their past record defines what message they offer for the future.[3]

The Daily Campaign Schedule

The daily campaign schedule becomes more hectic as primary or general election day approaches. The scheduler works closely with the campaign manager to plot the best places for the candidate to go. Campaign schedules tend to change as the election approaches because polling data show where the candidate has firm and weak support. The schedule may change to maximize the base of support for get-out-the-vote (GOTV) activities, to allow the candidate to attend events in areas where undecided voters may reside, or to do both. George McGovern's (D-SD) campaign schedule of June 1, 1972 demonstrates the frenzied activity of last-minute campaigning to win the California Democratic presidential primary in two regions of the state. (McGovern went on to win the Democratic presidential nomination that year). The following schedule shows the breakneck pace of campaigning in the states two largest media markets with interim periods filled with travel by bus or plane:

8:50–9:30 A.M.	Taping, "Newsmakers," CBS, Hollywood, CA
9:55–10:30 A.M.	Taping, "News Conference," NBC, Burbank, CA
12:00–1:00 P.M.	Senior Citizens Lunch and Rally, Bixby Park Band Shell, Long Beach, CA
2:00–2:45 P.M.	Fullerton Junior College, Speech, Fullerton, CA
3:00–4:45 P.M.	Motorcade and plane flight to Oakland, CA
5:40–6:45 P.M.	Private Dinner
8:30–9:15 P.M.	McGovern for President Rally, St. James Park, San Jose, CA
10:00–10:45 P.M.	Private Meeting
11:15 P.M.	Bus Arrives San Francisco Hilton, CA[4]

McGovern's day filled up with specific press events (two news interviews), rallies, and meetings. Furthermore, by traversing the two major population and media centers in the state (Los Angeles metropolitan and San Francisco Bay areas), McGovern's campaign ensured that he would receive significant news coverage. Accompanying McGovern was a large media contingent because of his status as Democratic frontrunner. The mammoth logistical operation that high-profile campaigns have to manage when plotting a schedule includes transporting large numbers of staff and press to multiple events in the same day.

WHERE TO CAMPAIGN

The strategic allocation of time is a primary concern of the campaign because the candidate's time is finite. Surrogates or running mates make appearances that are secondary targets on behalf of the candidates. Surrogates may be spouses, relatives, celebrity supporters, and well-known politicians. Campaigns compute the time and effort to determine the campaign schedule of candidates and their surrogates. The strategists evaluate states and jurisdictions in terms of size, need, and party potential. For example, in 1976, the Carter team used these variables in its allocation formula for percentages of campaign effort. The highest percentage allocated was for California (5.9 percent) followed by New York (5.1 percent), Illinois (4.1 percent), Pennsylvania (3.6 percent), Michigan (3.4 percent), Texas (3.3 percent), Ohio (3.0 percent), and New Jersey (3.0 percent). Carter was a former governor of Georgia, and the Democratic party was still competitive in southern states for presidential elections during the mid-1970s. Thus, many of the targeted states were outside and within his natural political base (i.e., in the South). Carter was successful enough in winning half the states from this list (New York, Pennsylvania, Michigan, Texas, and Ohio) to triumph over President Gerald Ford with a 297–241 electoral vote margin.[5]

National or statewide campaigns may allocate personal appearances by the candidate based on the percentage of effort out of the total number of potential scheduling appearances or "points." For example, if President George W. Bush's campaign rated Missouri 2.5 percent (effort) for 800 scheduling appearances for his 2004 reelection campaign, then the president would make 20 visits to locations

across the state. Those 20 location visits would not occur on different days but, rather, would be spread over five or six days spent
campaigning throughout the state at events.[6]

Sometimes the candidate appears with relatives or celebrities to
generate greater publicity. On November 3, 2000, rock star Sheryl
Crow headlined a last-minute tribute concert in St. Louis to honor
Governor Mel Carnahan (D-MO) who died in a plane crash just two
weeks earlier while running for the Senate. The governor's widow,
Jean Carnahan who agreed to serve in her husband's place (if elected
posthumously), and Vice President Al Gore (running a tight race for
president) appeared at the tribute concert. The Carnahan tribute concert featuring Crow, rock singer Don Henley, and actor Kevin Kline
was a de facto GOTV rally. Thousands of people attended the "tribute"
which was covered widely by the St. Louis local press. The concert
exemplifies how campaigns schedule events to build momentum
toward the end of a campaign. High-publicity events with celebrities
enable candidates to maximize attention to their campaign during its
critical final days of an election contest.[7]

TECHNIQUES OF CAMPAIGNING #1: CONNECTING TO THE POLITICAL AND SOCIAL CULTURE

Campaigning reflects how the personality of the candidate adapts to
their state or home district. Representatives adapt their personalities
to the district ("home"), which may differ from their Washington,
D.C. ("House") style according to political scientist Richard Fenno in
his book, *Home Styles: House Members in Their Districts*. For example,
Lyndon Johnson wore his Stetson cowboy hat often when campaigning in his home state of Texas, yet was the ultimate inside politician
in Washington, D.C. Congressman Daniel Flood (D), a flamboyant
member from coal-mining country in northeastern Pennsylvania
(1945–1947 and 1949–1980), campaigned in white tails, a top hat, and
could tap soft shoe for an audience. The techniques that work with
any jurisdiction depend on the local political culture. The candidate's style of campaigning has to fit with the constituency to be effective, whether it is homespun (e.g., Johnson) or flamboyant (e.g.,
Flood).[8]

Unconventional campaign tactics promote the candidate as a
populist and help attract media attention. Senator Bob Graham

(D-FL) campaigned for years using "work days" in his gubernatorial and senatorial campaigns. Graham worked at various jobs to show how cognizant he was of the daily life of Floridians. Graham labored a full day at jobs such as "policeman, railroad engineer, construction worker, sponge fisherman, factory worker, social worker, busboy, teacher and other occupations." In fact, many national and local candidates have copied Graham's "work days" for their own campaigns quite successfully. Pat DiNizio, the lead singer of the popular rock group the Smithereens, ran for New Jersey's U.S. Senate seat in 2000 as the Reform Party's candidate. DiNizio visited the homes of supporters "to give concerts—punctuated by political speeches . . . (going)into diners and getting attention by saying things like, 'Wake up! Life is not just veal parmigiana!'" DiNizio was not successful but his unusual style echoed another celebrity third party candidate two years earlier—Jesse Ventura.[9]

TECHNIQUES OF CAMPAIGNING #2: CAMPAIGN EVENTS TO GENERATE EARNED MEDIA

Campaigns use rallies, speeches, debates, and press conferences to generate grassroots support and attract media attention. Major national campaigns operate on a dual track: paid advertising enables the campaign to control its message to targeted voters, while an earned message appears in press that has a "spin" or twist that complements or accentuates the paid media message. For example, Bill Clinton's positive message of "change" reiterated at virtually every campaign appearance in 1992 signified a generational change in leadership and promised economic change. Clinton's paid advertising was iterating the same theme. The message has to be consistent or confusion ensues, inhibiting the effort to attract voter support to the candidate. Candidates tailor the message to audiences talking about various issues such as the economy, the environment, health care reform, or national security. For earned media, the filter of press coverage means that campaigns have to be creative to get a message across to voters. The George Bush, Sr. (1992), Bob Dole (1996), and Al Gore, Jr. (2000) presidential campaigns, in part, failed because of message inconsistency or change. Message alteration on the campaign trail implies that the current message is not getting traction from voters, no matter how spectacular the visuals on television.

Staged Events

Staged events, such as political rallies and speeches, help unify the party base behind the candidate. Rallies have been a staple of campaigns since the inception of political parties. Democratic candidates have traditionally completed their presidential campaign with an enormous rally accompanied by a torchlight parade in Chicago. Large naval bases in cities such as Norfolk, VA and San Diego, CA have served as backdrops for Republican candidates such as Senator John Warner (R-VA) and President George W. Bush to impress voters with pro-defense policies. College campus rallies at state universities such as Michigan and California-Berkeley have drawn tens of thousands of student supporters for Democratic candidates in key electoral states.

Rallies can take on their own persona, unravel out of control, and unwittingly work against a political party. The Paul Wellstone memorial tribute turned into a rally that backfired against the state Democratic party. Senator Paul Wellstone (D-MN), running for reelection in 2002, was killed when his twin-engine Beechcraft plane crashed in Evelyn, MN killing all aboard, including his wife on October 25, just ten days before the election. The memorial service that commemorated Wellstone's death turned into a campaign rally. An overflow crowd of 20,000 filled the Williams Arena in Minneapolis for the service. An audible "boo" rang out when Republican Senate Minority Leader Trent Lott of Mississippi and Minnesota Governor Jesse Ventura were introduced to the crowd. Senator Tom Harkin (D-Iowa) was the only elected politician to deliver a eulogy. "Harkin threw off his suit jacket and brought the crowd to its feet urging them to get behind the issues Wellstone believed in . . . education, health care . . . fighting for veterans' rights and family farmers." More partisan speeches followed including one by family friend Rick Kahn, who served as Wellstone's campaign treasurer. Kahn "urged the crowd to vote DFL [the name of the Democratic party in Minnesota] next week." Senator Lott, Governor Ventura and several others walked out disgusted by the tone of the proceedings, which mirrored a political rally. Many political observers believe that Wellstone's replacement on the ticket, former Vice President Walter Mondale, lost the campaign because the memorial service turned partisan and resonated negatively with many swing voters throughout the state who were watching it on television. The event galvanized angry Republicans and Independents to turn out and vote on election day. The result was a narrow come-from-behind victory by Republican Norm Coleman over Walter Mondale, 50–47 percent.[10]

Staged events are a critical part of the earned media communications process. The work of the "advance team" setting up candidate appearances at events (in advance, hence the term) is critical to a campaign. Local or national press coverage may focus on visual mistakes at an event, which become the news story of the day. The advance team choreographs nearly every move. The placement and height of the flags behind the podium, the height of the lectern, and the exact places where politicians stand on the platform illustrate how important advance work is. For instance, the advance team uses different colors of tape to correspond to each politician or writes the names of dignitaries on beige masking tape, to show each person where to stand on the platform. The advance team may position children near the front of the stage to greet the candidate after the address, making for great television. For an indoor rally, the advance team may deliberately integrate the crowd near the stage for photo ops, when the candidate delivers a speech about race relations. If the event recognizes veterans, campaigns are not above putting disabled veterans in wheelchairs close to the stage, for more than altruistic reasons. Campaigns want a photo op of veterans that will generate sympathy, respect, and honor. Even though the motive is crass, the goal of the advance team is to make the candidate look good.

Reporters seek conflict or controversy to sell stories to editors because the message from the stump speech rarely changes even if the visuals do. Staged events allow very little interpretive room by the press. The press' access is limited, and campaigns want reporters to write the story as they show and tell it. Sometimes this strategy goes awry because candidates do or say something stupid. George W. Bush's derogatory comment about *New York Times* reporter Adam Clymer made to his running mate, Dick Cheney, was caught over an open microphone minutes before a campaign speech in Naperville, Illinois. "There's Adam Clymer, a major league (fill-in the blank)" was the lead news story that night. His opponent Al Gore was prone to exaggeration. Several months earlier Al Gore had spoken before the Nashville City Club when it honored his mother Pauline. Gore told a story about how his mother accepted an invitation for lunch at the Nashville City Club's dining room, which had an all-male policy. She appeared at lunch, causing a "minor revolution" when she loudly complained that the dining room excluded women members. According to Gore, "a few days later, this city club was opened to women and the charter changed." The problem was that the club did not open its dining room to women until fourteen years later, according to *ABC News*. This contributed to the persona of Gore as a candidate who embellished the truth. Candidates have to remain on guard because anything they say is fodder for the press.[11]

The informal campaign or stump speech provides the candidate with an opportunity to speak before dozens, hundreds, or thousands of people. A charismatic candidate possesses the invaluable gift of oratory to captivate a crowd. Ronald Reagan, a former movie actor, used his training with great assurance and sincerity when delivering a stump speech. Reagan would glance down at his three-by-five cards to touch on something personal about the audience to whom he was speaking. Bill Clinton spoke in an extemporaneous style that was conversational and personal. The point is that the speechmaking style needs to fit the candidate naturally; otherwise, the delivery looks forced. Oratorical skill is perhaps the greatest natural trait that a candidate possesses because there is no greater advantage in politics than personal communication. Great orators inspire enthusiasm and belief that the future they seek is a positive and noble one.

Formal Addresses

Prepared announcement speeches, nomination acceptance speeches, and policy speeches by candidates to important host groups are an essential feature of campaigns. Presidential candidates often address the Council on Foreign Relations in New York, whose members include many former members of past administrations including secretaries of state and defense. Senate candidates are invited to statewide labor, small business, education, and veterans' conventions. John McCain, a Vietnam veteran spent seven years as a prisoner-of-war (POW) in Hanoi. Speaking before a New Hampshire Veterans of Foreign Wars (VFW) group in September 1999, as he campaigned for president, McCain told an engaged audience, "It doesn't take a lot of talent to get shot down. I was able to intercept a surface-to-air missile with my own airplane, which many of you know is no mean feat." McCain's self-deprecating sense of humor about a grievous personal travail connected him to an understanding audience. Personal anecdotes and candid remarks enable a candidate to relate directly to their audience as a real person.[12]

Local or state party events commemorating famous presidents give candidates the opportunity to show their wares in front of an official party forum. Jefferson-Jackson Day for Democrats or Lincoln's Day for Republicans represent the formal events where incumbents or prospective challengers speak to the party faithful. Senator John Kerry (D-MA), a candidate for his party's 2004 presidential nomination, gave the Jefferson-Jackson Day keynote address to the Michigan State Democratic Party on May 10, 2003. The cost per ticket to the dinner was $150. Private receptions with the candidates were available to party donors such as "Trustees" who donate at least $2,500 annually. Compare the Michigan State Democratic party function with the local Scott County, Illinois Republican Central Committee's Lincoln Day Dinner. The March 15, 2003 dinner featured a keynote address by Congressman Ray LaHood (R-IL), and the cost was a more modest $15. These dinners are party rituals whether they appear on the national or local level. Candidates make appearances at party functions in an off-year to remain visible and connected to supporters to build momentum for the ensuing election year.[13]

TECHNIQUES OF CAMPAIGNING #3: DEBATES

Texas political columnist Molly Ivins says, "political debates are sort of like stock-car races—no one really cares who wins, they just want to see the crashes. If there aren't any crashes, everyone votes the event a total bore." Without the "crashes," debates become disappointing because they generate little interest. Debates (or as some prefer forums since candidates may not address each other directly) provide voters a comparative medium to evaluate candidates. The modern world of television means that candidates speak for thirty seconds to two minutes rather than the lengthy and reflective responses characteristic of the famed Lincoln-Douglas debates of 1858. Television has put the emphasis on rehearsed answers and sound bites to communicate messages that resonate with persuadable voters in short time-bursts.[14]

Earned-Media Exposure Through Non-Televised Debates

Lack of television exposure makes the news of a local debate of great interest to hard-core political junkies, but not to typical voters. Local candidate debates among primary candidates pose the greatest challenges since the task of gaining valuable name recognition is difficult to achieve on a crowded dais. Unless a candidate makes a mistake, the story from the debate rarely makes news. Challengers often take an aggressive tack against incumbents or try something unusual to acquire press coverage to make a point. Congressman Sherrod Brown (D) from northeastern Ohio remarked on his debates during his first reelection bid in 1994: "there were no crashes in our debates, although perennial candidate John Michael Ryan did dress up like Paul Revere for one occasion." Dressing up as Paul Revere may help a candidate achieve notoriety in a local newspaper as a publicity stunt, but such a tactic is unlikely to draw substantive news coverage, which a challenger needs.[15]

Earned Media Through Televised Debates

Televised debates raise the ante for candidates because the audiences are much larger and the events garner more attentive media coverage. The first Bush-Gore debate in 2000 generated an audience of 46.5 million viewers, which was similar to the size of the first Clinton-Dole debate in 1996 (46.1 million viewers). The largest viewing audience for any debate was the lone Jimmy Carter–Ronald Reagan encounter in 1980 generating an audience of 80 million people! Furthermore, sound bites played on the networks several days after the debate replaying the highlights in snippets of ten seconds or less to viewers.[16]

The best-remembered televised debates in political history involve major personal errors made by the candidates. Governor Michael Dukakis (D-MA) running for the presidency in 1988 could not overcome the image that he was a cold technocrat. During his third presidential debate with George Bush, Sr., Dukakis' dispassionate response to a hypothetical question concerning what he would like to do to a man who raped and murdered his wife reinforced the notion that he lacked compassion. President Gerald Ford was portrayed as bumbling and ill-informed by the press. The second presidential debate of 1976 featured a discussion about foreign policy between Ford and his opponent Jimmy Carter. In response to a question about

DEBATES OF SUBSTANCE: THE KERRY-WELD MASSACHUSETTS
SENATE DEBATES OF 1996

The 1996 Massachusetts senatorial debates between Senator
John Kerry (D) and Republican challenger, Governor William
Weld (MA) were memorable for their edifying discussions of
substance. "They held seven debates altogether, literate rounds
of accusations and one-liners." Both candidates were Ivy
League educated, articulate, wealthy, and accomplished. The
seriousness and candor of discussion started in the first debate.
In response to a philosophical question, "why are people
poor?" Weld replied that the lack of job opportunities and the
culture of welfare handicapped the poor. He argued that a
smaller federal government and lower taxes could stimulate
the economy to increase job opportunities for the poor. Kerry's
more "emotional" response was that "the decks are stacked
against" those in poverty. The incumbent went further by stating that the political system actually worked against the poor
because the system was unfair and deliberately held them
back. Both candidates articulated their ideological philosophy,
Weld's concerning free markets and competition and Kerry's
regarding social justice. Furthermore, the *manner* of each response was important. Weld, whose political strength relied on
his personality and management of state government, gave an
intellectual response on national policies. Kerry, regarded as
more stoic and cerebral, gave an emotive response to demonstrate his humanity and character. Both candidates effectively
addressed a weakness in their candidate profiles in response to
the first question, demonstrating how poise, intelligence, and
message can impress viewers and reporters.[18]

the aspirations of people in Communist countries, Ford said "there is
no Soviet domination of Eastern Europe." Ford repeated the comment
when prompted again by an incredulous questioner even though the
Soviet Union's military and political sphere of influence extended
throughout Eastern Europe. Ford hurt his presidential aspirations
with claims about no Soviet domination, which seemed naïve to many
observers, particularly for a president during the Cold War.[17]

Debate Strategies

Debate strategies depend on the format, time limits, and issue context for discussion. The format may be a traditional joint news conference with candidates at separate podiums, a town hall debate with audience participation, or a single moderator sitting at a desk facing the candidates similar to Sunday morning talk shows. Time limits govern the length of introductory and closing remarks, responses, and rebuttals. The issue context determines whether the debate should concern one subject matter (e.g., drug policy), a broad policy area (e.g., the economy), or an open-ended discussion of many issues. The candidates, the sponsors, or both may set the rules for the debate. The more prominent the election contest, the greater the input candidates have in the format. The Democratic and Republican presidential candidates have greater input setting the rules for the general election campaign debates than do sponsors such as the Commission on Presidential Debates or the League of Women Voters.

Two-candidate debates are likely to encourage direct interaction between the contestants whereas multi-candidate debates may require the candidates to focus on a more specific strategy to establish a unique identity. Jesse Ventura running as an Independent in the 1998 Minnesota gubernatorial election played referee between his opponents, State Attorney General Skip Humphrey (D) and St. Paul Mayor, Norm Coleman (R) in the debates. Humphrey and Coleman savaged each other in personal attacks. One might think that Ventura's experience as a professional wrestler would motivate him to throw some verbal body slams in the ring. Instead, Ventura visibly shook his head as his counterparts verbally slugged each other. In one debate, Coleman accused Humphrey of unfairly prosecuting a window installation company: "You almost brought them to their knees," he said. Humphrey later retorted that Coleman, should "put money where your mouth is" to improve public schools. Ventura deliberately sat between the two candidates in the debates when he could: "It didn't hurt that . . . I'm a six-foot four monstrosity. . . . These guys were puny in comparison." Ventura related that he never used notes or "canned answers" as his opponents did. After the third debate, Coleman and Humphrey started to look for ways to opt out of further debates because Ventura was gaining steadily in the polls from his on-air exposure. The debates played an essential role in Ventura's-come-from behind victory raising his stature from celebrity to serious candidate.[19]

Debates enable candidates to portray strengths, address their own shortcomings, or highlight the weaknesses of an opponent. In a town hall debate of undecided voters in the general election race among Bill Clinton, George Bush, Sr. and Ross Perot (the Independent candidate), Clinton walked towards the audience when addressing them, closing the personal distance. Clinton's facial expressions such as nodding his head to reflect concern or rubbing his chin to ponder a question underscored that he "understood" the audience as people. How Clinton *listened* to questions by ordinary citizens was almost as important as how he answered those questions. Clinton's debate style emphasized a conversation with the audience. His ability to mesh personal appeal with substance made him difficult to attack.

George Bush, Sr. in the same debate showed how out-of-touch he was with the same audience. When asked by an African-American woman "how does the deficit affect you personally?" Bush stammered not seeming to understand the import of the question. His first attempt to answer the question in terms of national policy about the debt and interest rates brought a reminder from moderator Carol Simpson of *ABC News:* "She's saying you personally. Has it affected you personally?" Bush compounded the problem further saying, "Well, I'm sure it has. I love my grandchildren. I want to think. . . ." Bush's poorly conceived answer to this basic question demonstrated something more important; he seemed not to understand the problems of ordinary Americans as the economy struggled to come out of recession. Three months earlier an *ABC News* poll had pointed out the same problem. When registered voters were asked, "are you satisfied that Bush understands the problems of average Americans well enough to serve effectively as President," 34 percent said "yes," and 62 percent said "no." The debate only intensified those feelings. According to *ABC News* polling analyst Gary Langer, "Bush's mistake was in insisting that recovery had occurred—technically it had; the recession ended in March 1991. But practically, the recovery did not reach Main Street until years later, in the mid-1990s." The debate revealed the President disconnected from the personal problems faced by ordinary voters.[20]

Gimmicks are a high-risk strategy that candidates behind in the polls occasionally use, but they rarely work. A gimmick is a prop used by a candidate to rattle an opponent. The 2000 New York senatorial race between Republican Rick Lazio and First Lady Hillary Rodham Clinton demonstrated how a gimmick backfires in a debate.

Lazio walked across the stage, stood directly in front of Clinton, placed a letter into her hands, and demanded that she sign it. The letter pledged that both candidates would disavow the use of "soft money" or unregulated campaign contributions spent on their behalf by political party organizations. Lazio's campaign had prepared the letter, which he had already signed. Clinton stated that she would need time to examine the contents before responding. Lazio's ploy flopped as noted by one focus group member watching the debate: "Oh, cute . . . Sight unseen, you don't sign a document like that." Clinton's calm response and the perception that Lazio had invaded her personal space hurt the Republican. The tactic backfired because it drummed up sympathy for Clinton, which is the last thing that Lazio wanted to do.[21]

Consultants try to impress candidates that personal appearance, grooming, and visual cues can leave a lasting image with viewers. Television debates heighten visual cues because voters can react to the clothes, makeup, and personal demeanor of the candidates. John Kennedy and Richard Nixon appeared on the stage for the first televised presidential debate on September 25, 1960. Kennedy was well-rested, coifed, immaculately dressed, and self-possessed. Nixon looked tired and haggard, with dark circles under his eyes from a recent hospital stay. Nixon who had "five o'clock shadow" from his heavy beard applied a "light coating of Lazy Shave," which did little to hide the stubble on his face. Both candidates were highly articulate. The audience who watched the debate thought Kennedy had beaten Nixon, whereas those who had listened on radio thought Nixon won. The viewing audience was far larger than the number of listeners. Kennedy was the first candidate to understand that visual perceptions influence voters' judgments. The debate enhanced Senator Kennedy's stature as "presidential" material qualified to defeat the experienced and world-traveled Vice President, Richard Nixon.[22]

Visual cues can point out a particular character feature or flaw of a candidate that can have serious repercussions. George Bush, Sr. looked at his watch several times toward the close of the second presidential debate in 1992 as if expressing his impatience that the debate was not yet finished. Ross Perot's running mate, former Admiral James Stockdale, wandered around his podium seemingly lost near the end of his vice presidential debate with Democrat Al Gore and Republican Dan Quayle in 1992. Perot was the Reform Party candidate and participated in the presidential debates while

Stockdale participated in the lone vice presidential debate. Viewers were not sure whether Stockdale was disoriented or had a misconception about when the debate was going to end. The episode did not enhance Perot's viability as a third party option when his vice presidential candidate appeared not up to the task of debating.

Debate Preparation

Debate preparation is essential to success. Some candidates are introverts, some extroverts; some are fast learners, others not. The style of preparation, the amount of preparation, debate experience, and candidate self-possession are part of candidate training for debates. George W. Bush went through numerous mock debates with his debate coach, Andrew Card playing the role of Al Gore in 2000. Self-possessed, relaxed, knowledgeable, and glib candidates such as John McCain and Bill Clinton might need less formal preparation. In fact, Clinton maintained a hectic campaign schedule just prior to a debate. Clinton could not resist meeting an audience or attending rallies even on the day of a debate because crowds energized him.

A briefing book prepared by the campaign staff helps to train many presidential, senatorial, and gubernatorial candidates for a debate. The book includes important facts, figures, and themes to communicate with voters, as well as techniques to answer questions. The book might also suggest possible attacks by the opponent and canned responses that would resonate effectively in the debate. Candidates spend substantial time memorizing information and lines for sound bites. Jimmy Carter's debate briefing book apparently ended up in the possession of the Ronald Reagan campaign in 1980, according to *The Washington Post*. Congressman David Stockman (R-IL) and campaign staffer David Gergen used this material to prepare the former California governor for the debate.[23]

Familiarity with the debate setting is important. The candidate and campaign staff should conduct a walk-through of the stage to ensure that debate preparations are completed. Putting the candidate at ease by walking around the stage and familiarizing them with their surroundings is essential for success. Staff members test the sound and alter the height of the candidate's microphone. Adjusting the lights, the height of chairs and the room temperature for the comfort of the candidates often requires negotiation to control for candidate size differential and how much one candidate might sweat on stage. Bright lighting alerts the campaign that the candidate should wear darker colors to minimize glare and reflection. Subdued lighting means that the candidate can wear bolder colors. Minimizing distractions enables a candidate to focus on the substance of the debate rather than their surroundings.

THE ROLE OF EARNED MEDIA

Campaigns plant sound bites in candidate speeches, press conference statements, debates, and talk show appearances to gain positive coverage on network newscasts. Thirty years ago, the average sound bite lasted one minute; today, it is approximately eight seconds. Attention spans of viewers have shortened because the remote control facilitates channel surfing for the bored television watcher. The increased number of cable and satellite stations makes competition even keener for a discerning audience. ABC, CBS, and NBC had a near monopoly on television viewership before the growth of cable television in the 1980s and 1990s. Today, only about half of the television viewing audience watches the evening news on the three major networks each night. Networks and their local affiliates realize that the pace of coverage on the news has much to do with ratings. Television news has become faster-paced in order to maintain its share of viewers throughout the broadcast, which means that long excerpts from candidate speeches are out of vogue.[24]

Broadcast media coverage of campaigns has changed from covering events to political commentary. The Center for Media and Public Affairs (CMPA) found that while the amount of campaign coverage on the networks diminished only slightly between 1996 and 2000, commentary increased at the expense of candidates' talking about their campaigns. "Over six times as much campaign talk came from news anchors and reporters as from candidates themselves (74 percent versus 12 percent)." CMPA also found that *Late Night with David Letterman* gave presidential candidates George W. Bush and Al Gore the lengthiest forum (13 minutes) to talk about their campaigns during the 2000 election. The results indicated that more commentary about the "horse race" (in 71 percent of stories) than about issues (in 40 percent of stories) drove news coverage. More active and judgmental reporting has supplanted the passive non-judgmental reporting by television reporters from decades past. The implication is that television journalists play a greater role in filtering the news from campaigns to viewers today.[25]

Print journalism has followed a similar route as television focusing more on the events, personalities, and attributes of candidates than on the policies they espouse. Christopher Hanson, writing in the highly respected *Columbia Journalism Review,* described how 2004 campaign stories focused primarily on process (frontloading or early appearance of primaries on the calendar) and candidate foibles around the country. *The Washington Post* covered a Democratic presidential candidate forum on January 23, 2003. "Senator John Edwards, D-NC, was observed chewing gum while rival candidates spoke. Senator John Kerry of Massachusetts applied lip balm during the same event." *The Associated Press* reported on February 1, 2003 that former Vermont Governor Howard Dean received the endorsement of actor Martin Sheen who plays the President of the United States on the television series *The West Wing.* The propriety of how media outlets cover candidates is debatable; however, the fact that candidates have to adapt to the vagaries of press coverage is not debatable.[26]

RELATIONSHIP OF THE PRESS AND CANDIDATES

"What's your sense of the meaning of a personality-driven campaign? Good? Bad? Is it something that we're evolving to because of our enormous prosperity and because there's no risk of war?" Al Gore's rhetorical reply to *New York* magazine writer Michael Wolff on how he would perform against the personable John McCain if the latter were the Republican presidential nominee in 2000 describes the dilemma many candidates feel when running for office. The relationship between candidates and the press is tenuous at best, but it could best be termed *symbiotic.* Candidates need an outlet to express their views by earning media coverage, and the press needs a story every day to sell print or broadcasting advertising space. Today, media conglomerates such as Rupert Murdoch's *News Corporation* own television networks (Fox and Fox News Channel), important daily newspapers (*New York Post*), politically influential magazines (*The Weekly Standard*) and one of the nation's largest publishing

STYLE OVER SUBSTANCE: COVERAGE OF NATIONAL
WOMEN CANDIDATES

Cultural norms and biases inherent in news coverage pose greater obstacles for women candidates than for men on the campaign trail. Women candidates face stereotypical attitudes not only on issues but also on personal appearance. One highly regarded study on women candidates for governor and state attorney general found that 16.9 percent of paragraphs in newspapers discussed personal attributes compared with 12.3 percent of paragraphs for men during the 1998 campaign. Comments are often sexist, whether the intent is positive or negative: "A grandmotherly redhead dressed in a sensible suit climbs out of the back seat . . . If anyone in the lobby recognizes Gov. Jane Hull (R-AZ) . . . they don't let on." The press critiqued Senator Hillary Rodham Clinton's diet (eating "little more than a lettuce leaf during fund-raisers") during her 2000 New York Senate campaign. The perception of an assertive, take-charge woman versus a man tends to gain negative press coverage as well. Colorado's 1998 Democratic gubernatorial candidate Gail Schoettler was portrayed as "not a schmoozer . . . She's also been called a 'Nazi' for taking charge at interminable school board meetings." The barriers to election for women candidates are greater because they have to overcome the cultural stereotypes that men do not face. Working with the press is more complex for women candidates because the scrutiny of their personal appearance or habits is greater than it is for men, distracting coverage from the substance they offer.[28]

houses (HarperCollins). Corporations such as Disney (owners of ABC) and General Electric (NBC) buy networks, including news divisions, to make profits. Television ratings and newspaper sales drive up advertising rates, which in turn generate more profit. Most candidates, consultants, and campaign staff accept the fact that business aspects drive the news today. Campaigns that fail to do so have unrealistic expectations.[27]

EFFECTIVE EARNED MEDIA STRATEGIES

Campaigns seek to maximize positive coverage of their candidates by preempting the opposition, by controlling personal access to the candidate, by using daily news coverage, and by managing crises. Campaigns need to be flexible because of changes occurring on the election front (e.g., the Kerry campaign's response to his prostate cancer surgery of 2003) and from the world (e.g., the effect of September 11 on the 2001 Virginia gubernatorial election). Campaigns must address questions about their own ineffective management (e.g., George McGovern's presidential bid in 1972), candidate misstatements (e.g., Bob Dole's calling World War II a "Democrat war" while running for vice president in 1976), or a candidate's personal scandal (e.g., Clinton's addressing Vietnam draft-dodging charges in 1992).

Preempting the Opposition

Preemption helps to inoculate the candidate against attack or to take the initiative on an important policy issue. Communicating that message through a speech, press conference, press release or utilizing the press secretary can be particularly useful.

George W. Bush made numerous speeches on literacy, vouchers, and economic opportunities that correlate with a strong education as he campaigned across the country during the spring of 2000 after wrapping up the Republican presidential nomination. The national press traveled with Bush as he made an important education speech on public school integration in Little Rock, AK. Bush's speech generated major print and nightly broadcast coverage across the country because a southern Republican was addressing the issue of racism at Central High, "a school synonymous with the desegregation fights of the 1950s and, '60s." Furthermore, Little Rock was the home turf of President Bill Clinton whose Vice President, Al Gore, would be the Democratic presidential nominee. Both moves signaled to the press that Bush, running as a "compassionate conservative," would attempt to cut into a traditional Democratic party strength on education. Exit polling data from the election showed that Bush did cut sharply into the margin that Democrats normally possess on the education issue. Among voters who said education mattered most, 52 percent voted for Gore and 44 percent for Bush. Bush's successful use of earned media on the education issue helped portray his views in the political mainstream.[29]

Controlling Access to the Candidate

Two theories exist regarding how much access the press should have to a candidate: the more access the better, or the more access the worse. Candidates who are prone to verbal foibles (such as Ronald Reagan) or who dislike the press (such as Richard Nixon) shield themselves from reporters. Presidential campaigns can use Secret Service and advance teams to cordon off access to the candidate from the national press. Glib politicians such as Senators Orrin Hatch (R-Utah), Chuck Hagel (R-NE), and Chris Dodd (D-CT) are naturals before the camera. The 1998 New York Senate race between incumbent Al D'Amato (R) and challenger Chuck Schumer (D) matched two bare-knuckled candidates who loved the press limelight. During one debate on local television, both candidates were so out of control that the moderator pleaded: "Gentleman, gentleman this is getting out of hand. . . . As the presiding officer, I am in charge here, temporarily." Candidates such as D'Amato and Schumer are not controllable by their campaign staffs, which can result in overexposure to the press.[30]

Most senatorial, gubernatorial, and presidential candidates use their press secretary as a conduit between themselves and reporters. As noted in Chapter 4, the press secretary serves as the official spokesperson for the campaign. The press secretary's (or communications director's) role becomes even more critical as the election approaches. The press secretary works more closely and spends more time with reporters than does any other member of the campaign staff. The tension becomes palpable particularly in a close election contest. The campaign becomes more parsimonious in providing access to the candidate because staff members fear that a blunder or an off-hand remark could lose the election. The press, meanwhile, has a certain expectation of access, which they have become accustomed to during the campaign. The press secretary is in the middle of this storm. George Stephanopoulos, the 1992 Clinton communications director, stated that the campaign felt tremendous pressure near the end of the race because the Arkansas governor appeared headed for victory. Stephanopoulos said, "I was so on edge with some reporters, that I lashed out at E.J. Dionne [of *The Washington Post*] and stormed away from the table over a single adjective he

used in an otherwise straight piece." The self-discipline that characterizes campaigns earlier sometimes results in overreaction when
under pressure.[31]

Utilizing Daily News Coverage

Candidates opt for local news coverage to bolster their candidacies
in an era when paid media are becoming more expensive. Even presidential candidates are spending less time with the national press
and more with local affiliates and newspapers because most consumers read or watch local media.

California's 36th Congressional District race between Jane Harman (D) and Steve Kuykendall (R) provides an excellent example of
how to use local media. The district extends south from Venice Beach
(Los Angeles) toward Long Beach. Jane Harman was running to
regain the seat she vacated in 1998 when she ran and lost the Democratic primary for California governor. The 2000 election pitted
Harman against first-term member Steve Kuykendall. Kuykendall's
communication team decided to plant numerous minor stories "that
had nothing to do with our major message" in local and neighbor-
hood newspapers based on opposition research "with help from the
National Republican Congressional Committee." The purpose was to
throw the Harman team off by responding to inconsequential information appearing in community newspapers and avoiding large
media outlets such as *The Los Angeles Times*. By creating "noise" in the
political environment, Kuykendall's communication consultants,
Adam Mendelsen and Chris St. Hilaire, helped the freshman member
take the offensive in the race. The strategy solidified Kuykendall's
standing in the polls although he eventually lost to Harman by 4,000
votes. Mendelsen and St. Hilaire's strategy of giving exclusives to
community papers was contrary to conventional wisdom about not
playing favorites in the press. In a large media market where there are
many competitive congressional races, attracting earned media on a
daily basis requires ingenuity by the campaign staff.[32]

Managing Scandal

Scandal concerning a candidate's personal life or public record is one
of the worst nightmares that a campaign experiences. Campaign
consultants always ask a prospective client: "Is there anything in

your background that I should know that would cause you or your family profound embarrassment?" (See Chapter 3). After all, the consultants are professionals who want to win and to maintain a good professional reputation. Furthermore, the campaign needs to release all relevant information as soon as possible or revert to damage control, which can have lasting effects. George W. Bush's senior advisor and spokesperson, Karen Hughes was aware of his arrest in 1976 for driving-under-the-influence (DWI). The story became public five days before the election. The campaign's tentative response that evening helped the story fester in the press for a critical 24 hours consuming the campaign, until Bush appeared the next evening with his wife Laura by his side and admitted the truth. The story obscured the campaign's message for two days in the last critical week of the campaign.

Admitting the truth of a scandalous allegation immediately addresses the issue and can even result in a political plus for the candidate. Governor Grover Cleveland of New York ran for the presidency in 1884 on the platform that a "Public Office is a Public Trust." During the summer, a story broke in the *Buffalo Telegraph* that Cleveland had fathered a ten-year old boy out-of-wedlock. Cleveland was informed of the story and he immediately wired back the following message to Democratic party leaders: "WHATEVER YOU DO, TELL THE TRUTH." The admission was immediate even though it was terribly embarrassing. The Cleveland campaign let the press know that the New York Governor also helped provide for the youth's upbringing to put a positive "spin" on the story. The press reaction to the Cleveland admission was mostly positive across the nation. Cleveland's confession put the issue behind him well enough, to win the presidency. [33]

Preempting an allegation is another damage control strategy. Al Gore's admission that he had smoked marijuana in college came within days "after Supreme Court Justice not-to-be Douglas Ginsberg admitted to smoking the illegal narcotic" in 1987. Gore's admission could have derailed his first presidential campaign bid in 1988; however, his disclosure barely registered in the public domain, and the Gore campaign was surprisingly pleased that almost no one cared.[34]

Other crisis management strategies entail a higher risk such as denying allegations, refusing to respond to allegations, demanding proof of the charge, and providing evasive responses to reporters or attacking the press. Bill Clinton's evasive "I did not inhale" response, when asked whether he had ever smoked marijuana, damaged his credibility over something relatively minor. Congressman Wes Cooley (R-OR) denied allegations that he lied on his resume about serving in the Special Forces in Korea. (The Special Forces did not exist at the time Cooley said he served in them. He actually served stateside from 1952–1954.) The allegations became public in the spring of 1996. Reporters then investigated whether Cooley's wife collected veterans' benefits from her first husband, after she had remarried Cooley, by concealing the date of their marriage so that she could collect $900 a month. Cooley met with constituents and bashed reporters within a week of winning his primary in May 1996. State and national Republican party leaders pressured Cooley over two months to quit the race until he relented on August 6, 1996. Republicans saved the seat by replacing Cooley on the ticket with former Congressman Bob Smith (R-OR) who easily won the election. A federal jury convicted Cooley of lying on official documents about his service in 1997. Scandals about incumbents tend to generate more news since they are elected government representatives or a scandal may have remained hidden for years until publicly exposed.[35]

Press conferences, news shows, and talk show appearances give candidates the opportunity to discuss a personal scandal before a regional or national audience to generate sympathy. The candidate has to appear sincere and remorseful, which Bill Clinton did convincingly enough on CBS's *60 Minutes* regarding an extramarital affair with Gennifer Flowers. The interview helped stem the erosion of his support prior to the 1992 New Hampshire primary. Furthermore, the timing of the interview or press conference is essential. The candidate must seize the moment to come clean or as consultants James Carville and Paul Begala would say, "fess up." Carville and Begala suggest that public figures admit that they are wrong, and, if necessary, make amends for their actions. Campaigns offer candidates a very narrow time-frame to make such decisions before the problem snowballs in the public destroying their candidacy. Former actor Ben Jones, who played Cooter on the 1970s television show, *The Dukes of Hazzard* ran for Congress from Georgia in 1988. Stories circulated that Jones had been a womanizer and drank heavily. Instead of lying, Jones sought redemption by admitting the truth: "It's true. I used to spend ninety percent of my money on whiskey and women. The other ten percent I just wasted." Jones was able to put the issue behind him and later won the election. The Carville-Begala sugges-tion provides the best solution to limiting the damage from a scandal or crisis. Public appearances remain the best vehicle for admitting wrongdoing because written statements seem to imply that the candidate is afraid to discuss the issue directly with the press and voters.[36]

THE HOME STRETCH: HOW CAMPAIGNS FINISH

Every race for political office is a marathon. Candidates campaign 12–18 hours a day for weeks, months, and sometimes years. Fatigue, desperation, and euphoria are common feelings by candi-dates toward the end of a campaign. Senator Bob Dole (R-KS) trav-eled "10,534 miles and touched down in 20 states" during the last 96 hours of his losing presidential bid in 1996 to Bill Clinton. Historians estimate that William Jennings Bryan (D-NE) made over 600 speeches (10 to 20 a day) and traveled 18,000 miles (by train) during his campaign of 1896. Bryan gave stump speeches from trains, halls and streets, wherever crowds gathered on his campaign journey across the country. Bryan's grueling pace was amazing even by modern standards. The campaign's exhausting final efforts to communicate and mobilize voters require stamina and the willing-ness to change tactics to campaign wherever necessary to mobilize support.[37]

Candidates and Campaigns

"'We love you! We love you! We love you!'" the crowd chanted as Clinton, who stopped on his way out to snap his fingers to the beat of Aretha Franklin's 'Respect,' disappeared from view." This was *not* Bill Clinton campaigning for the presidency. Bill Clinton was eagerly campaigning for Bill McBride, the 2002 Democratic nominee for Florida governor, just two years after leaving the White House. The former president was blitzing south Florida on behalf of McBride three days before the election visiting Miami, Miami Beach, and Fort Lauderdale. The more Clinton campaigned the more animated he became. Even though energized by large and friendly crowds, many candidates become so fatigued that they make verbal or mental er-rors in the last days of the campaign. President George Bush, Sr., had closed to within a few points of the lead late in the 1992 campaign.

Campaigning in Michigan five days before the election, a fatigued president called Bill Clinton and Gore "bozos." Tracking polls showed Bush slipping the next day. Sometimes a campaign becomes even nastier as candidates try to win late deciders. Democrat Chuck Schumer (D-NY) increased the rapidity of his claim that incumbent Senator Al D'Amato (R-NY) had told New Yorkers "too many lies, for too long" during the home stretch of their 1998 senate contest. Schumer unseated D'Amato by a nine-point margin. More often than not, campaigns go positive to get their core supporters out to vote. Approximately, 80 percent of senatorial and gubernatorial races and 90 percent of congressional races are decided by a 10 percent margin or greater. Attack strategies work during the home stretch only when a large percentage of undecided voters remain in a close race as in the Schumer-D'Amato contest.[38]

Mobilizing Voters: How Political Parties Helped Candidates in 2002

Candidates operationalize get-out-the-vote (GOTV) efforts with state parties and relevant interest groups (see Chapter 4). The 2002 midterm elections provide a particularly useful illustration of GOTV efforts by both parties down the home stretch. The case study demonstrates how skillful Republican planning and the willingness to make adjustments paid off on election day. Republicans took note of the successful Democratic party and organized labor GOTV efforts in 2000. Those efforts helped Al Gore win the popular vote and Democrats gained four U.S. Senate seats. Turnout by African-Americans, union members, environmentalists and women—key Democratic constituencies—was unexpectedly high in 2000. Steve Rosenthal, the political director of the AFL-CIO's GOTV operation estimated that union workers consisted of 26 percent of all individuals who voted on election day 2000, "surpassing its share of the overall population." Democrats spent $15 million and the AFL-CIO spent $20 million on GOTV for 2002. As a result, Republican party officials allocated $20 million to counteract the efforts of Democratic GOTV activities in 2002.[39]

Republicans instituted state-of-the-art phone banks in key states calling potential supporters numerous times in the weeks leading up to election day. The National Republican Congressional Committee (NRCC), the official party organization dedicated to electing

Republican House members, instituted the Strategic Task Force to Organize and Mobilize People (STOMP) program. Under STOMP, Republicans from safe districts contributed staff and volunteers to work in competitive congressional races across the country.[40]

Republicans coordinated their GOTV operation with a cross-country blitz by President George W. Bush during the last week of the midterm campaign. Bush visited fifteen states in the last five days of the campaign, making the midterm election a referendum on himself. For example, he attended rallies with Republican candidates in highly competitive senatorial races (Arkansas, Iowa, South Dakota, Missouri, North Carolina and Texas), gubernatorial races (Florida and Texas), and congressional races (Kentucky and Pennsylvania). Bush hop-scotched across the country at a dizzying pace, visiting Iowa, Missouri, Arkansas, and Texas on the Monday before the election.

Democrats countered the Bush blitz with former President Bill Clinton and former Vice President Al Gore stumping for Democratic candidates in New Jersey, Florida, and Maryland. However, the media attention paid to President Bush overshadowed any attempt made by Democrats to change the focus from the president's agenda to their issues of prescription drug benefits, Social Security, and jobs. Republicans regained control of the Senate and increased their margin by six seats in the House of Representatives. Bush was the first president since Franklin Roosevelt (1934) to have his party gain seats in the U.S. House and Senate during his first term in office. Party-centered rather than candidate-centered activities served as the basis for GOTV operations by Republicans in 2002 because the GOP made the elections a referendum on the Bush presidency.

THE AFTERMATH

Campaigns are very personal because it means that 100,000, 1 million, or 100 million adults accept or reject your job application for the position of representative, senator, governor, or president. Voters serve as the hiring committee vetting resumes, watching candidates being interviewed, and comparing them to make a decision. The most qualified candidate, the best looking, or the most honest does not necessarily win. The candidate who is the *best fit* for that jurisdiction, that state, or the nation at a particular time wins the election.

Darwinian as that may sound the fact remains that a candidate's fate is ultimately in the hands of voters. Losing presidential candidates such as Gerald Ford, Jimmy Carter, George Bush Sr. and Al Gore have a particularly difficult time adjusting to defeat. Ford, Carter, and Bush, Sr., lost presidential reelection bids whereas Gore won the popular vote. Overcoming the bitterness take years, and sometimes losing candidates suffer from depression. Candidates remonstrate about the factors leading to their losses. Incumbents are often defeated because of a mediocre job approval rating, personal scandal, or a national tide of support for the opposing party carries them out of office. In most cases, campaigns are for incumbents to lose, rather than for challengers to win. Challengers have a far more difficult task because they tend to have lower name recognition and fewer resources. Their rationalization for defeat is much simpler, but no less painful.

Winners celebrate with the adrenaline of victory by raising hands, slapping backs, or even gesturing thanks to a higher authority. Hillary Rodham Clinton said in her victory speech, "Sixty-two counties, sixteen months, three debates, two opponents, and six black pantsuits later, because of you [the voters], here we are." Victory also reminds national politicians of the sobering responsibilities of governing. Bob Ehrlich (R) elected Maryland governor in 2002, a strongly partisan Democratic state, jokingly remarked: "When you're a Republican in Maryland you tend not to make commitments." Governing means that campaign commitments made are tempered by the reality of governing. Candidates become elected officials and move from campaign mode to governing mode. Campaign staff may move to Washington, D.C., or to a state capital to help the newly elected official set up shop. The campaign consultants move on to their next race. James Carville remarked, "I am nowhere as in love with victory, as I am fearful of defeat . . . To me that is ecstasy." Victory brings the sobriety of responsibility. Defeat brings abject sadness.[41]

CONCLUSION

The pace of campaigns is a whirling dervish of activity that gives little time for reflection. Campaigns that plan effectively for contingencies are best-suited adapting to the inevitable problems that arise on the campaign trail. The daily coverage of campaigns often is the greatest source of publicity for candidates, good or bad. Campaigns that plan events, speeches, or memorable lines from debates can get their message to voters through earned media. No candidate wants to be a Bill McBride, the 2002 Democratic gubernatorial nominee from Florida. McBride pulled nearly even with Florida's Republican governor Jeb Bush. During an October 22 debate, McBride failed to answer "moderator Tim Russert's flurry of questions how he would pay for his plan to reduce class size in public schools." McBride's ambiguous response pointed out his inexperience and lack of ability to think on his feet at a crucial juncture of the campaign. There is no excuse when a candidate fails to have a canned answer how to pay for a program that serves as the centerpiece of their campaign. Planning cannot anticipate all the problems and contingencies on the campaign trail; however, the exercise of planning enables a candidate to think more nimbly and to improvise, which is necessary when running for office. The crescendo of activity in a campaign's final days gives a candidate an adrenaline rush that few individuals experience in their lives. Whether the outcome is victory or defeat, candidates feel the energy of the large and boisterous crowds greeting them in the last days of the campaign. Those memories may be embellished in time but remind a candidate that there is much worthwhile about running for office.[42]

STUDY/DISCUSSION QUESTIONS

What attributes make for an effective candidate on the campaign trail?

How is the amount of time and effort by the candidate and surrogates determined by the staff?

What are some effective earned media strategies that campaigns use?

How can debates play a critical role in a campaign? Does the amount of press attention to the debate make a difference?

What additional hurdles or barriers do women candidates face that men do not face when campaigning?

How should a candidate manage a personal crisis or scandal when campaigning?

SUGGESTED READINGS

Achenbach, Joel. *It Looks Like a President, Only Smaller: Trailing Campaign 2000*. New York: Simon & Schuster, 2001.

Crouse, Timothy. *The Boys on the Bus*. New York: Ballantine Books, 1973.

Farnsworth, Stephen J., and S. Robert Lichter. *The Nightly News Nightmare: Television's Coverage of U.S. Presidential Elections 1988–2000*. Lanham, MD: University Press of America, 2002.

Fenno, Richard F., Jr. *Home Style: House Members in Their Districts*. Boston: Little, Brown, 1978.

Iyengar, Shanto, and Richard Reeves, eds. *Do the Media Govern: Politicians, Voters, and Reporters in America*. Thousand Oaks, CA: Sage, 1997.

Jamieson, Kathleen Hall. *Everything You Think You Know About Politics . . . and Why You're Wrong*. New York: Basic Books, 2000.

Jamieson, Kathleen Hall, and David S. Birdsell. *Presidential Debates: The Challenge of Creating an Informed Electorate*. New York: Oxford University Press, 1988.

Kerbel, Matthew Robert. *Edited for Television: CNN, ABC and the 1992 Presidential Campaign*. Boulder, CO: Westview, 1994.

Moore, James C., and Wayne Slater. *Bush's Brain: How Karl Rove Made George W. Bush Presidential*. New York: John Wiley & Sons, 2003.

Simpson, Dick W. *Winning Elections: A Handbook of Modern Participatory Politics*. New York: HarperCollins, 1996.

Stephanopoulos, George. *All Too Human: A Political Education*. Boston: Little, Brown, 1999.

NOTES

1. Anita Dunn, "The Best Campaign Wins," in *Campaigns and Elections American Style*, eds. James A. Thurber and Candice J. Nelson (Boulder, CO: Westview, 1995), 119 for all references.
2. Philip D. Duncan and Christine C. Lawrence, *Politics in America 1996* (Washington, DC: Congressional Quarterly Press, 1995), 1406, quotation; Michael Barone with Richard Cohen, *The Almanac of American Politics 2002* (Washington, DC: National Journal, 2001), 1612, background on the 5th Congressional District of Washington, Galusha Gow, and 1615, 2000 election.

3. See Dick W. Simpson, *Winning Elections: A Handbook of Modern Participatory Politics* (New York: HarperCollins, 1996) to understand the difficulties faced by running against an entrenched congressional incumbent (Dan Rostenkowski) in a party primary (chap. IX); David Mayhew, *Congress: The Electoral Connection* (New Haven, CT: Yale University Press, 1974) on "credit claiming."

4. Timothy Crouse, *The Boys on the Bus* (New York: Ballantine Books, 1973), 16 and 23, for McGovern morning and afternoon/ evening schedules.

5. Martin Schram, *Running for President: A Journal of the Carter Campaign* (New York: Pocket Books, 1977), 428–30.

6. Ibid; see page 431 for the allocation of site visits used for the Carter campaign.

7. "Jean Carnahan to Announce Decision," *The Associated Press*, October 30, 2000; "Get out the vote efforts energized," *Associated Press*, November 2, 2000, both on Carnihan tribute concert.

8. Richard F. Fenno, Jr., *Home Style: House Members in Their Districts* (Boston: Little, Brown, 1978).

9. "Florida Governors' Portraits: Bob Graham," Florida Division of Human Resources, State of Florida. Accessed May 12, 2003 at *www.dhr.dos.state.fl.us/governors/graham.html*; "At the margins: unusual candidates, unusual tactics," *Associated Press*, November 6, 2000, regarding DiNizio.

10. Pat Burson, "Tears and Cheers for Senator Wellstone," *Newsday*, October 30, 2002. Accessed November 8, 2002 at *www.newsday.com*, first quote; Tom Scheck, "Wellstone staff apologizes for memorial service rhetoric," *Minnesota Public Radio*, October 30, 2002. Accessed November 8, 2002 at *www.news.mpr.org/features*, second quote; Kavita Kumar et al. "Republicans decry service as partisan," *Minneapolis Star-Tribune*, October 30, 2002. Accessed November 8, 2002 at *www.startribune.com/stories*.

11. Jake Tapper, "A 'major league asshole,'" September 4, 2000. Accessed May 12, 2003 at *www.salon.com*; Moynihan quote from "Moynihan endorses Bradley, says Gore 'can't be elected,'" CNN.com, September 23, 1999. Accessed May 4, 2000 at *www .cnn.com/ALLPOLITICS/stories/1999/09/23/president.2000/bradley .moynihan*.

12. "Sen. McCain on the Trail," *Online PBS NewsHour: A NewsHour with Jim Lehrer Transcript*, September 1, 1999. Accessed May 12, 2003

at *www.pbs.org/newshour/bb/election/july-dec99/mccain_9-1.html*, all references.

13. Jefferson/Jackson Day Dinner. Hosted by the Michigan Democratic Party. Accessed May 12, 2003 at *www.mi-democrats.com/topics/jeff-jack2003.htm;* Scott County Republican Lincoln Day Dinner featuring Congressman Ray LaHood (R-IL). Accessed May 12, 2003 at *www.illinoisleader.com/calendar/calendarview.asp?e=1595.*

14. Sherrod Brown, *Congress from the Inside* (Kent, OH: Kent University Press, 1999), 200, citing Molly Ivins.

15. Ibid.

16. "Bush-Gore debate draws big audience," *Associated Press,* October 4, 2000, for all data.

17. Jules Witcover, *Marathon: Pursuit of the Presidency 1972–1976* (New York: Viking Press, 1977), 597, on Ford.

18. Michael Barone and Grant Ujifusa, *Almanac of American Politics 2000* (Washington, DC: National Journal, 1999), 774, on Kerry-Weld debates and first quote on "one-liners"; "Why Are People Poor?" Harvard University report. Accessed May 13, 2003 at *www.digitas.harvard.edu*, regarding all references to the first Kerry-Weld debate on "why are people poor?"

19. "Guv Candidates Debate in Hibbing: No New Initiatives Announced During Latest Issues Discussion," *Associated Press,* October 7, 1998. Accessed May 13, 2003 at *www.channel4000.com/news/stories/news-campaign98-981007-080052.html,* regarding the Hibbing debate with Coleman and Humphrey comments; Jesse Ventura, *I Ain't Got Time to Bleed* (New York: Villard, 1999), 165, quote and discussion of how responses given on page 164.

20. Ron Faucheux, "Debate Watcher's Guide: How to Score Candidate Performances," *Campaigns and Elections,* October/November 1996, 30. (All Clinton/Bush quotes on the 1992 debate.) Gary Langer, "New Blame Game," ABCNews.com, January 4, 2002. Accessed May 23, 2003 at *www.abcnew.go.com/sections/politics/DailyNews/daschle_poll020104.html.*

21. Martha M. Moore, "Viewers: 1st round to 1st lady," *USA Today,* September 14, 2000, 9A, all references.

22. Theodore H. White, *The Making of the President 1960* (New York: Pocket Books, 1961), 344.

23. Howard Kurtz, "Choreographers Had Plan for Every Step in 1980 Debate," *The Washington Post,* July 2, 1983, A3, concerning

memorizing facts, figures, and lines; Martin Schram, "Justice Dept. Asks FBI to Join Probe of Briefing Papers," *The Washington Post*, July 1, 1983, A1. Articles accessed May 13, 2003 at *www.museum.tv/debateweb/html/history/1980/headlines.htm*.

24. Daniel Hallin, "Sound Bite News: Television Coverage of Elections," in *Do the Media Govern: Politicians, Voters, and Reporters in America*, ed. Shanto Iyengar and Richard Reeves. Thousand, Oaks, CA: Sage, 1997, 60–61, on sound bite length and the pace of coverage; Stephen Ansolabehere, Roy Behr, and Shanto Iyengar, *The Media Game: American Politics in the Television Age* (New York: Macmillan, 1993), 43.

25. "Campaign 2000 Final: How TV News Covered the General Election Campaign," Center for Media and Public Affairs' *Media Monitor*, November/December 2000. Accessed May 13, 2003 at *www.cmpa.com/Mediamon/mm111200.htm*. All data citations; Hallin, 61, on passivity of the press.

26. Christopher Hanson, "The Invisible Primary: Now Is The Time For All-Out News Coverage," *Columbia Journalism Review*, March/April 2003. Accessed May 13, 2003 at *www.cjr.org/year/03/2/hanson.asp*, quoting *The Washington Post* and *Associated Press*.

27. Gore's reflection about a "personality-driven campaign" is found in Michael Wolff, "How I Got Over My Al Gore-a-phobia," *New York Magazine*, February 21, 2000. Reprinted online. Accessed May 13, 2003 at *www.newyorkmetro.com/nymetro/news/media/columns/medialife/2198/index.html*.

28. James Devitt, (report). *Framing Gender on the Campaign Trail: Women's Executive Leadership and the Press* (New York: The White House Project, 1999), statistical data from page 5, descriptions of Jane Hull and Gail Schoettler from page 17; Jennifer L. Pozner, March 13, 2001. "Cosmetic Coverage." Accessed May 13, 2003 at *www.alternet.org/story.html?StoryID=10592*. Pozer is the Women's Desk editor from Fairness and Accuracy in Reporting (FAIR), a media watchdog.

29. Suzi Parker, "Deep in the Heart of Clinton Country," Salon.com, March 25, 2000. Accessed May 14, 2003 at *www.salon.com/politics2000/feature/2000/03/25/bush/index.html*, regarding the Little Rock visit; Voter News Service, national exit poll results from 2000, when 13,130 respondents were interviewed on voting preferences and issues. Accessed February 1, 2001 at *www.cnn.com/ELECTION/2000/*.

30. Joel Siegel, "Al, Chuck Hit Hard," *New York Daily News*, October 26, 1998. Accessed November 9, 1998 at *www.nydailynews.com*.
31. George Stephanopoulos, *All Too Human: A Political Education* (Boston: Little, Brown, 1999), 100, quote, on lashing out at E. J. Dionne.
32. Adam Mendelsen and Chris St. Hilaire, "Getting Press Coverage in Campaigns," *Campaigns and Elections*, May 2001, 60.
33. Morgan Stewart, "Damage Control," *Campaigns and Elections*, March 1994, 25; H. P. Jeffers, *An Honest President: The Life and Presidencies of Grover Cleveland* (New York: HarperPerennial, 2000), 106–108, including quote regarding Cleveland.
34. Stewart, 26.
35. Ibid, 26 on types of damage control; "Cooley Struggles to Clear His Name," CNN's AllPolitics, May 29, 1996. Accessed May 22, 2003 at *www.cnn.com/ALLPOLITICS/1996/news/9605/29/cooley/index.shtml*; "Fake Service Claims," *VFW* magazine, November 2001. Accessed May 22, 2003 at *www.vetsexpo.org/frauds.htm*. Accessed May 22, 2003; Philip D. Duncan and Christine C. Lawrence, *Politics in America 1998* (Washington, DC: Congressional Quarterly, 1997), 1200, on marriage allegations.
36. James Carville and Paul Begala, *Buck Up, Suck Up . . . and Come Back When You Foul Up: 12 Winning Secrets From the War Room* (New York: Simon & Schuster, 2002), 177, on "fessing up", and 182, the Ben Jones story.
37. "Bridge to 2000," *Newsweek Special Election Issue*, November 18, 1996, 124, references to Dole's travel during the last 96 hours of the campaign; Paul F. Boller, Jr., *Presidential Campaigns* (New York: Oxford University Press, 1984), 170, references on the Bryan campaign.
38. Mike Allen and Manuel Roig-Franzia, "Presidents Clash over Florida Governor's Race," *The Washington Post*, November 3, 2002, A4, on Clinton campaigning for Bill McBride; see references in chap. 4 regarding the Schumer slogan, on issue typologies.
39. Dan Balz and David Broder, "Close Election Turns on Voter Turnout," *Washington Post*, November 1, 2002, A1.
40. Jonathan E. Kaplan, "Republicans discount possible House losses." *The Hill*, October 30, 2002. Accessed November 7, 2002 at *www.hillnews.com*.
41. Barbara Mikulski et al., *Nine Women and Counting* (New York: HarperPerennial, 2001), 207, regarding Hillary Rodham Clinton;

Craig Whitlock and Lori Montgomery, "Quick Start, Ready Help for Ehrlich," *Washington Post*, November 7, 2002, A42; James Carville and Mary Matalin, *All's Fair: Love, War, and Running for the White House* (New York: Random House, 1994), 470.

42. Allen and Roig-Franzia, A4, citing Russert's question to McBride.

CHAPTER 9

Campaigns and American Democracy

Democracy is the only system that persists in asking the powers that be whether they are the powers that ought to be[1]
—**Sydney J. Harris, Journalist**

The dramatic telephone exchange with Governor George W. Bush and Vice President Al Gore, Jr. that began this book characterizes the norms and reality that reflect candidates in their quest for public office. The quest begins with a personal desire to hold public office and (or) to bring about political and social change. Reality tempers that quest, as every candidate has personal and professional strengths and weaknesses. A good campaign organization recognizes, enhances, and protects its candidate. Campaigns for national or statewide office execute a plan to win an election through the public airwaves and on the ground by highlighting the virtues of their candidate and (or) by reflecting on the limitations of the opponent.

The presentation of self, as political scientist Richard Fenno would say, or the presentation of the opponent's self, has been generalized by many press observers as simplistic, immoral, and manipulative. Journalist Jules Witcover has contended that "money and hired guns" have corrupted politics. Yet, politics has never been pure going back to the very foundations of our nation, when Jeffersonian Republicans and Adamsonian Federalists engaged in a sometimes profane and, what we would deem today, an unpatriotic name-calling campaign (see Chapter 1). Thus, the dynamic of competition brings out the best and worst in candidates including the Founders. The worst is well-documented in newspapers, magazines, history books, and writings on current affairs. Here we shall focus on the less publicized but undervalued argument that campaigns and political choices serve democracy imperfectly but well.[2]

THE PERMANENT CAMPAIGN

The United States has an extraordinary number of elections compared with the rest of the world. Professor Anthony King argues "U.S. elected officials in many cases have very short terms of office *and* face the prospect of being defeated in primary elections *and* have to run for office more as individuals rather than standard-bearers *and* have continually to raise large sums of money to finance their own elections." The amount and frequency of electoral entrepreneurship engaged in by candidates make the process servile to self-interest. The "permanent campaign," according to King implies that politicians adapt and change to the environment to protect against their own "vulnerability." The theater of campaigns is merely for show and not tied to any rational purpose for governing. Candidate-centered politics, given these modern conditions of campaigning, only debases the democratic process.[3]

The citizen-based model of politics assumes that campaigns are responsive to voters' interests. Citizens are information seekers who search for knowledge based on their interest, time, and effort. Information-seeking entails costs but the payoff is higher. Not only does the quality of information matter, so does the *quantity*, according to political scientist Samuel Popkin. Citizens get reacquainted with politicians every two years through paid media, earned media, and personal campaigning. Popkin argues that undervaluing the symbolic nature of campaigns fails to reflect the importance of rituals and practices that tie Americans to their historical roots and political traditions.[4]

Criticism by journalists and academics regarding the use of the American flag as a political prop has frequently been justified. The flag came back in vogue during the 1980s as Ronald Reagan's presidency infused the nation with a sense of patriotism. Some candidates continue to use the flag as a backdrop to inoculate themselves against charges of being unpatriotic. However, the flag appeared in political campaigns for the first one hundred fifty years of American history. It fell out of vogue in the post-Kennedy era of Vietnam and Watergate when trust in our political institutions fell to their nadir.

Political symbols such as the flag, even when crassly used in American politics, do tie citizens to their democratic traditions. The heterogeneous cultures that inhabit the United States mean that political symbols connect citizens to campaigns, representatives, and government, more importantly than in homogenous democracies such as Germany, France, and Britain, which share centuries of a common culture. Americans willingly accept the political ritual of campaigning for office because it utilizes symbols that commonly connect people of diverse backgrounds to a shared political culture. How those symbols appear in campaigns is test-marketed for appeal, but that does not make them devoid of value.[5]

THE CHANGING MOSAIC OF AMERICAN POLITICS

The changing mosaic of American politics is the interaction of diverse cultures and 21st century technology. The interaction is often messy, confusing, and full of mistakes. The diverse characteristics shaping American culture continue to change and politicians will have to adapt to those changes. Today, 31 percent of the nation's population is non-white. By 2060, the majority of the American population will be non-white according to demographer Leon Bouvier. Because of the rapid demographic shift, politicians may have to diversify appeals culturally. George W. Bush and Al Gore were the first presidential candidates to record messages in Spanish. Bilingual campaign appeals are now commonplace in states with large Latino populations such as Arizona, California, Colorado, Florida, and New Mexico. The Latino population in the United States increased from 8.9 percent to 12.5 percent from 1990–2000, as Latinos are now the largest minority group in the country. The prevalence of bilingual national advertising and earned media appeals will become more common in future decades.[6]

The rapid pace of technological change only facilitates interaction with voter groups, as campaigns are able to target them more precisely. Technology has increased the types of media available to campaigns to interact with voters including newspapers, radio, television, direct mail, websites, and e-mail. Venues of advertising are likely to increase rather than decrease, in the future. The marketplace reflects a variety not only among the media but also within each medium (e.g., in radio, classical, jazz, rap, country, classic rock, hip-hop, news, talk radio, and international stations). The implications are that communications tools used by campaigns will be continually refined to reach voters in one of the most culturally diverse nations in the world.

THE REMAINING CONSTANT

Despite all of the changes and adaptations that take place, the motivations and reasons why individuals run for office remain constant. The motivation to seek public office has remained relatively unchanged over the course of American political history. Controversial issues, compelling personal reasons, civic duty, career advancement, and ego are motivational incentives to compete. For politicians in a democracy, the notion of free competition permits for some altruistic candidate motivation.

Competitive elections enable voters to exercise some restraint over elected politicians in a democracy, no matter how imperfect. Even the great British Prime Minister Winston Churchill, who saw Britain through its darkest days during World War II was ousted from power less than half a year after the war ended by Labour Party leader Clement Atlee. President George Bush, Sr. was ousted from office by challenger Bill Clinton a mere 18 months following the first Persian Gulf War, when the United States decisively defeated Iraq and pushed it out of Kuwait. No one could have predicted that electoral outcome when George Bush, Sr., recorded an astonishing 89 percent job approval in the April 1991 Gallup poll. Bush's perceived inability to improve a slumping economy resulted in his 1992 defeat. Bush's sense of duty and political experience motivated him to run, but he failed to convince enough voters with a rationale to reelect him.[7]

Tempering the motivation is the reality of running for office. The ability to receive important political endorsements, raise money, or self-fund the campaign alerts candidates to the prospective hardships of seeking election. Candidates must also withstand scrutiny by the press and opponents regarding their personal backgrounds and still believe they are electable. Finally, candidates must address family concerns in determining whether to run for election or reelection. These factors not only shape a candidate's decision-making process on whether to run for office, but also determine the dynamic of an electoral contest for other prospective candidates.

CAMPAIGNS AND AMERICAN DEMOCRACY

The interaction within the campaign among the candidate, consultants, and staff creates a world of politics within the campaign. Candidates and their campaign managers must manage the internal machinations of the campaign so that the external campaign against the opponent is waged effectively. The internal squabbling on the Dole presidential campaign in 1996 (see Chapter 4) between campaign manager Scott Reed and media consultants Mike Murphy and Don Sipple took time and attention away from the campaign's main target, President Bill Clinton.

Teamwork within the campaign is essential to minimize internal conflict and keep the attention on the opponent. The George W. Bush campaign of 2000 was quite successful in this regard because strategist Karl Rove had authority in and the final say about the campaign. The last three individuals elected President vested one person to run their campaign: George Bush, Sr. in 1988 with Jim Baker, Bill Clinton in 1992 with James Carville, and George W. Bush in 2000 with Karl Rove. Campaign organizations exist to win elections; but are often not managed democratically. However, the output of well-run message driven campaigns does promote democracy because the clear articulation of ideas crystallizes choice rather than muddies them. Polling, paid advertising, earned media, and now the Internet are tools that facilitate messages to voters in a culture driven more by technology than personalization. The simplicity of appeals to targeted audiences reflects a modern world, where the sources of information stimuli are increasing. The campaign's difficult task requires attracting attention to the candidate through the permeation and repetition of a campaign message that wins votes through the media or on the campaign trail.

Political scientists and journalists question the values of campaign consultants because the tone and endless continuum of modern campaigns seem to sully the democratic process. Promoting permanent campaigns, as Anthony King discussed earlier, would seem to focus the business of politics on marketing and selling rather than policymaking. If consultants encourage pandering to constituents in order to maximize a candidate's chances at winning, then representation becomes a means to a more important prospective end, getting elected. Nevertheless, the very nature of campaigning through events, debates, speeches, press releases, and even sound bites contributes information to voters, as Popkin articulated. The fact is that voters have more information before them today than ever before, which may create greater confusion. However, in a democracy it is *their* responsibility to assimilate that information and make the best decision possible given an imperfect world. No matter how odious, brazen, annoying, or disingenuous a candidate's claims may be during an election contest, the next election follows shortly thereafter to make a necessary correction. The emergence of the Republican party in the mid 1850s to challenge the Democratic party made elections competitive. Since 1860, Democrats have maintained a majority in the House of Representatives 58.1 percent of the time, whereas Republicans have occupied the White House 59.1 percent of the time. The result has been that the party-centered politics before 1960 and the candidate-centered politics since 1960 have produced turnover, often uncomfortably or for the wrong reasons. Yet, in the long-run those choices have served the nation well because they have been made by voters. As famed political scientist V. O. Key said nearly forty years ago, "Voters are not fools."[8]

STUDY/DISCUSSION QUESTIONS

How do campaigns contribute to the democratic process?

How much responsibility do voters have in the electoral process? Do you believe it is greater than, the same as, or less than the responsibility of the candidates running for office?

Write a memorandum to the chair of the Republican National Committee or Democratic National Committee suggesting how to improve political campaigns.

SUGGESTED READINGS

Kamber, Victor, and Paul Simon. *Poison Politics: Are Negative Campaigns Destroying Democracy?* Cambridge, MA: Perseus Books, 1997.

Key, Vladimir Orlando, and Milton Cummings. *The Responsible Electorate.* Cambridge, MA: Belknap Press of the Harvard University Press, 1966.

King, Anthony S. *Running Scared: Why America's Politicians Campaign Too Much and Govern Too Little.* New York: Free Press, 1999.

Ornstein, Norman J., and Thomas E. Mann, eds. *The Permanent Campaign and Its Future.* Washington, DC: AEI Press, 2000.

Popkin, Samuel L. *The Reasoning Voter: Communication and Persuasion in Presidential Campaigns.* Chicago: University of Chicago Press, 1991.

Witcover, Jules. *No Way to Pick a President: How Money and Hired Guns Have Debased American Elections.* New York: Routledge, 2001.

NOTES

1. QuoteGarden.com. Accessed May 16, 2003 at *www.quotegarden .com/election/election-day.html.*
2. Richard F. Fenno, Jr., *Home Style: House Members in Their Districts* (Boston: Little, Brown, 1978); Jules Witcover, *No Way to Pick a President: How Money and Hired Guns Have Debased American Elections* (New York: Routledge, 2001) quote on money and hired guns.
3. Anthony King, "Running Scared," in *Taking Sides: Political Issues,* 11th ed., George McKenna and Stanley Feingold (Guilford, CT: Dushkin, 1999), 31–40, quote on page 32.
4. Samuel L. Popkin, "The Reasoning Voter," in *Taking Sides: Political Issues,* 11th ed., George McKenna and Stanley Feingold (Guilford, CT: Dushkin, 1999), 22–30.
5. Ibid; Popkin discusses how symbols are very important in politics.
6. "State and County" Quick Facts, U.S. Census Bureau. *www.quickfacts.census.gov* (regarding the percentage of non-whites and Latinos in 2000); Leon Bouvier, *Peaceful Invasions: Immigration and Changing America* (Lanham, MD: University Press of America, 1992), on majority-minority population; "Table 1. United States— Race and Hispanic Origin: 1790–1990," United States Census Bureau (report). Accessed May 19, 2003 at *www.census.gov/ population/documented/twps00561tab.01pdf;* provides the Latino population of the United States in 1990.
7. "Bush Approval at 89 Percent, Highest in Polling History," *The Gallup Monthly Poll,* March 1991, 2; survey taken February 28– March 3, 1991.
8. Vladimir Orlando Key, Jr., with the assistance of Milton Cummings, Jr., *The Responsible Electorate* (Cambridge, MA: Belknap, 1966), 8.

The 2004 Iowa Caucus and New Hampshire Primary

Elections are most often lost, not won. The early lessons from the 2004 Democratic presidential nomination demonstrate how voter preferences can change dramatically, in the course of several weeks, altering the dynamic of a presidential nomination contest.

THE PRE-NOMINATION FIGHT

Early in 2003, the presumptive leader of the pack was Senator John Kerry (D-MA). Kerry, a Vietnam War hero serving in his fourth U.S. Senate term, was regarded as a formidable candidate to face President George W. Bush in the 2004 elections because of his war experience and foreign affairs expertise. These candidate attributes seemed necessary in the wake of 9/11 and the wars in Afghanistan and Iraq to inoculate a Democrat against charges of being weak in national security affairs. The Kerry campaign did not get off to a fast start—the candidate would often ramble for 25–30 minutes in front of small group audiences and give excruciatingly long answers to questions from citizens or reporters. Furthermore, the candidate did not articulate a clear message why he was running for president. Kerry's support for the Iraq war resolution and then his subsequent displeasure with the war seemed contradictory to many Democratic voters.

Dr. Howard Dean (D-VT), the former governor of Vermont, shrewdly positioned himself as the anti-Iraq war candidate in the Democratic party for president. Activists from the populist wing of the Democratic party furious about U.S. intervention in Iraq and President Bush's controversial victory in the 2000 election gravitated towards the Dean campaign. Furthermore, Dean's campaign manager, Joe Trippi, had built a campaign organization through the

Internet on a scale never-before seen in modern politics. By January 2004, Howard Dean's campaign raised $41 million and his organization claimed more than 180,000 volunteers. Dean led in some state polls by 30 percent and seemed poised to lap the entire Democratic field. Furthermore, the Democratic party establishment led by former Vice President Al Gore and former senator and presidential candidate Bill Bradley endorsed Dean's candidacy. Dean was the prohibitive favorite to win his party's nomination.[1]

Several other prominent Democrats were also contending for the Democratic presidential nomination: former House Minority Leader, Rep. Dick Gephardt (D-MO), Senator John Edwards (D-NC), and former General Wesley Clark (D-AR). Gephardt had tremendous union support. The charismatic Edwards argued that only a southern Democrat could win the White House (the last three Democrats to win the presidency were from the South). Former NATO commander, General Wesley Clark, had successfully managed a war in Kosovo (1998). Clark argued that he alone had the appropriate national security credentials to beat President Bush in the fall election. Three candidates—Senator Joseph Lieberman (D-CT), Congressman Dennis Kucinich (D-OH) and community activist Al Sharpton (D-NY)—rounded out the field.

TROUBLE FOR THE DEAN CAMPAIGN

The sudden decline of Howard Dean's candidacy was predicated on two major factors: the candidate's miscues and questions whether he could beat President George W. Bush if nominated to be president. The Dean campaign, which was playing offense from April until mid-December 2003, suddenly found itself playing defense.

The Dean candidacy unraveled quickly as Iowa voters began scrutinizing him in early January before the nation's first caucus took place. (A caucus is a series of thousands of party meetings throughout a state on a designated evening that begin a process to select delegates to the party's national convention). Candidates were attacking Dean both publicly and on the airwaves, particularly Congressman Dick Gephardt running a close second to Dean in the polls. The Dean campaign struck back with its own attack ads claiming that Dean was the outsider who could change Washington while the other candidates were part of the establishment supporting the Iraq war. Dean's own outspokenness became an issue in the campaign.

Furthermore, Dean stumbled during an Iowa debate in mid-January while answering a question about race from opponent Al Sharpton (D-NY). Sharpton asked why no minorities served as cabinet officers while Dean was governor of Vermont (1991–2003), a state with a predominantly white population (97 percent non-minority). Instead of answering the question directly, Dean stated that a senior member of his gubernatorial staff had been a minority. Dean's brusque and evasive answer seemed to contrast with his populist campaign image, raising questions about his character and judgment. The debate did nothing to stem Dean's freefall of support in the days before the Iowa caucus—losing nearly 10–20 points in the last three weeks of the campaign, according to polls.

THE IOWA AND NEW HAMPSHIRE RESULTS

On January 19, 2004 Dean received only 18 percent of the support of Iowa Democratic caucus attendees, lagging far behind Senator John Kerry (D-MA) with 38 percent and Senator John Edwards (D-NC) with 32 percent. Pro-labor Congressman Dick Gephardt received only 11 percent of caucus-goers support in a heavily union state. (He dropped out of the race the next day.) Entrance polls of caucus attendees found that electability, or beating President Bush, was the dominant factor that influenced their choice. Most Iowa Democrats thought the often-blunt Dean acted less presidential than the experienced Kerry or the glib Edwards. Kerry and Edwards had emerged out of nowhere to defeat the frontrunner by a substantial margin. Both Kerry and Edwards used positive advertising in the weeks leading up to the caucus emerging from third and fourth place in the polls just weeks before the primary. Finishing third, Dean spoke to his Iowa supporters seemingly unaware that a national audience would be watching. Dean's "I Have a Scream" speech was punctuated with a "YEE-AH!!" to rally his supporters. It seemed surreal and bizarre to many viewers and pundits and was replayed often during the following week leading up to the New Hampshire primary.

Eight days later (on January 27), the new frontrunner, John Kerry, won a decisive victory in New Hampshire winning 39 percent of the vote with Dean finishing a distant second at 26 percent. (New Hampshire is the nation's first primary.) Third and fourth place finishers Wesley Clark and John Edwards hoped to rebound the following week in two southern primaries (South Carolina and Oklahoma). Dean's war chest was nearly depleted (only $5 million remained), as he pulled all his advertising from the airwaves in February 3 primary states. In addition, Dean asked his campaign staff to defer their paychecks for two weeks. Dean's campaign manager Joe Trippi resigned from the campaign after facing a demotion. The former Vermont governor replaced Trippi with Washington insider Roy Neel, a Gore protégé.[2] However, none of the remaining candidates could ever gain enough momentum to challenge Kerry.

KERRY'S COMEBACK

John Kerry's comeback from the political abyss (he was at six percent in an Iowa poll just five weeks before the primary) was predicated on two factors. First, the candidate became more disciplined and circumspect on the campaign trail offering a message of fighting to take back America from special interests and the powerful. The fighting motif was based on Kerry's war service and voting record as a progressive in the senate. Second, the campaign's advertising that focused on John Kerry's personal story of combat valor, courage, and political experience resonated with Iowa and New Hampshire voters. The lesson from Iowa and New Hampshire was that one major candidate could adapt (Kerry) to a fast changing political environment, while the other failed to do so (Dean). Kerry went on to win 35 of the first 38 primary or caucus contests. By mid-March he seemed poised to win the nomination as all major opponents had exited the race.

NOTES

1. *Meetup.com* reported that Dean had 186,000 volunteers and organizers as of January 30, 2004; Sharon Theimer, "Howard Dean Sees Campaign Funds Dwindle As Losses Mount; John Kerry Reaps Benefits of Victories," *Associated Press,* January 30, 2004 on the Dean campaign finances.
2. Ibid, Theimer.

Index